杜人

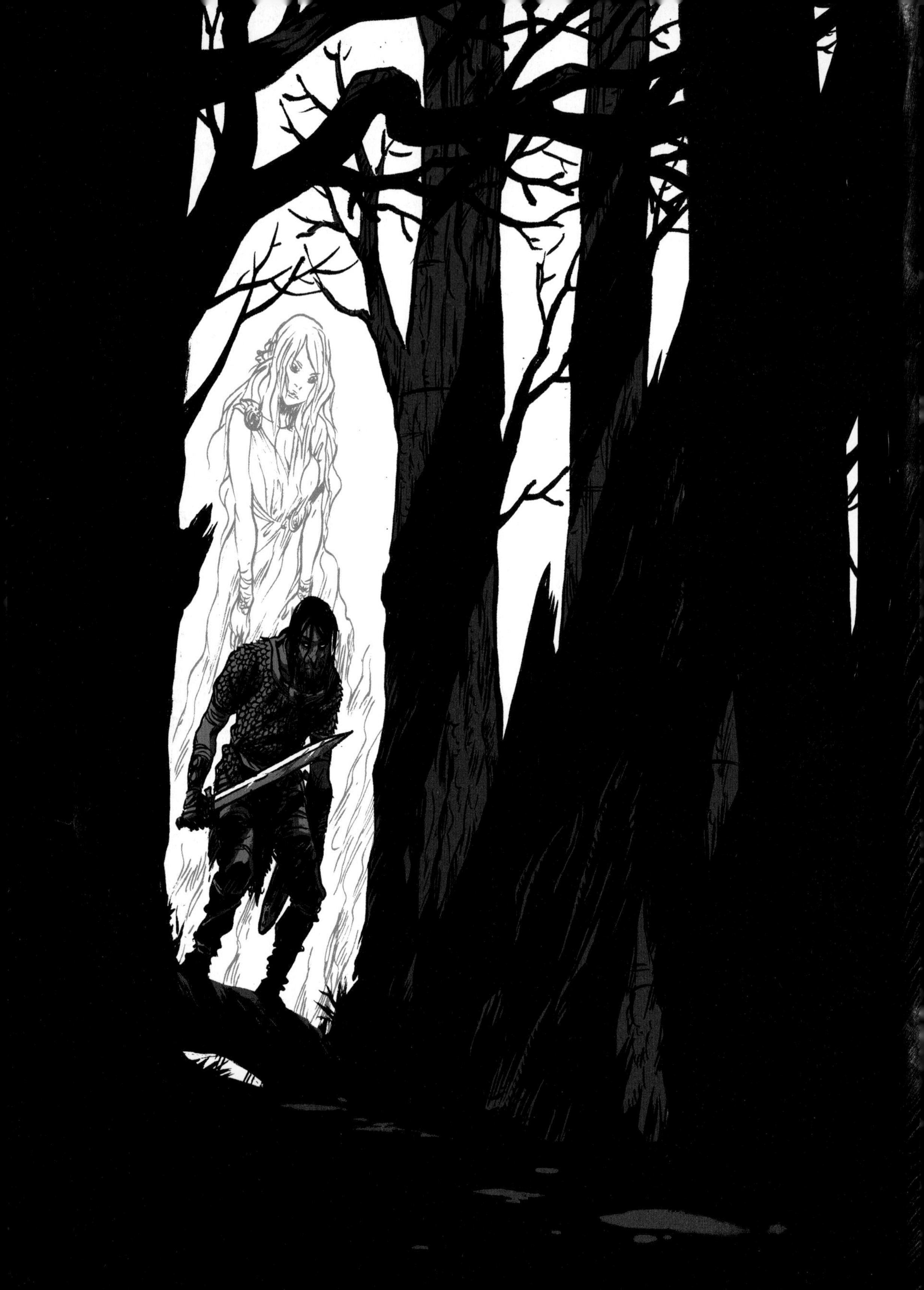

*When bones, when blood, when limbs are broken,*
*Bone to bone, blood to blood, limb to limb,*
*Let them be bonded.*

# By Chance or Providence

### STORIES BY BECKY CLOONAN
#### WITH COLORS BY LEE LOUGHRIDGE

® **IMAGE COMICS, INC.**

**Robert Kirkman**—Chief Operating Officer
**Erik Larsen**—Chief Financial Officer
**Todd McFarlane**—President
**Marc Silvestri**—Chief Executive Officer
**Jim Valentino**—Vice President
**Eric Stephenson**—Publisher/Chief Creative Officer
**Jeff Boison**—Director of Publishing Planning
& Book Trade Sales
**Chris Ross**—Director of Digital Sales
**Jeff Stang**—Director of Direct Market Sales
**Kat Salazar**—Director of PR & Marketing
**Drew Gill**—Art Director
**Heather Doornink**—Production Director
**Nicole Lapalme**—Controller

**IMAGECOMICS.COM**

BY CHANCE OR PROVIDENCE. Second printing. August 2019. Published by Image Comics, Inc. Office of publication: 2701 NW Vaughn St., Suite 780, Portland, OR 97210. Copyright © 2019 Becky Cloonan. All rights reserved. "By Chance Or Providence," its logos, and the likenesses of all characters herein are trademarks of Becky Cloonan, unless otherwise noted. "Image" and the Image Comics logos are registered trademarks of Image Comics, Inc. No part of this publication may be reproduced or transmitted in any form or by any means (except for short excerpts for journalistic or review purposes), without the express written permission of Becky Cloonan or Image Comics, Inc. All names, characters, events, and locales in this publication are entirely fictional. Any resemblance to actual persons (living or dead), events, or places, without satiric intent, is coincidental. Printed in the USA. For information regarding the CPSIA on this printed material call: 203-595-3636. For international rights, contact: foreignlicensing@imagecomics.com.

ISBN: 978-1-5343-0186-3

DEDICATED TO
THOSE OF YOU WITH
CRUSHES ON YOUR
CHARACTERS.

# I.

# Wolves

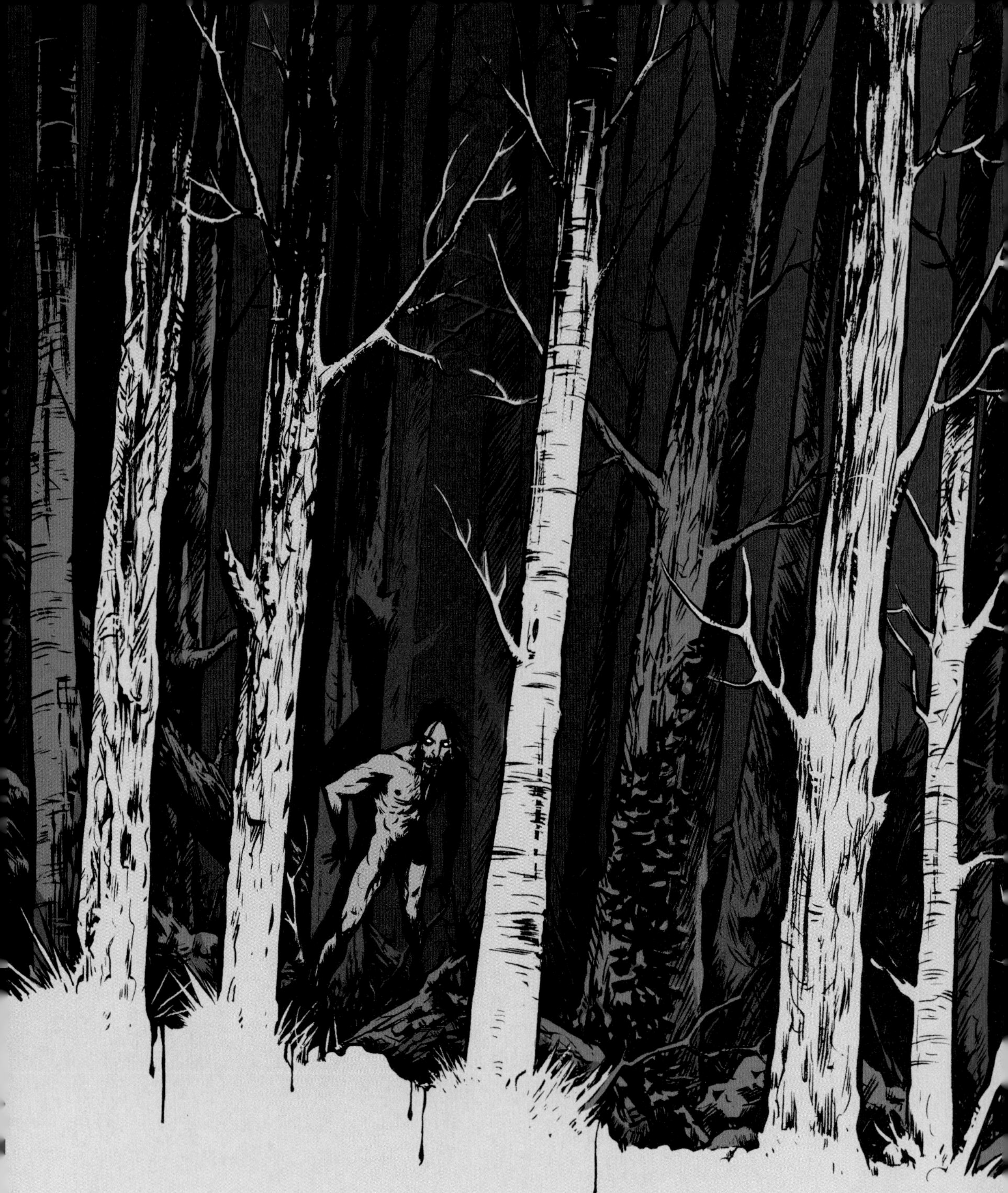

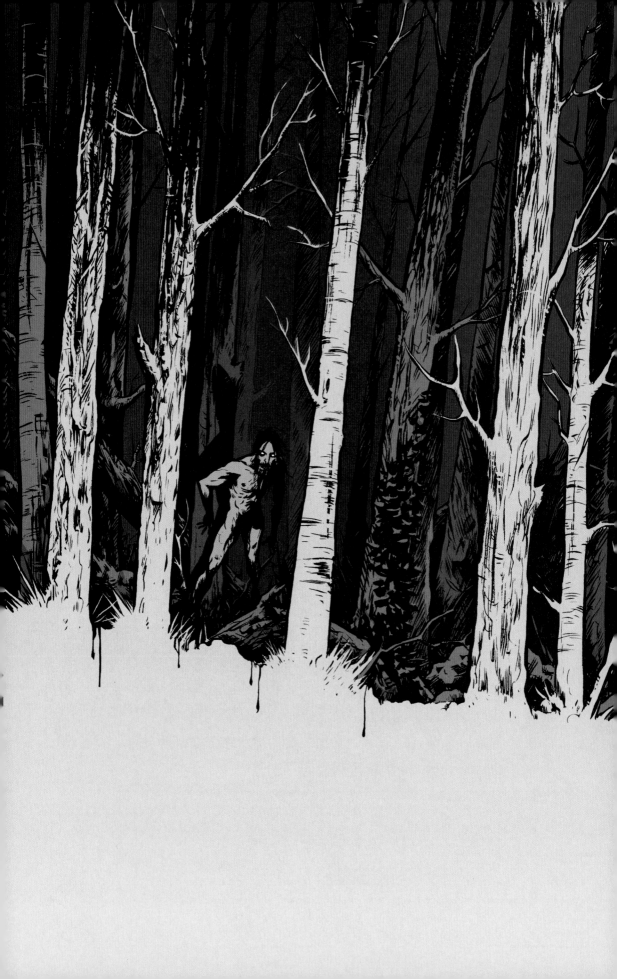

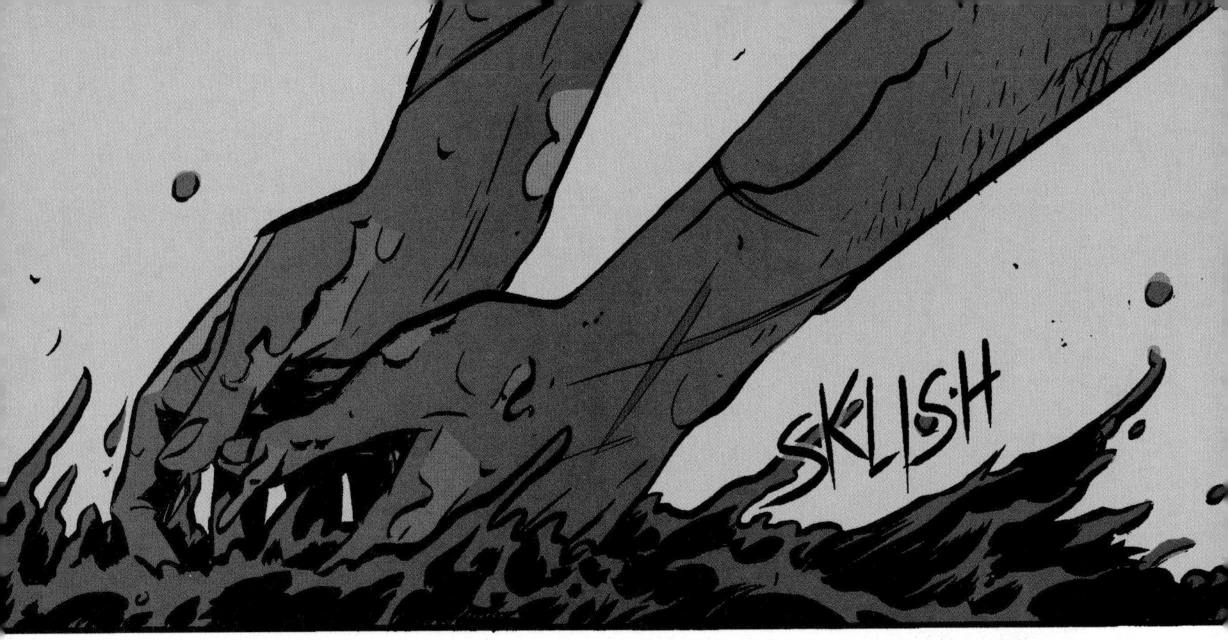
SKLISH
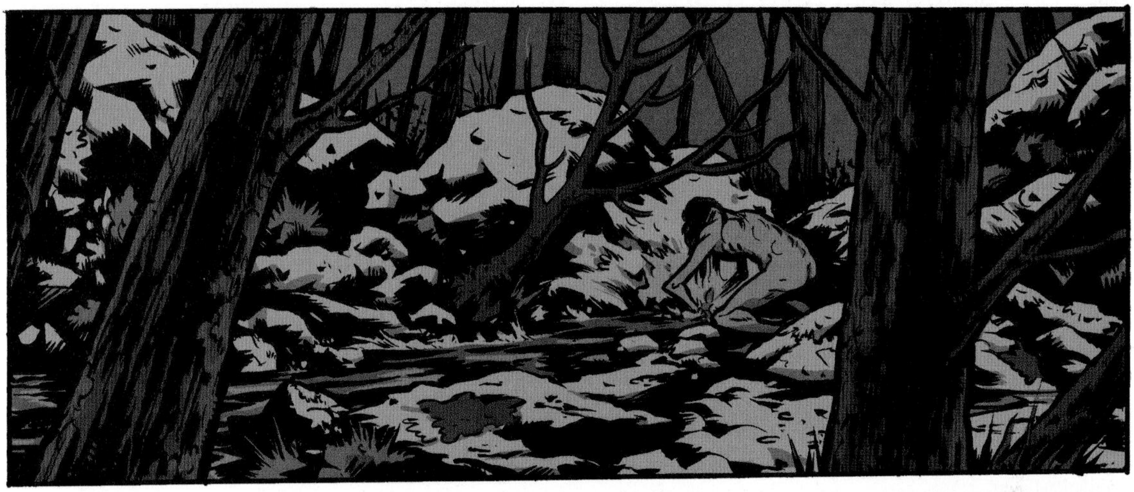
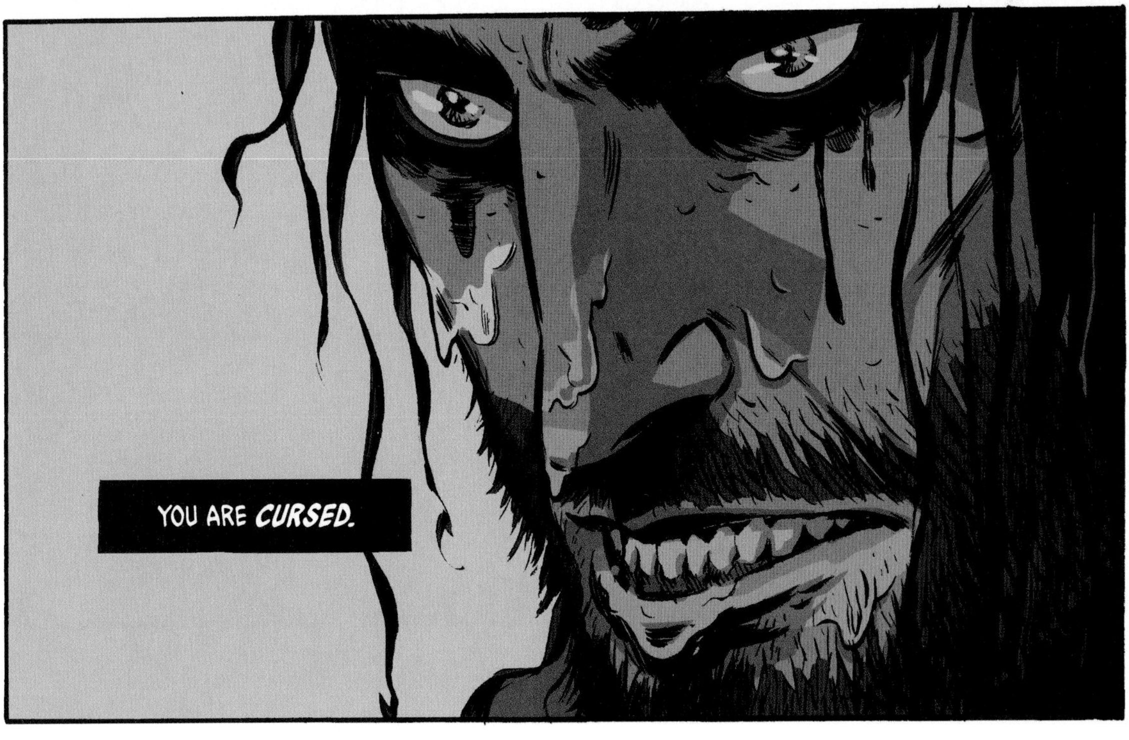
YOU ARE CURSED.

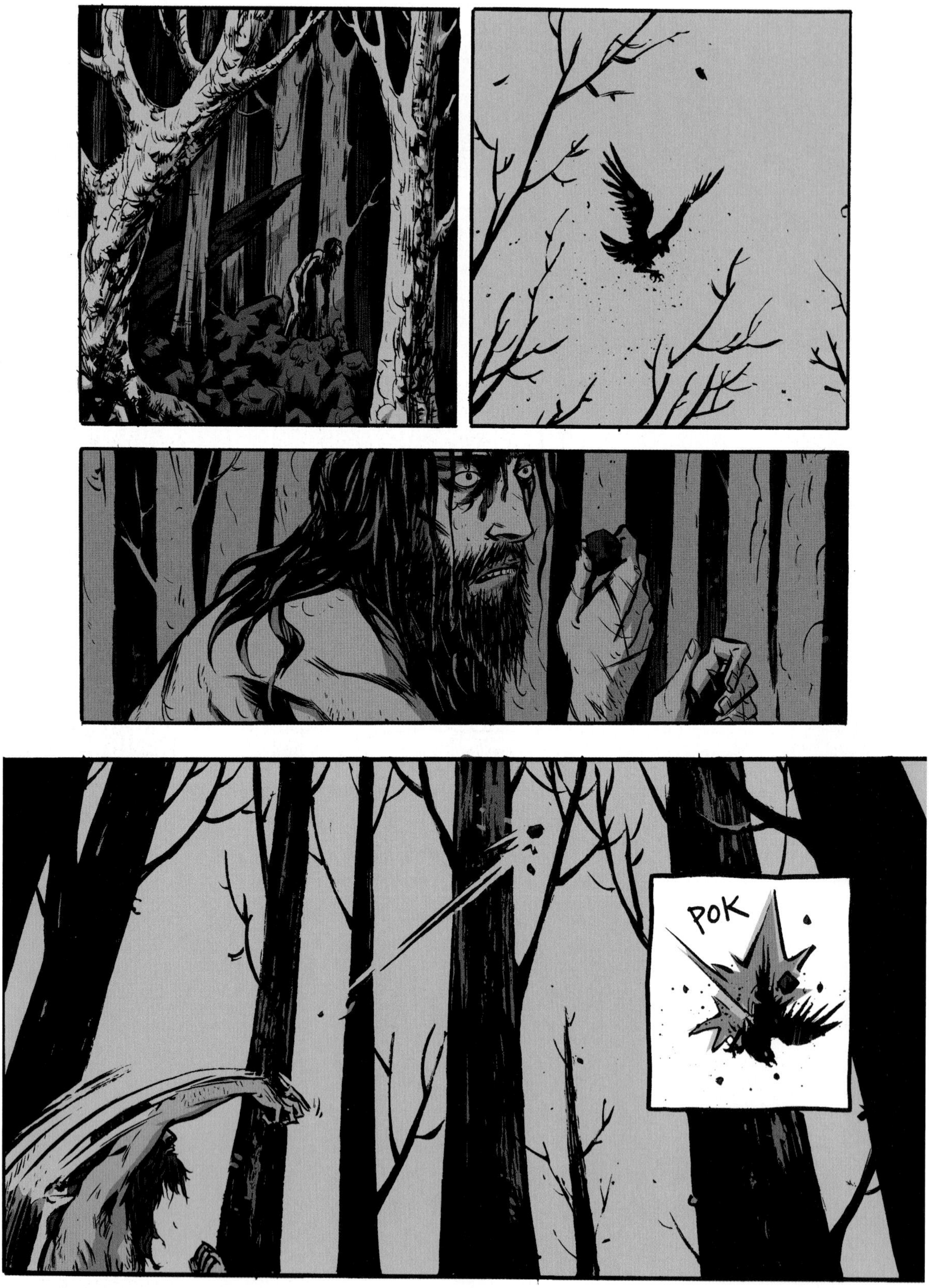
POK

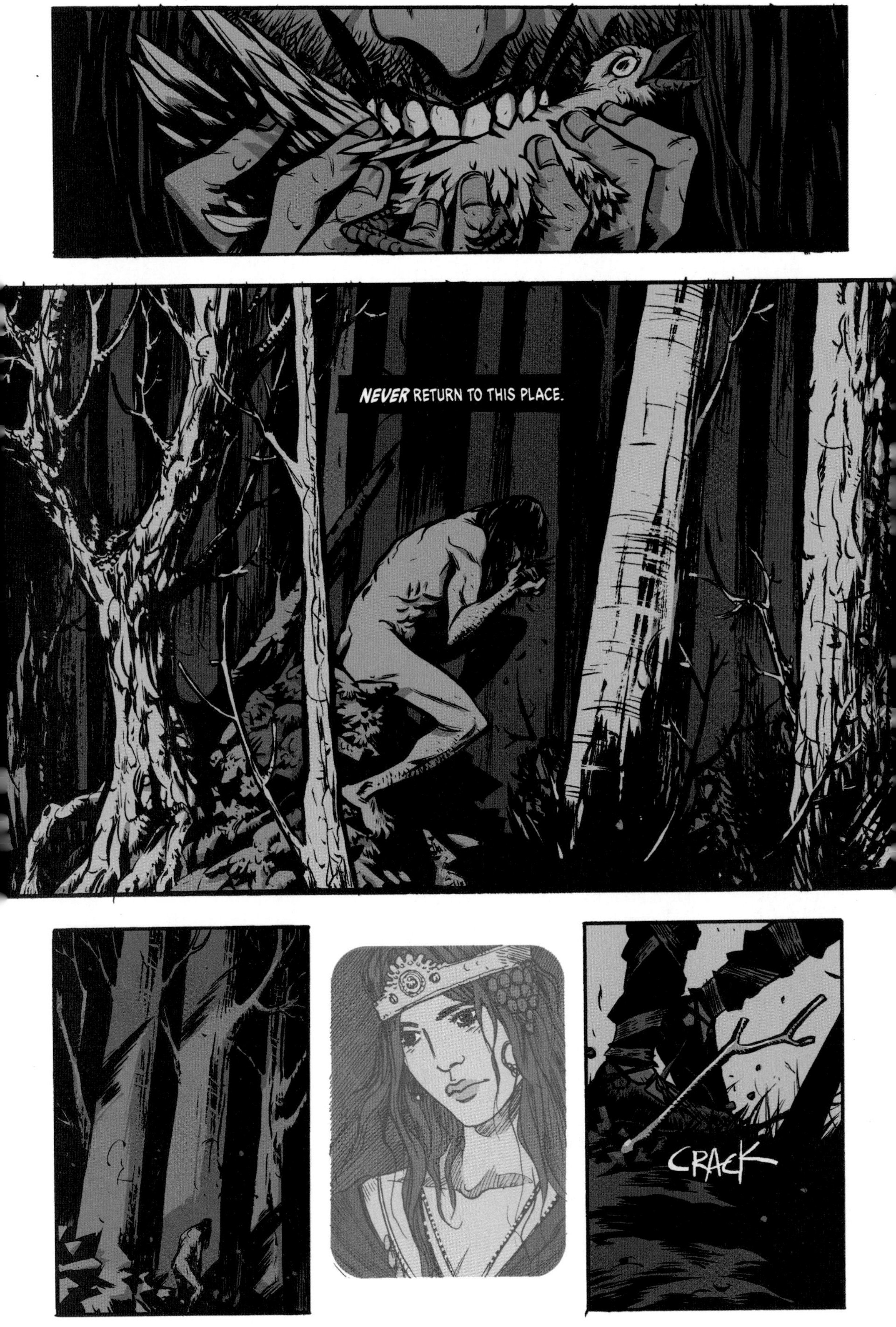
NEVER RETURN TO THIS PLACE.
CRACK

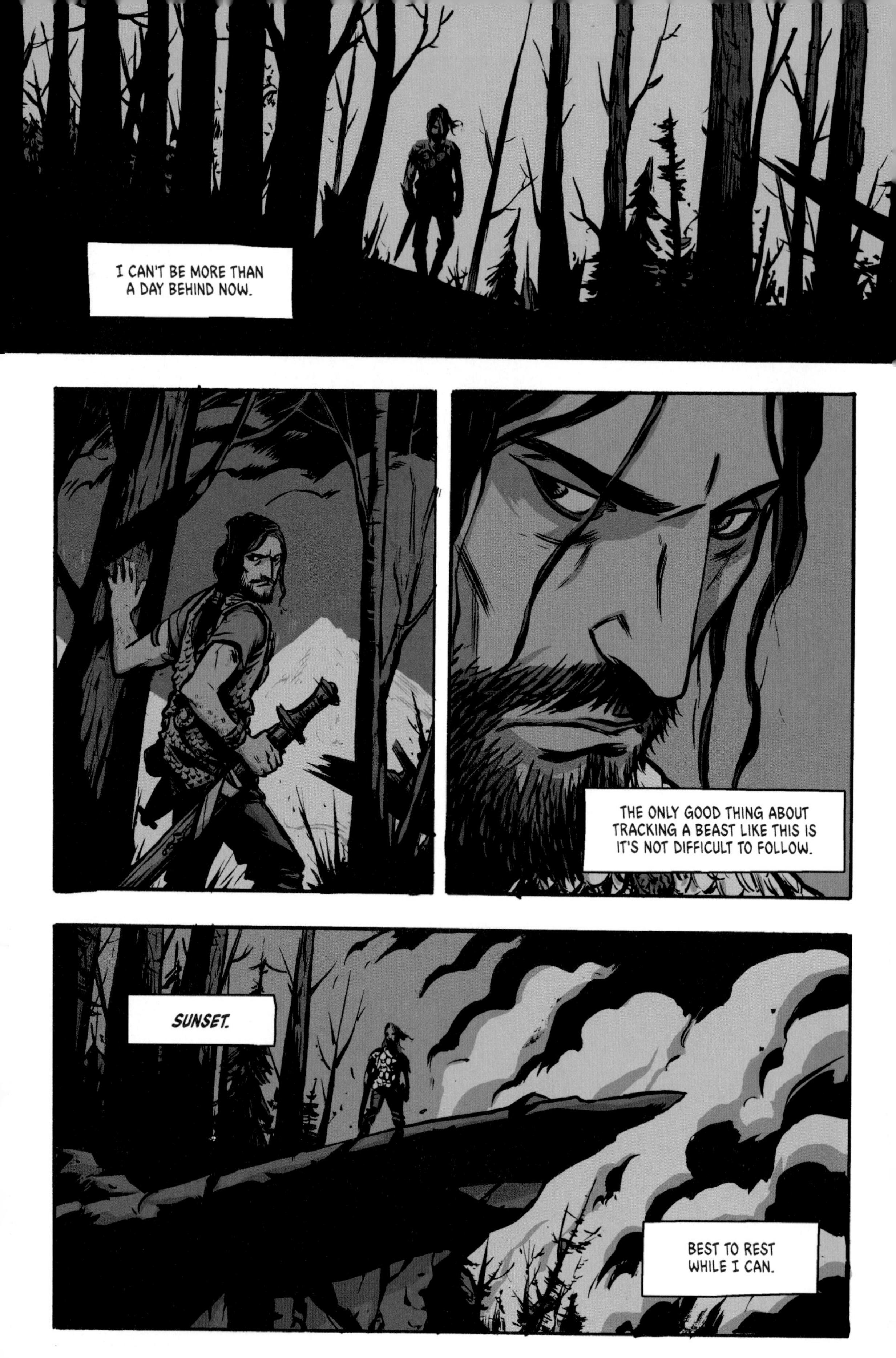
I CAN'T BE MORE THAN A DAY BEHIND NOW.
THE ONLY GOOD THING ABOUT TRACKING A BEAST LIKE THIS IS IT'S NOT DIFFICULT TO FOLLOW.
SUNSET.
BEST TO REST WHILE I CAN.

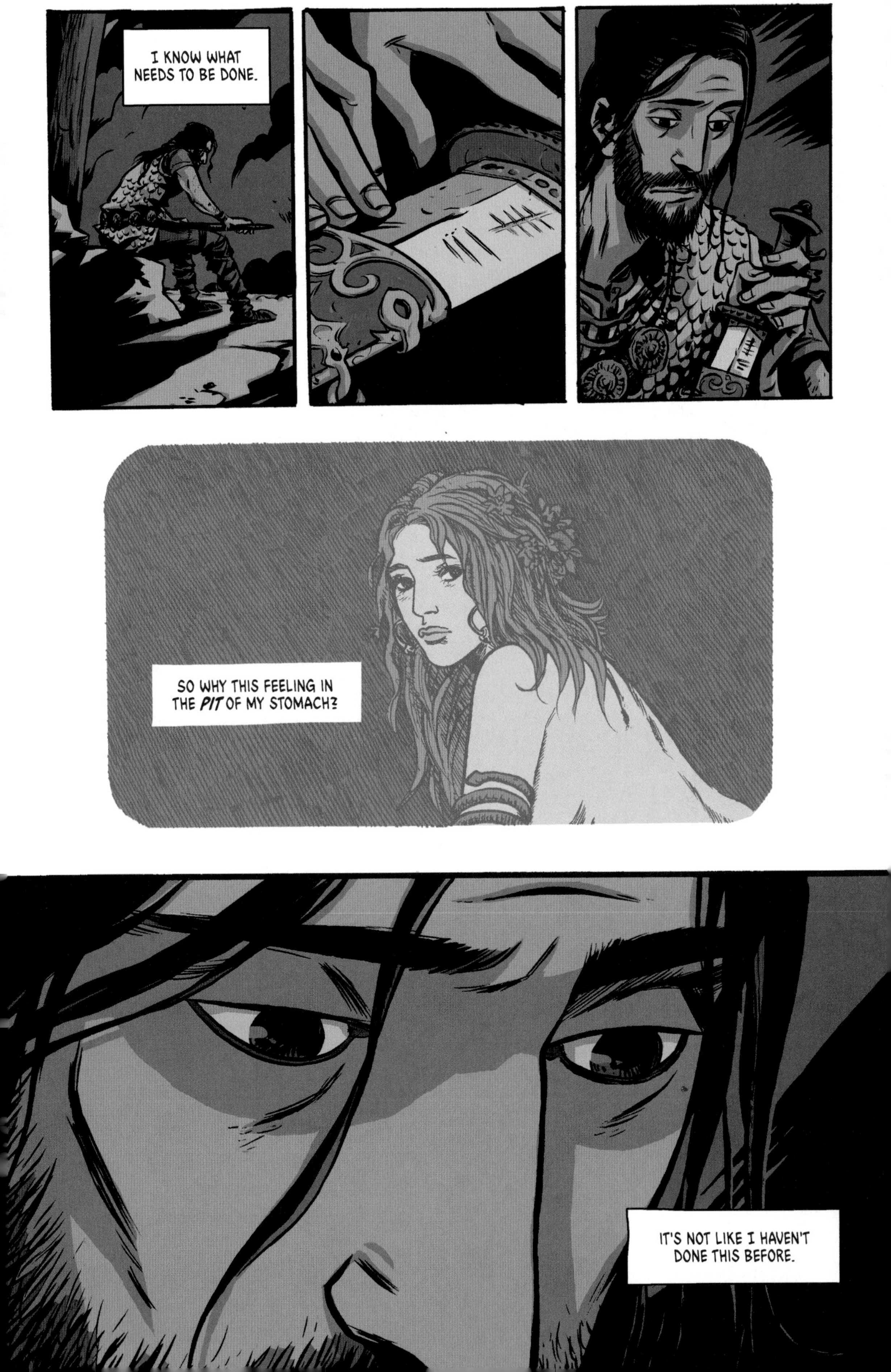
I KNOW WHAT NEEDS TO BE DONE.
SO WHY THIS FEELING IN THE *PIT* OF MY STOMACH?
IT'S NOT LIKE I HAVEN'T DONE THIS BEFORE.

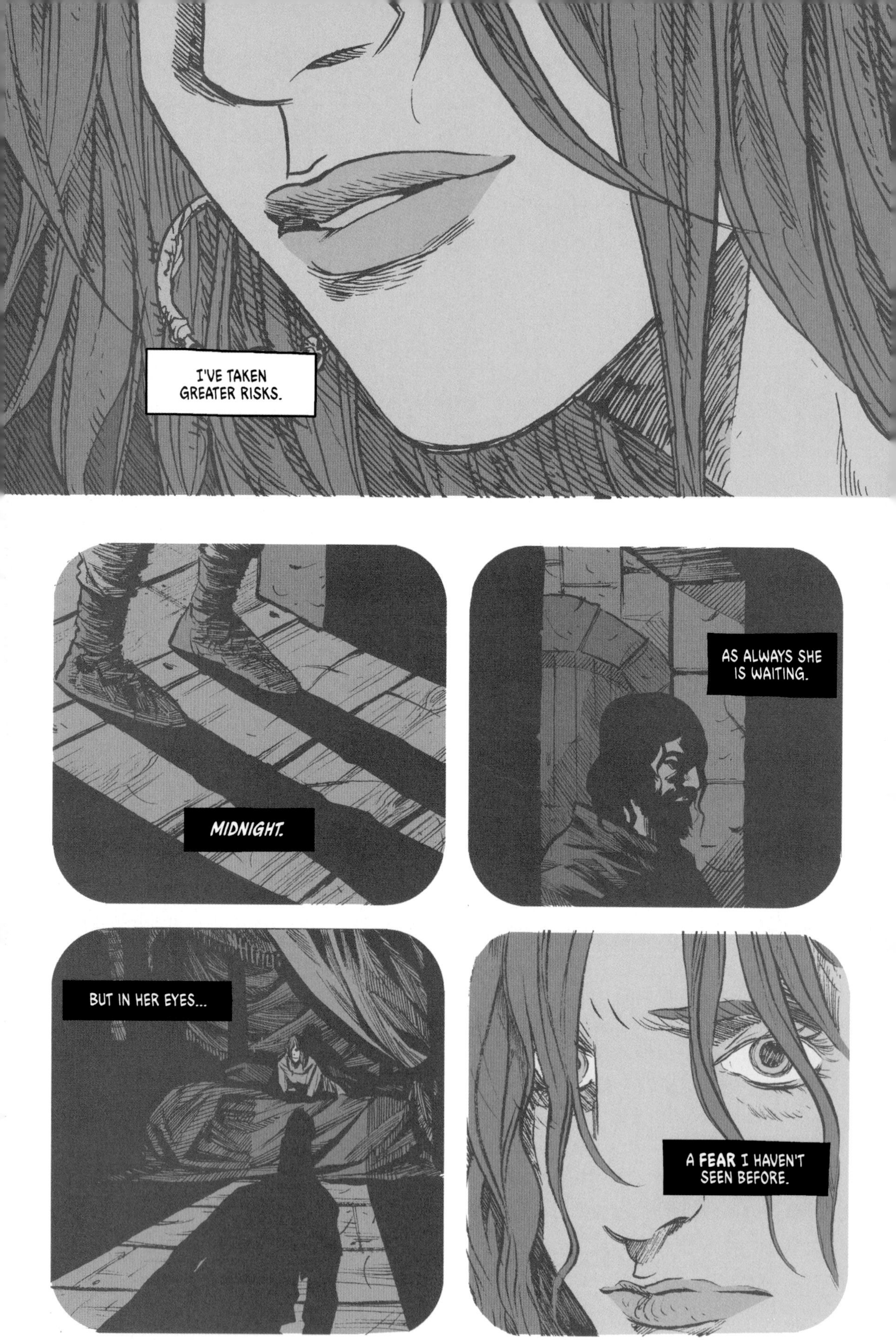
I'VE TAKEN GREATER RISKS.
MIDNIGHT.
AS ALWAYS SHE IS WAITING.
BUT IN HER EYES...
A FEAR I HAVEN'T SEEN BEFORE.

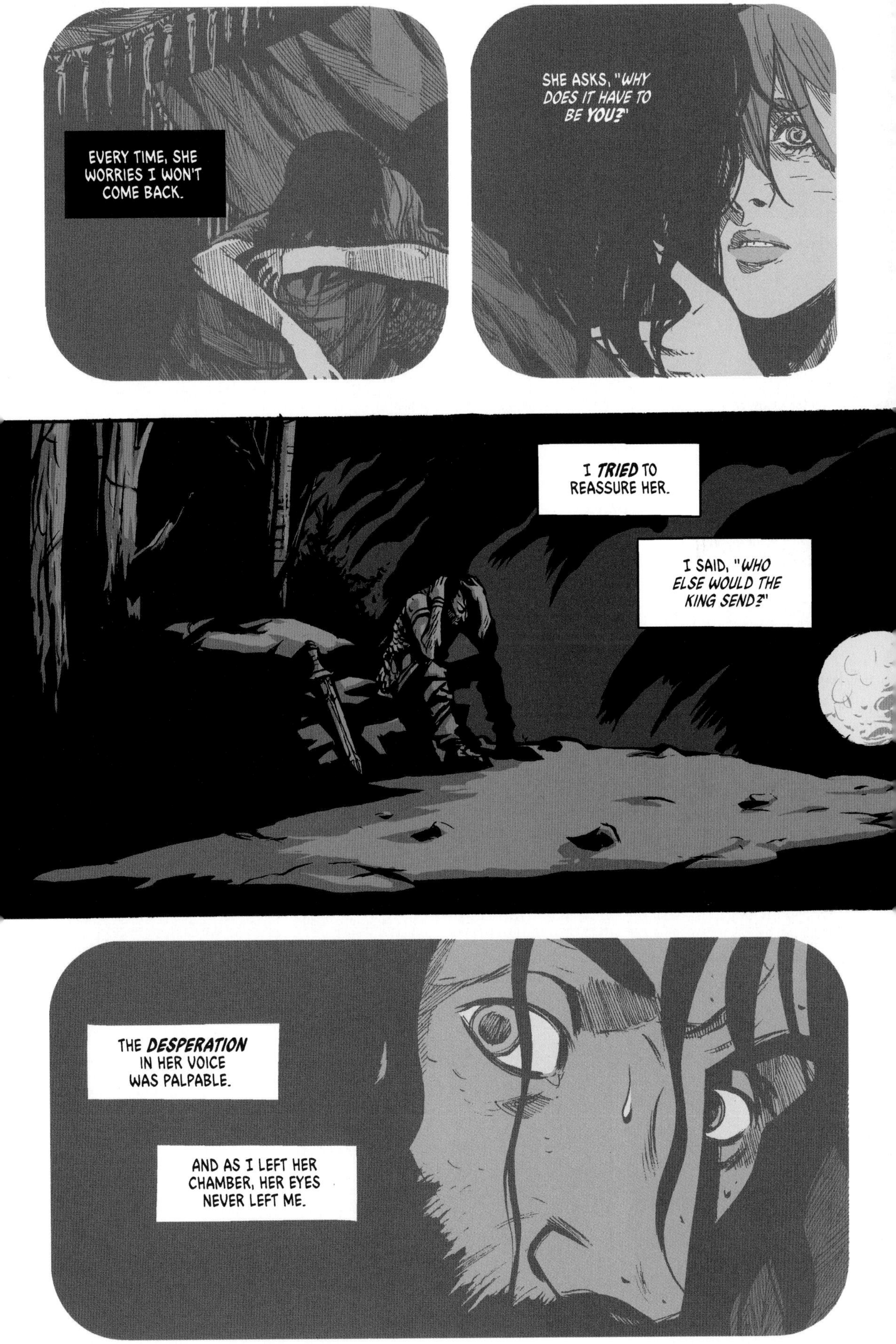
EVERY TIME, SHE WORRIES I WON'T COME BACK.
SHE ASKS, "WHY DOES IT HAVE TO BE YOU?"
I TRIED TO REASSURE HER.
I SAID, "WHO ELSE WOULD THE KING SEND?"
THE DESPERATION IN HER VOICE WAS PALPABLE.
AND AS I LEFT HER CHAMBER, HER EYES NEVER LEFT ME.

NIGHTFALL.

MY MEMORIES HAVE LEFT ME PRONE.

IT HAS MY SCENT.

SO I SCATTER THE WARDS FOR PROTECTION.

POK PIK

TAK

PAKT SKT

AND I *SACRIFICE* MY BLOOD.

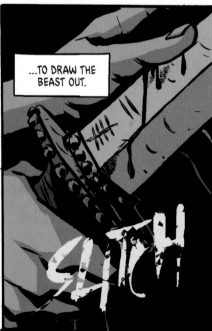

...TO DRAW THE BEAST OUT.

SLTCH

TCH.

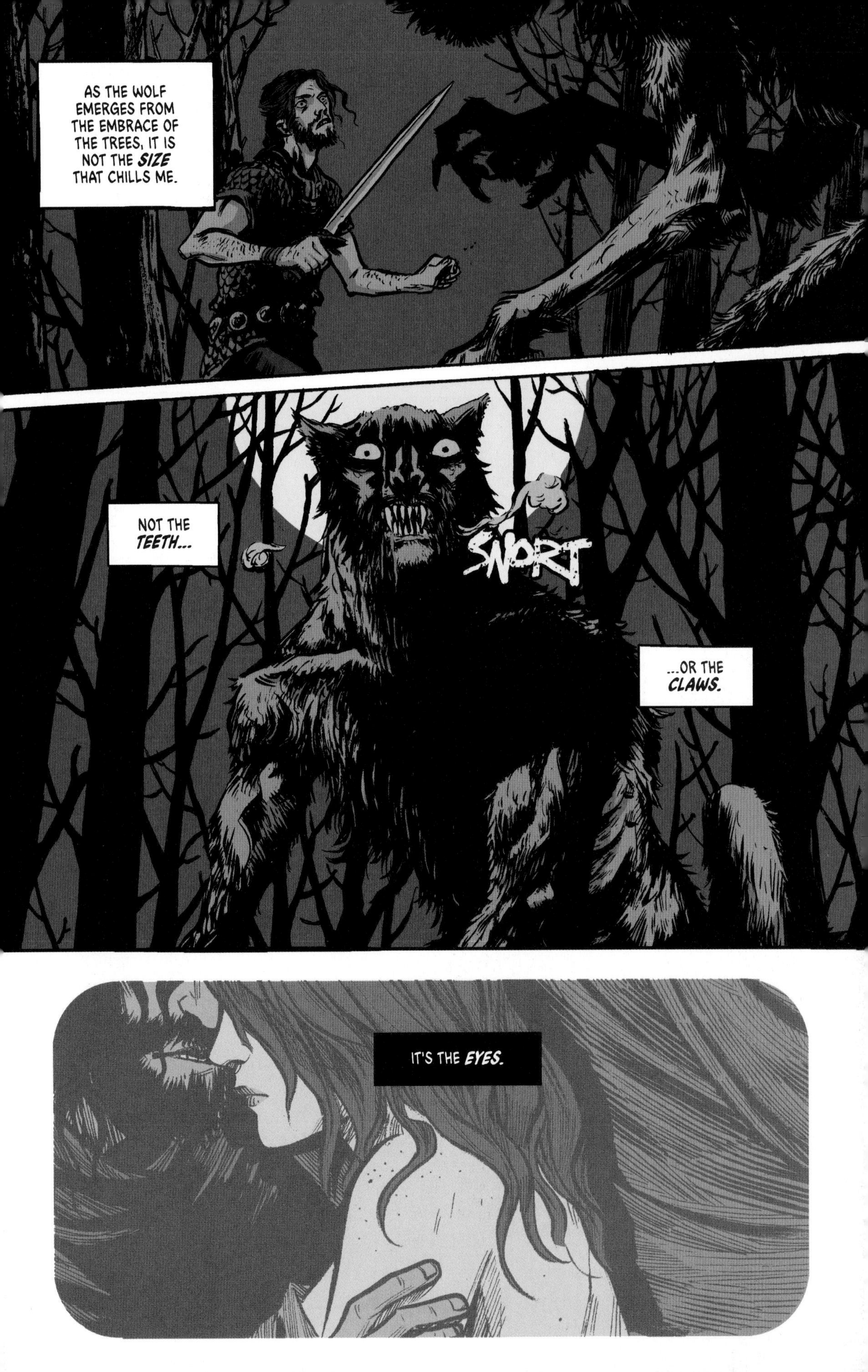
AS THE WOLF EMERGES FROM THE EMBRACE OF THE TREES, IT IS NOT THE *SIZE* THAT CHILLS ME.
NOT THE *TEETH...*
SNORT
...OR THE *CLAWS.*
IT'S THE *EYES.*

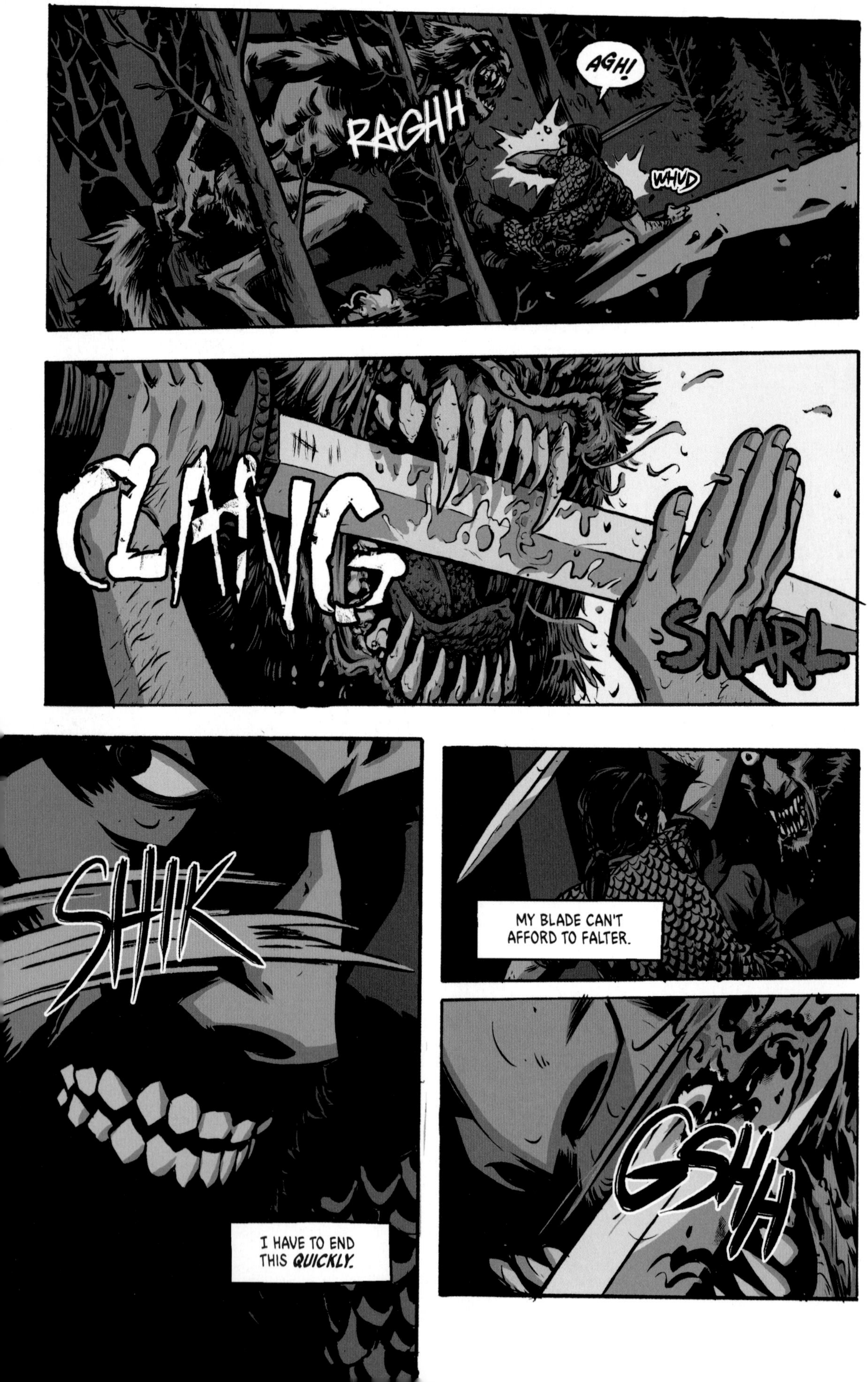
RAGHH
AGH!
WHUD
CLANG
SNARL
SHIK
I HAVE TO END THIS *QUICKLY.*
MY BLADE CAN'T AFFORD TO FALTER.
GSHH

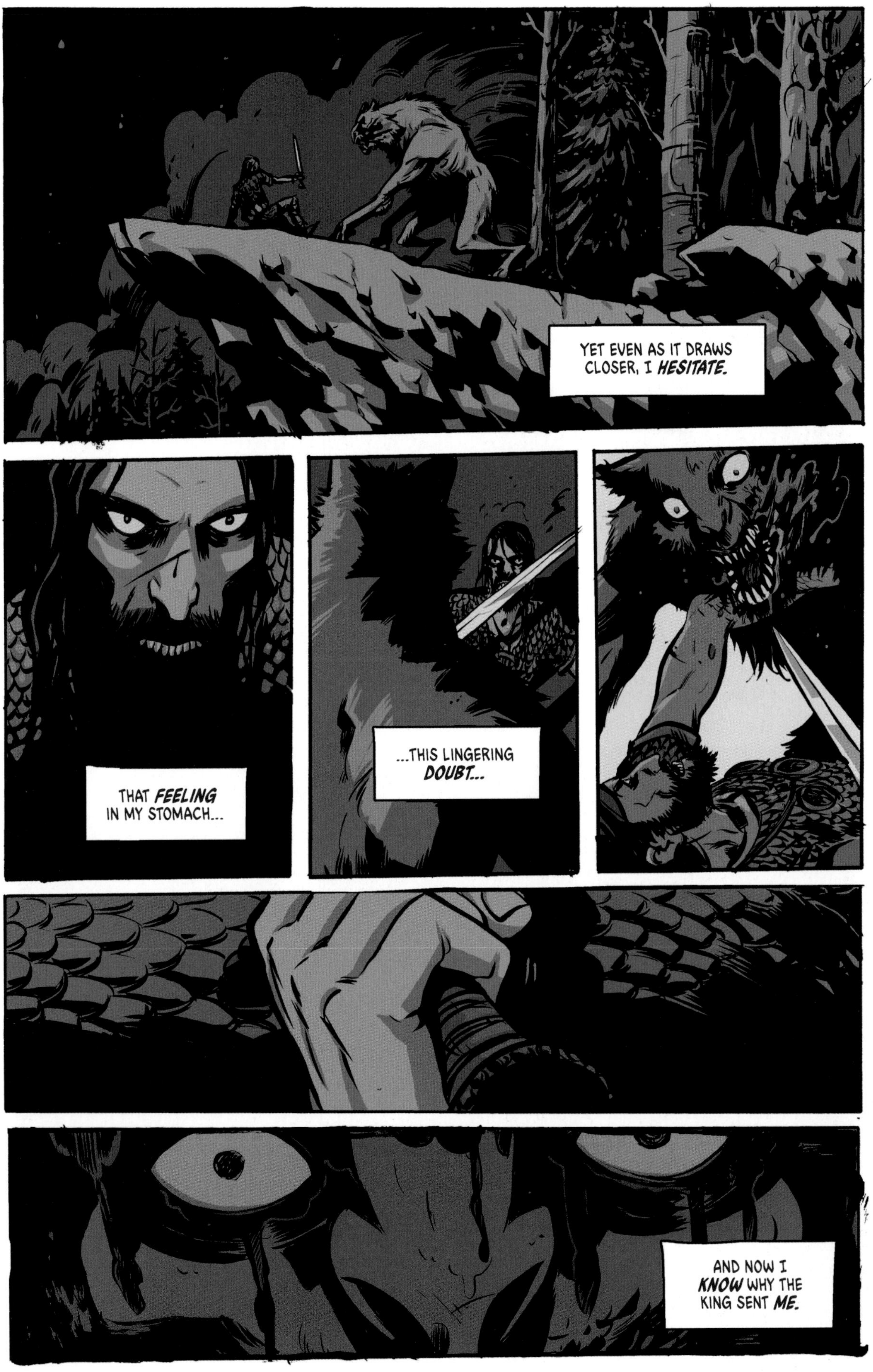
YET EVEN AS IT DRAWS CLOSER, I *HESITATE.*
THAT *FEELING* IN MY STOMACH...
...THIS LINGERING *DOUBT...*
AND NOW I *KNOW* WHY THE KING SENT *ME.*

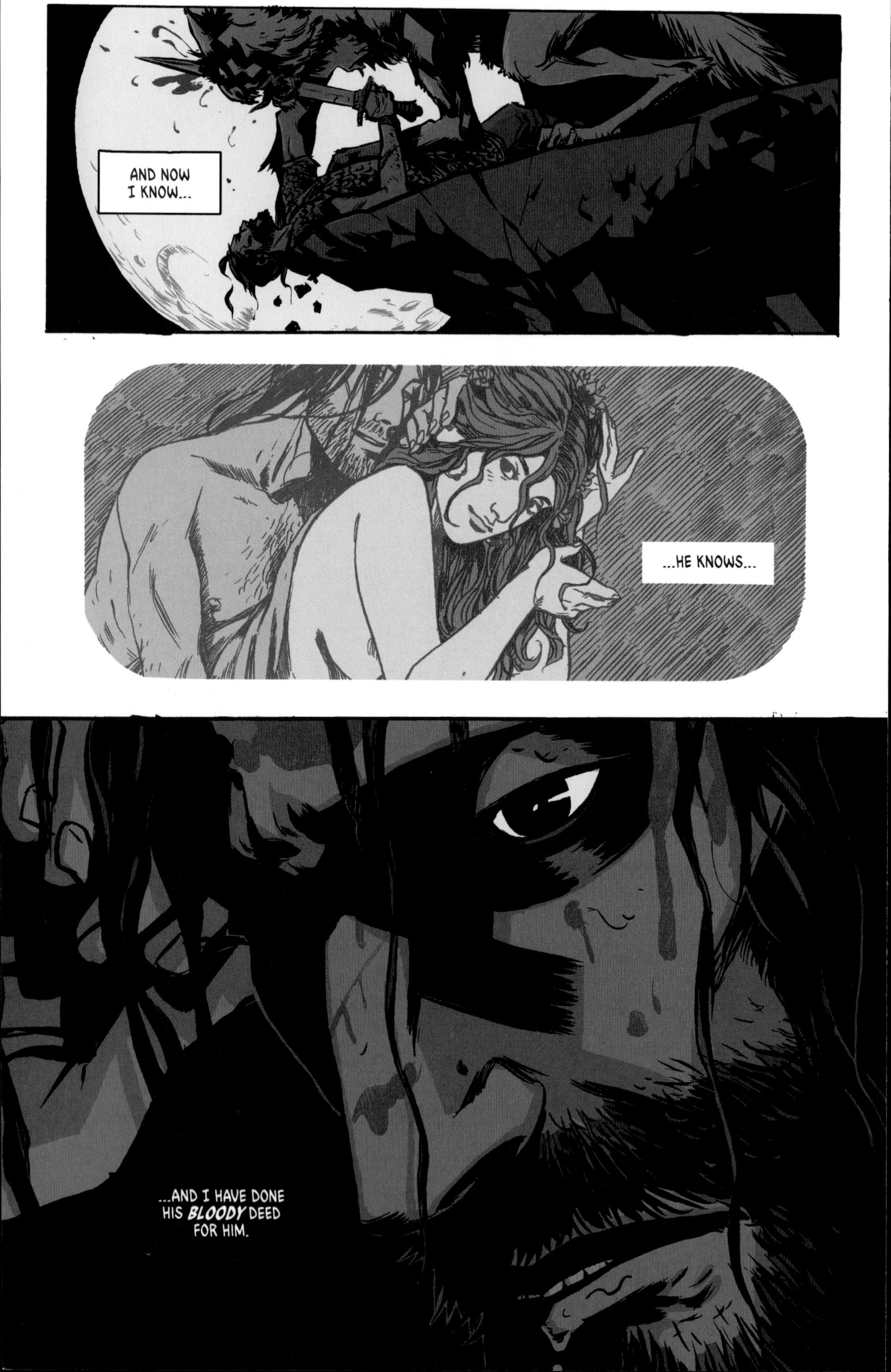
AND NOW I KNOW...
...HE KNOWS...
...AND I HAVE DONE HIS BLOODY DEED FOR HIM.

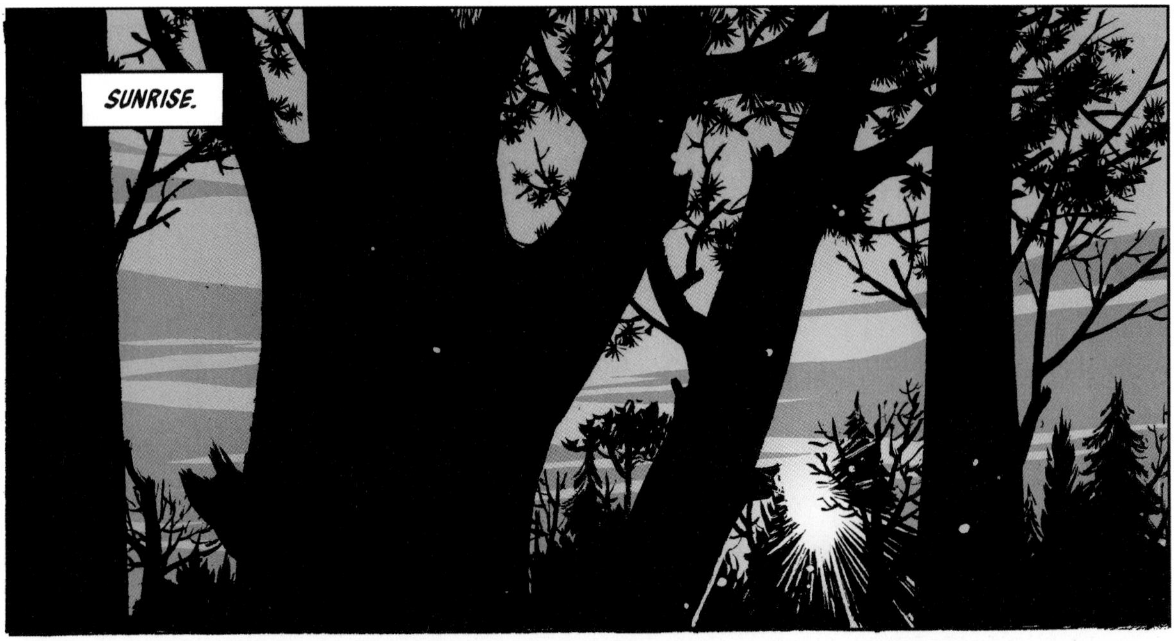
SUNRISE.

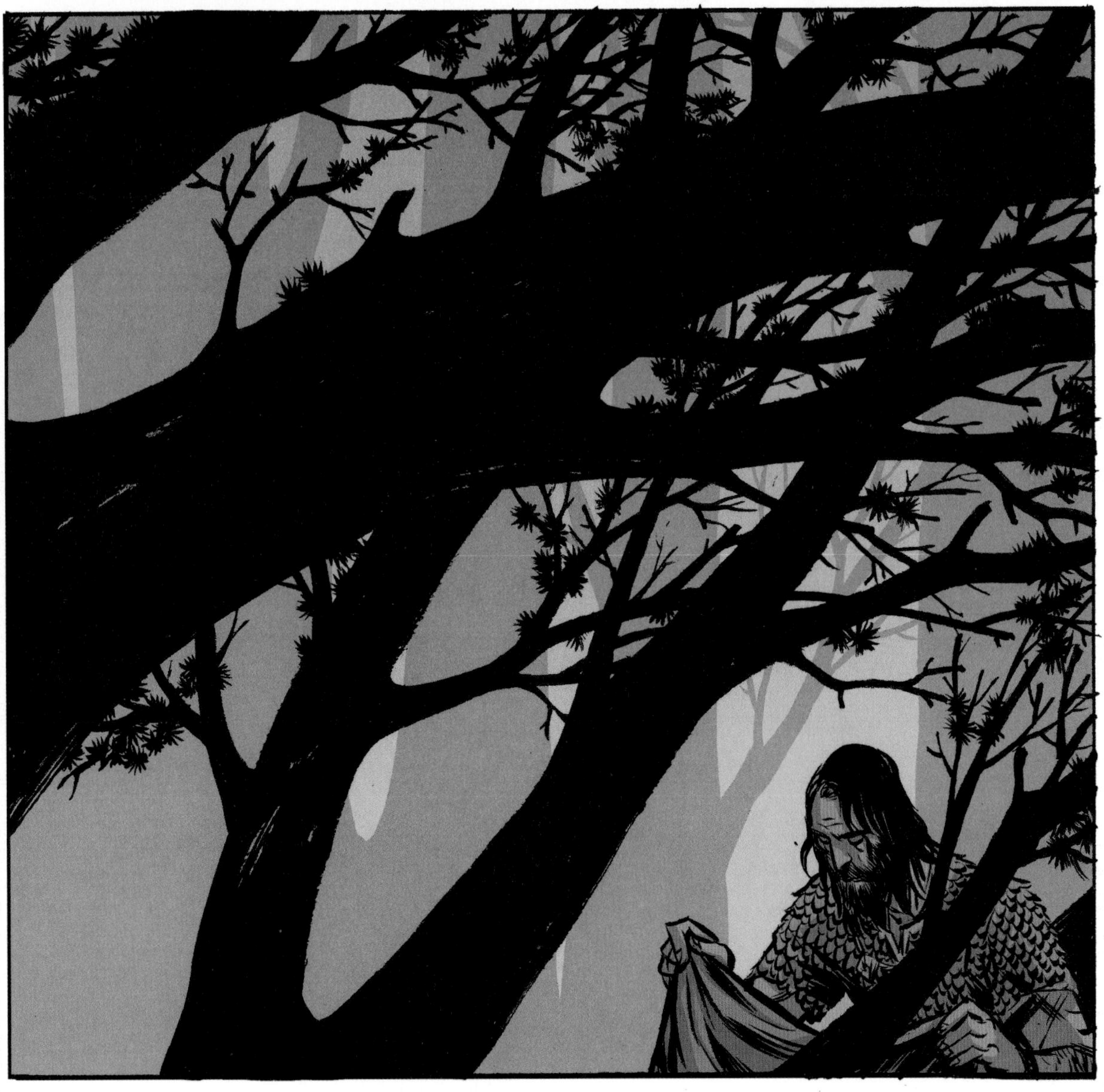

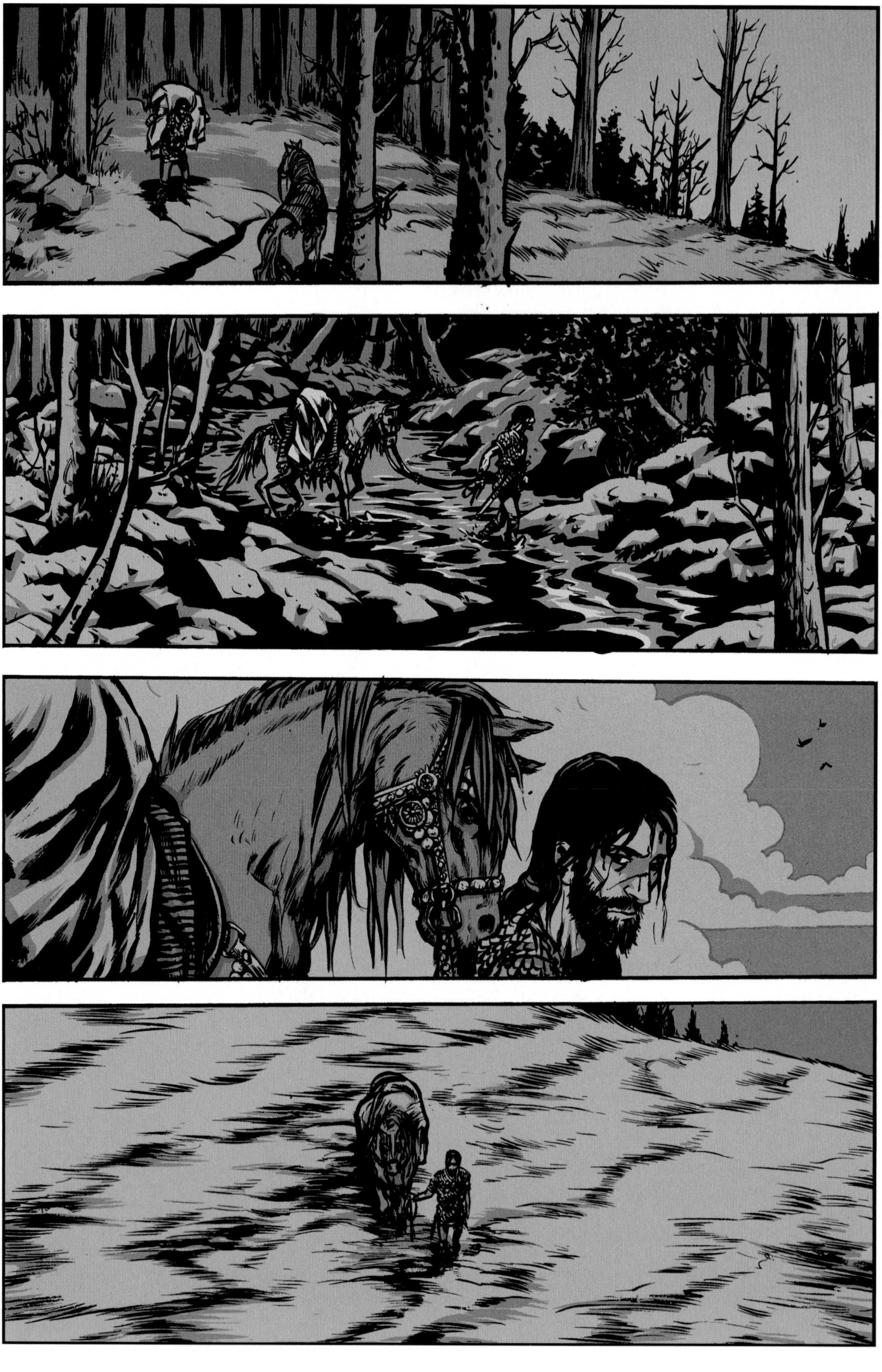

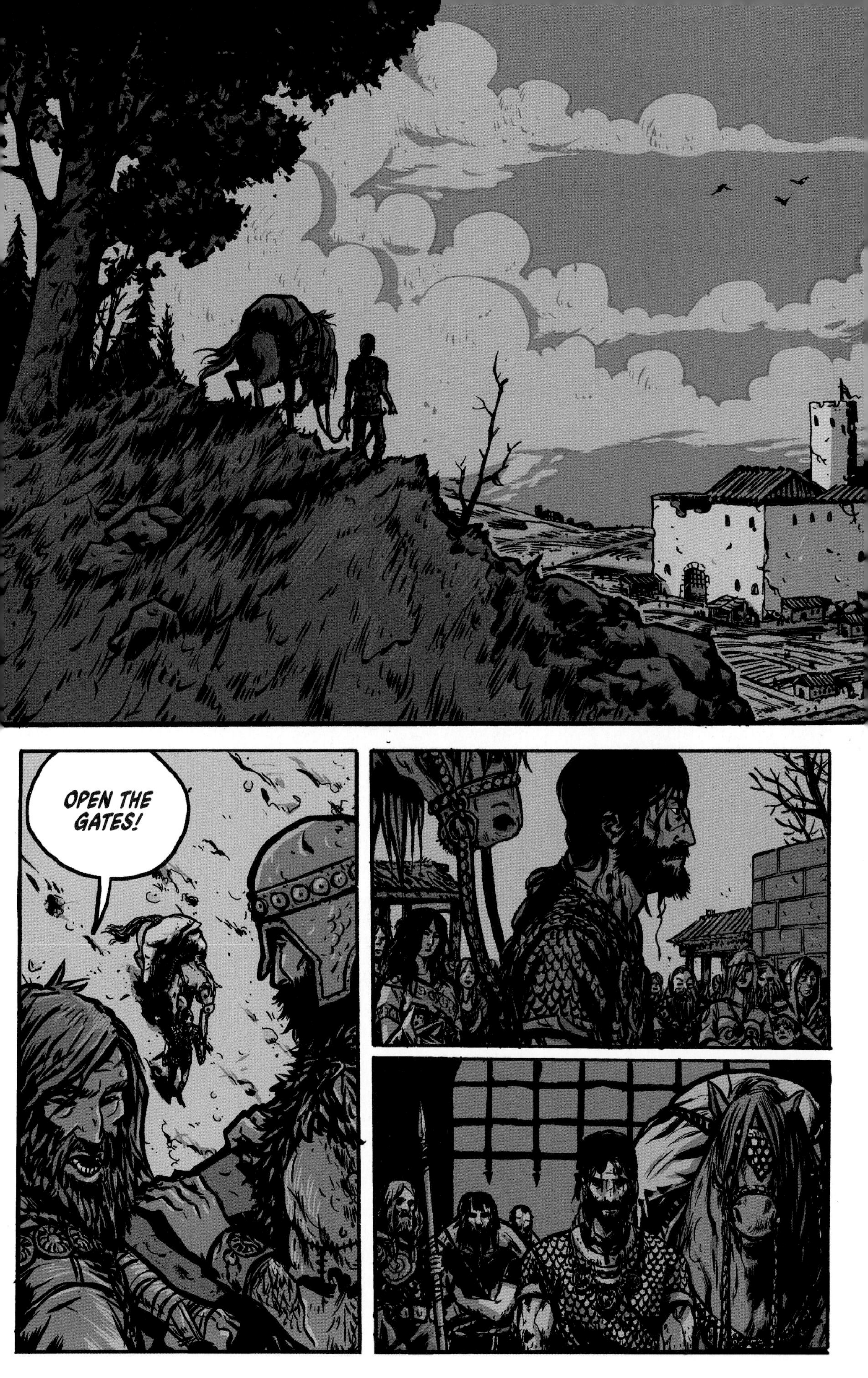
OPEN THE GATES!

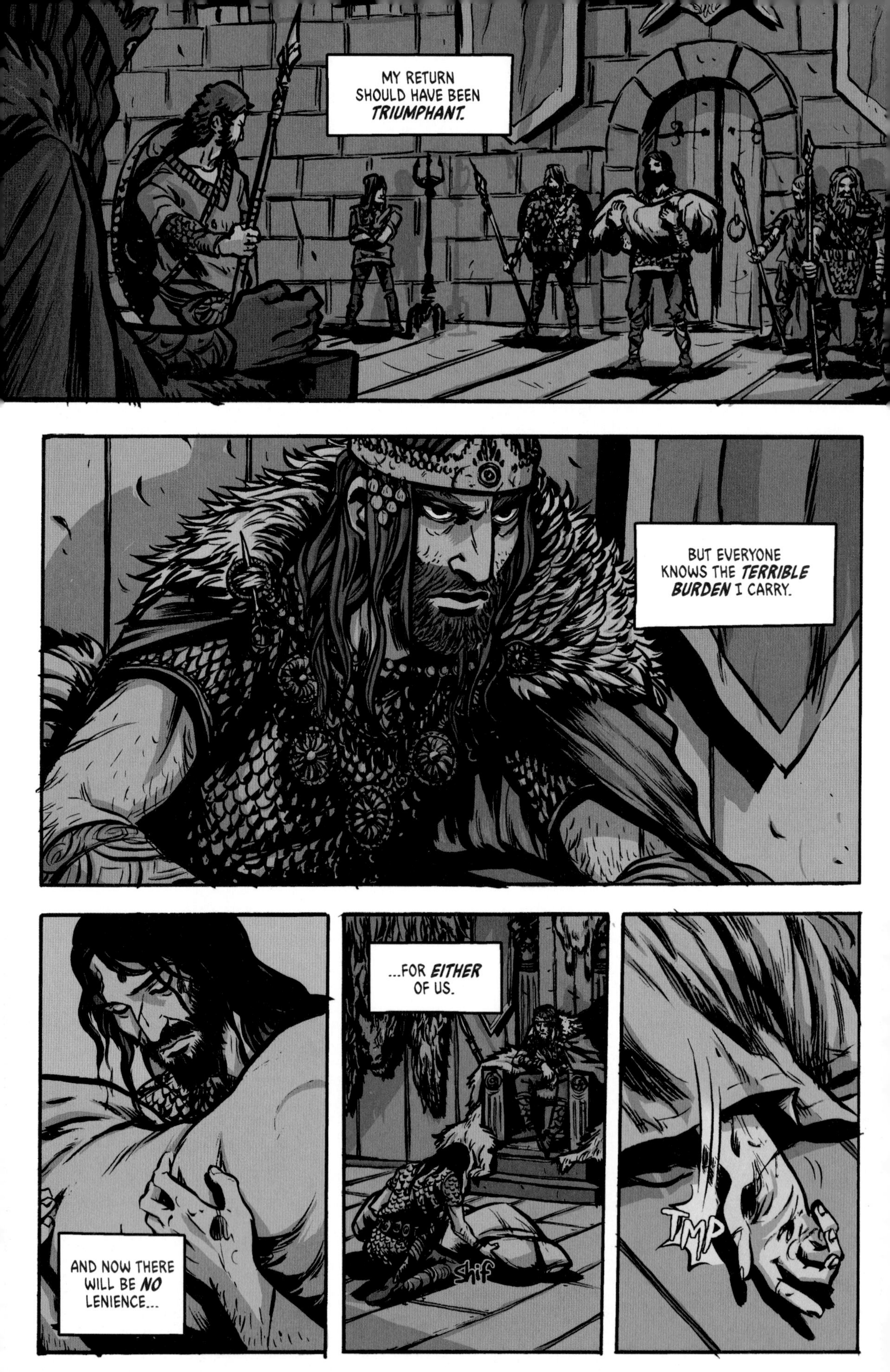
MY RETURN SHOULD HAVE BEEN TRIUMPHANT.
BUT EVERYONE KNOWS THE TERRIBLE BURDEN I CARRY.
AND NOW THERE WILL BE NO LENIENCE...
...FOR EITHER OF US.
SHIF
TMP

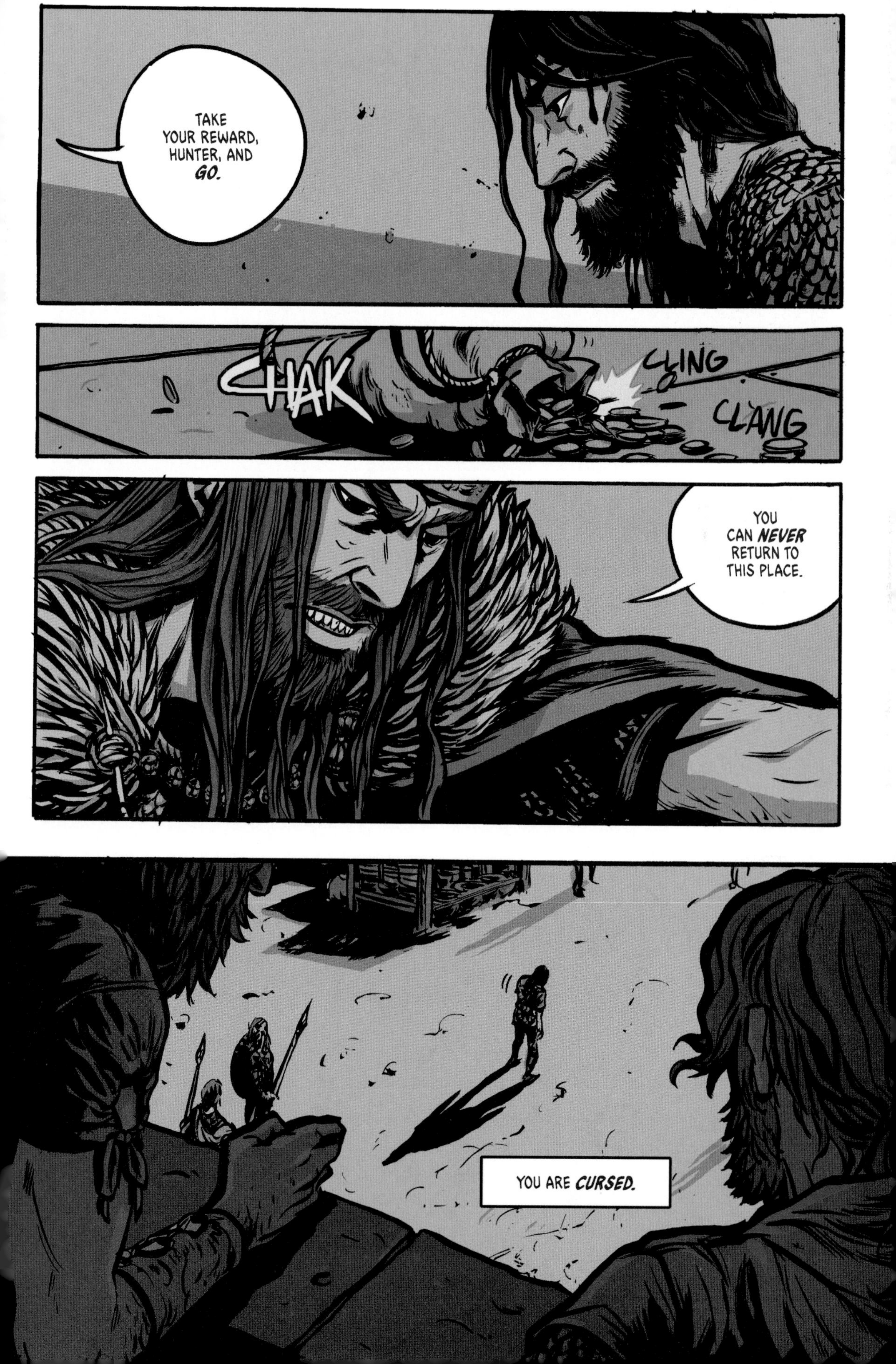
TAKE YOUR REWARD, HUNTER, AND GO.
CHAK
CLING
CLANG
YOU CAN NEVER RETURN TO THIS PLACE.
YOU ARE CURSED.

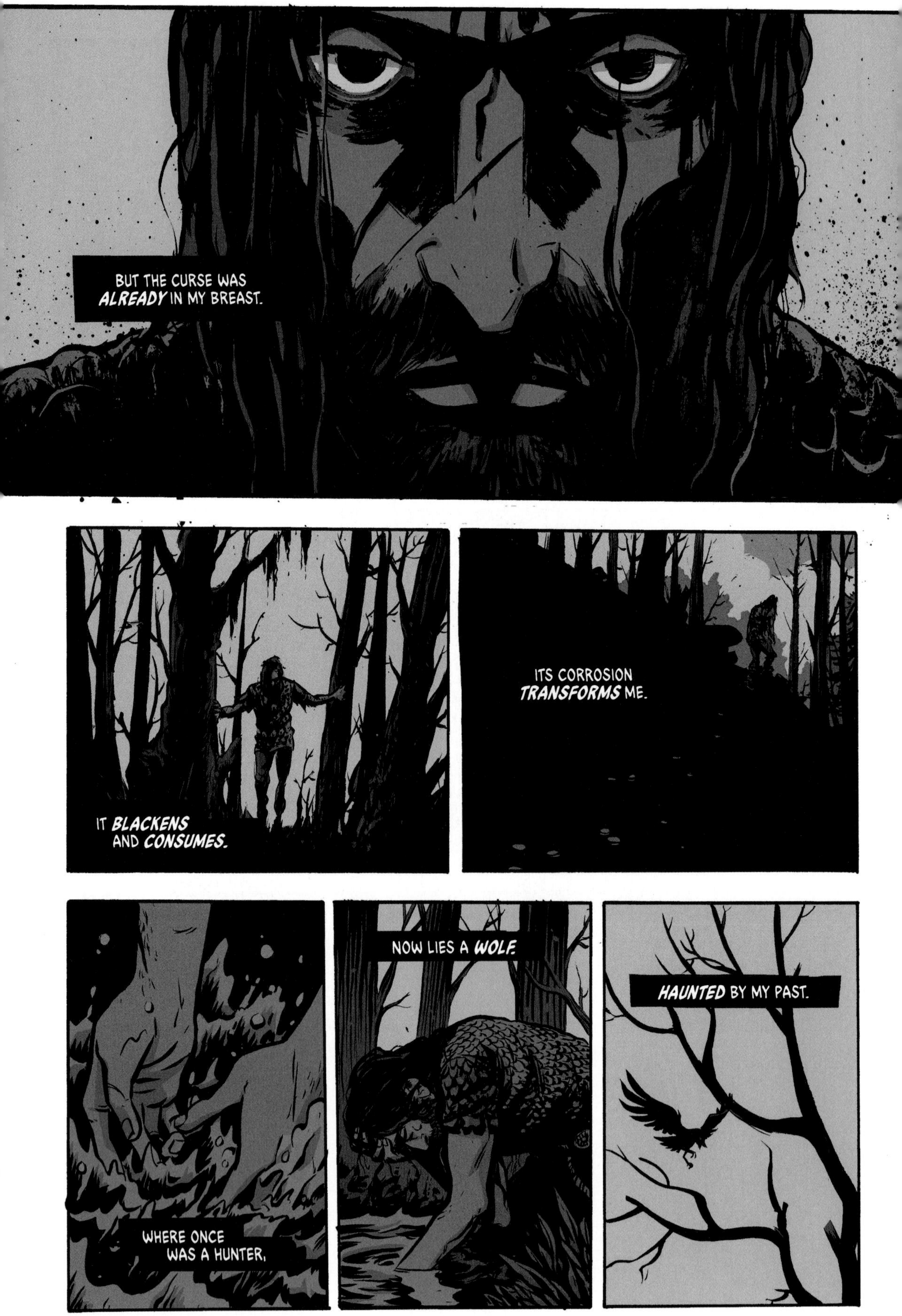
BUT THE CURSE WAS ALREADY IN MY BREAST.
IT BLACKENS AND CONSUMES.
ITS CORROSION TRANSFORMS ME.
WHERE ONCE WAS A HUNTER,
NOW LIES A WOLF.
HAUNTED BY MY PAST.

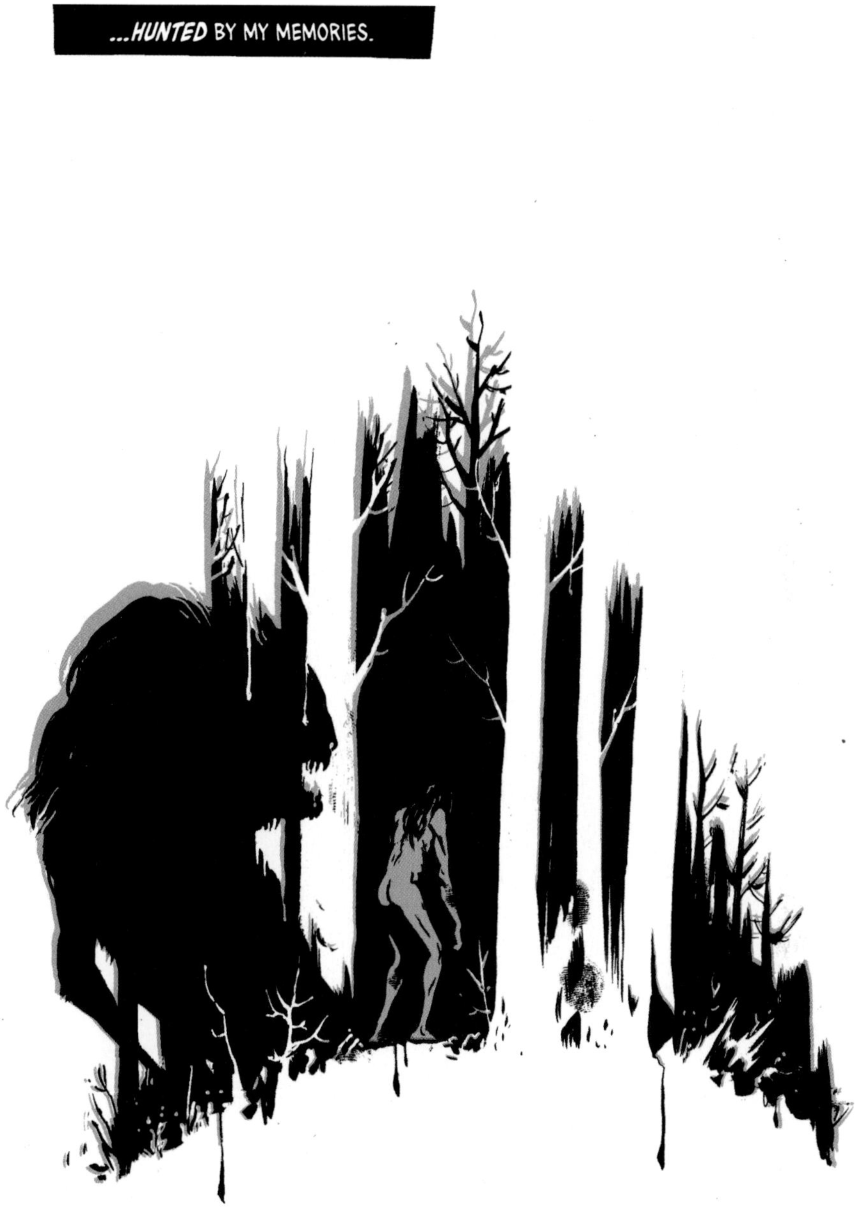
...HUNTED BY MY MEMORIES.

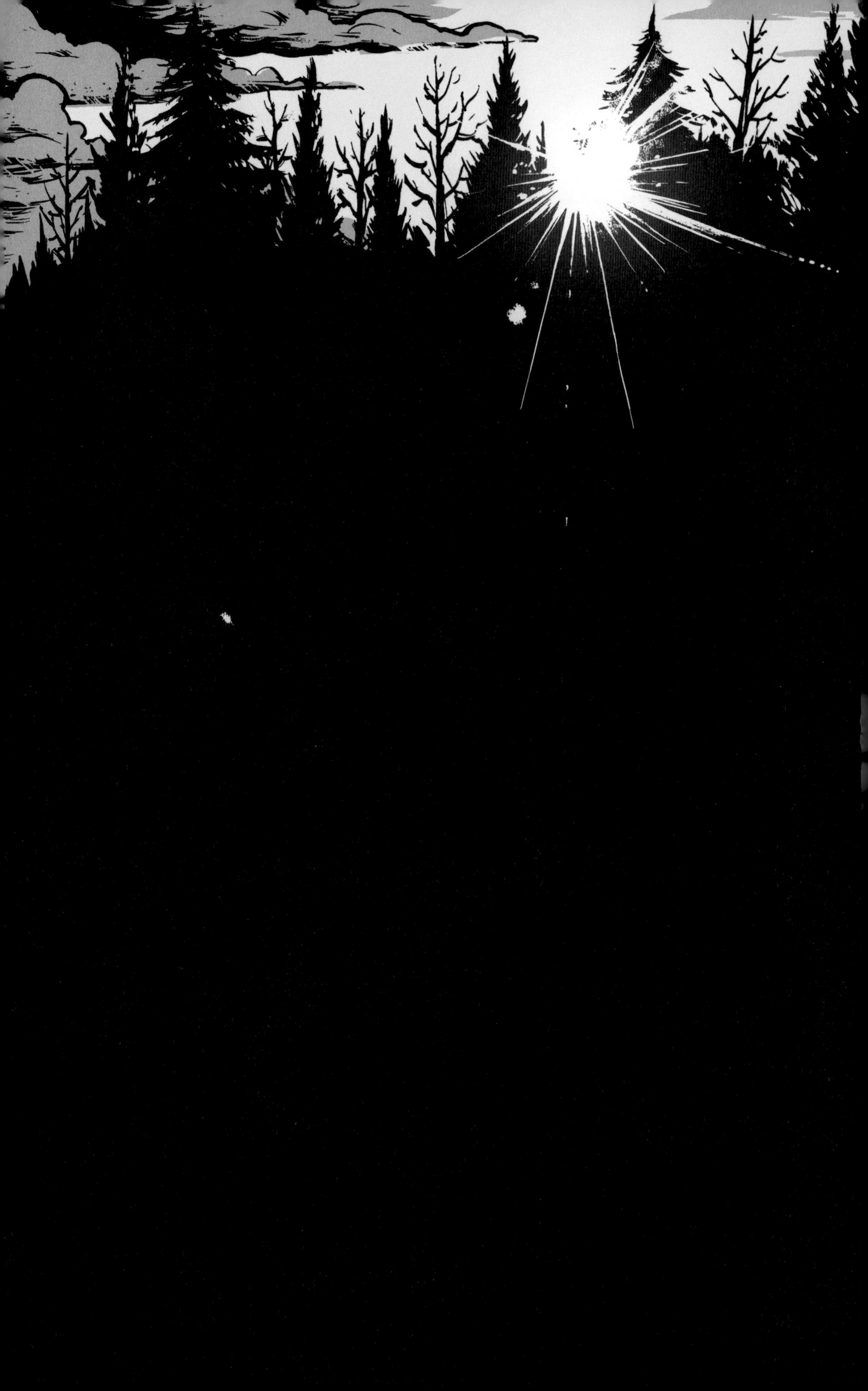

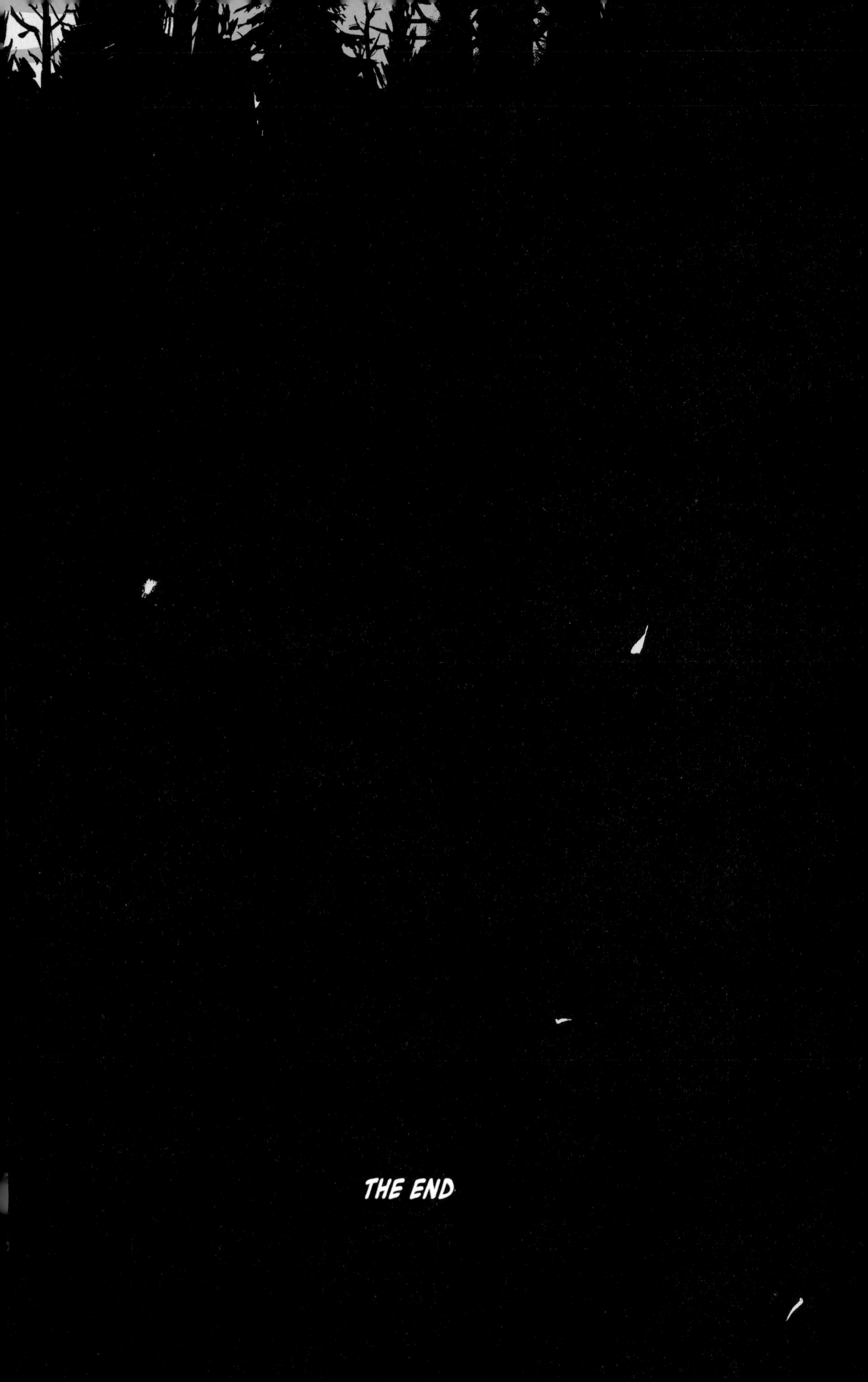
THE END

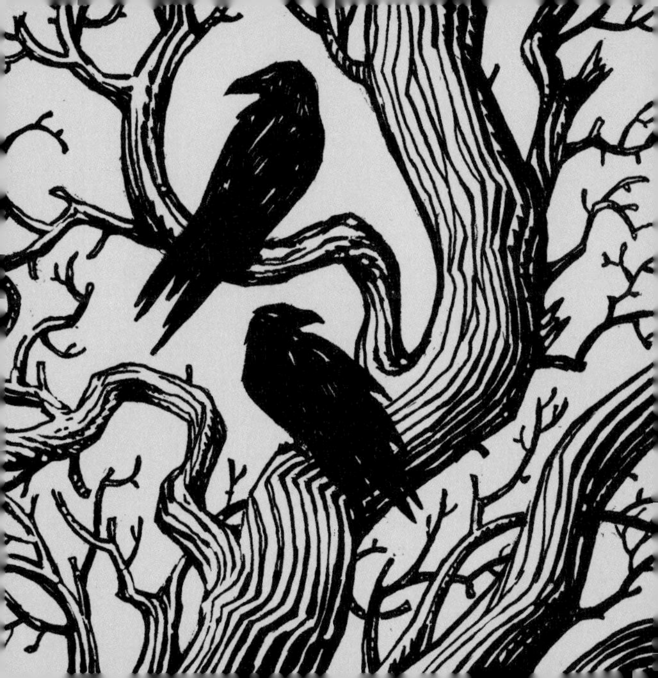

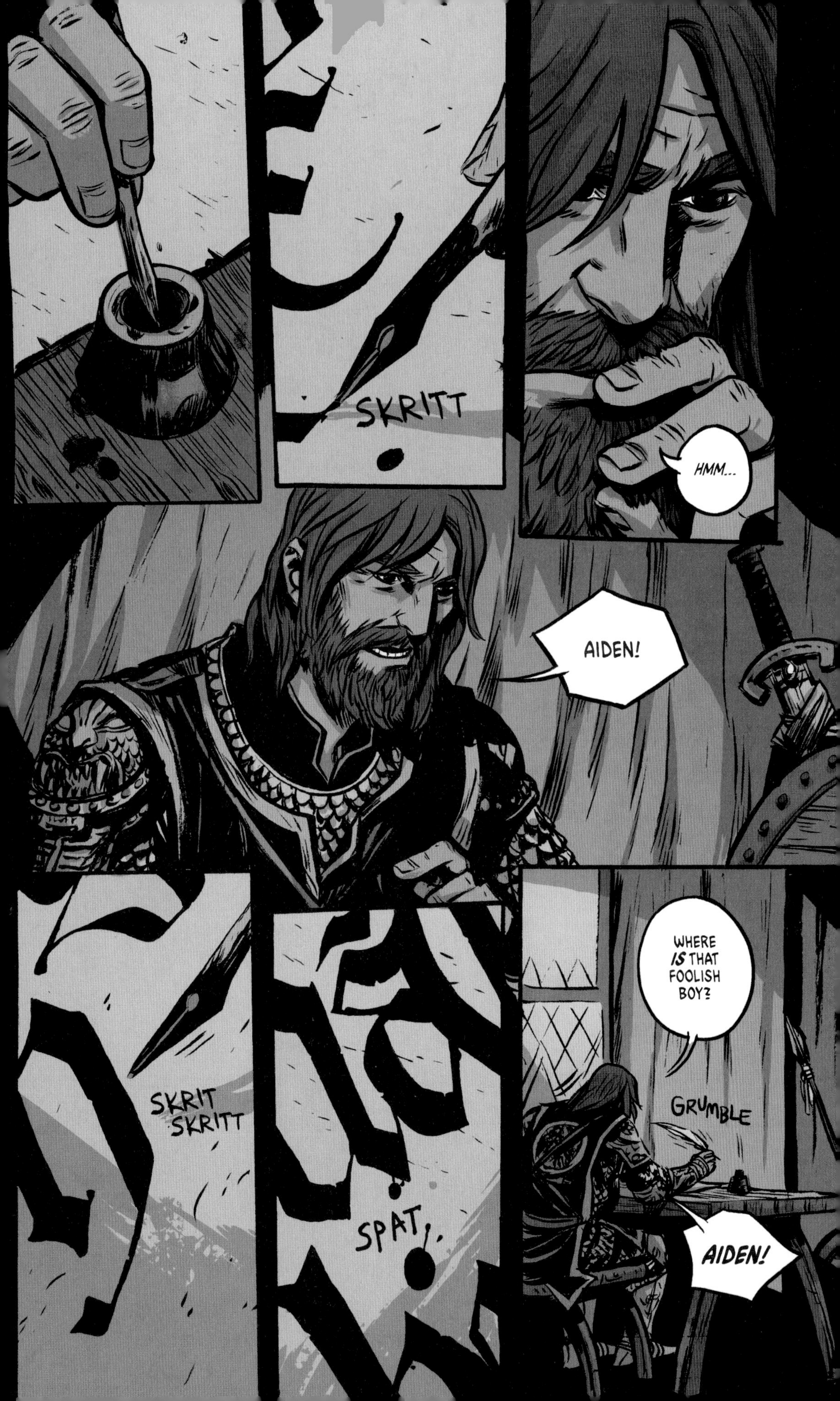
SKRITT
HMM...
AIDEN!
SKRIT SKRITT
SPAT
WHERE IS THAT FOOLISH BOY?
GRUMBLE
AIDEN!

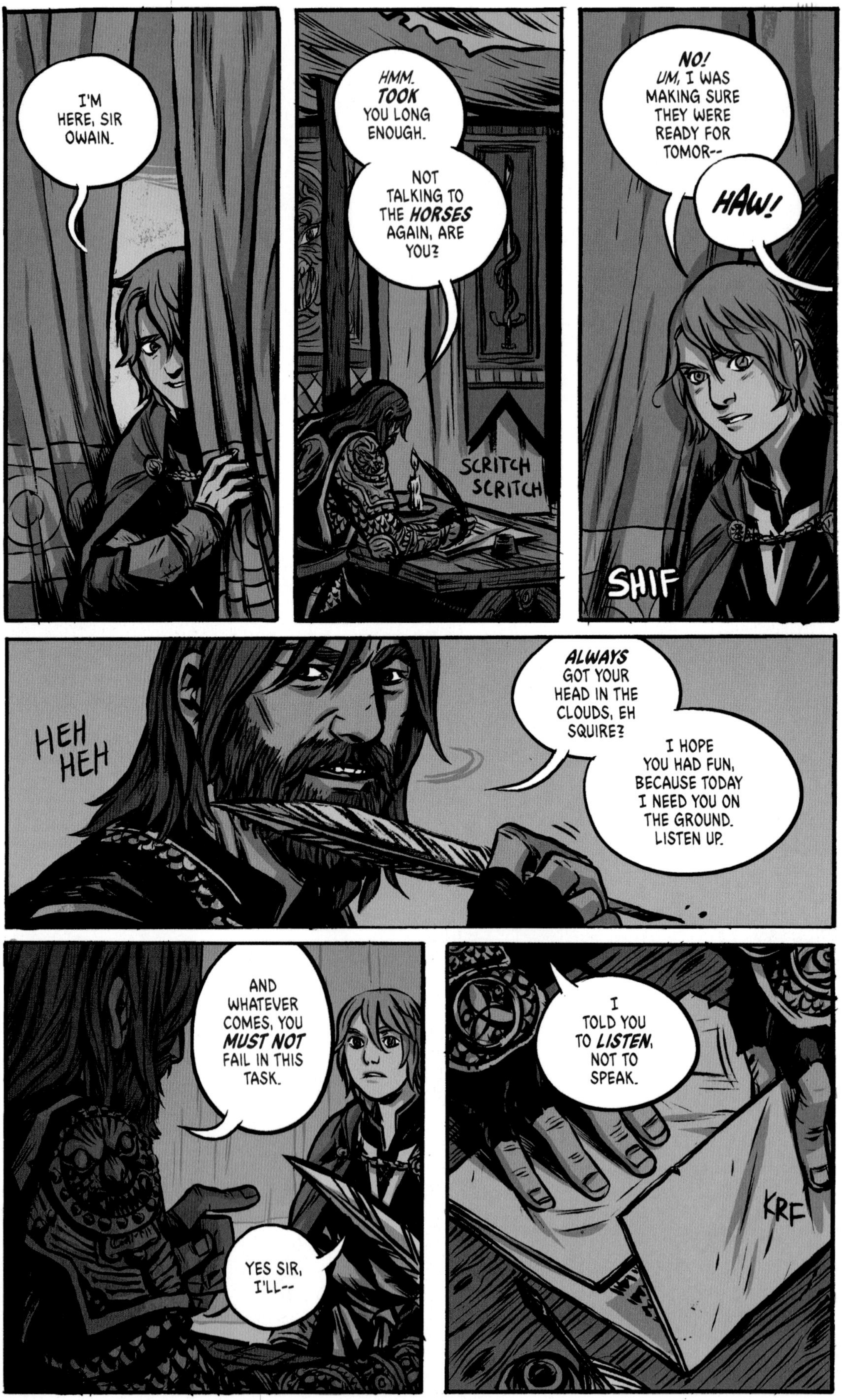
I'M HERE, SIR OWAIN.
HMM. TOOK YOU LONG ENOUGH.
NOT TALKING TO THE HORSES AGAIN, ARE YOU?
SCRITCH SCRITCH
NO! UM, I WAS MAKING SURE THEY WERE READY FOR TOMOR--
HAW!
SHIF
HEH HEH
ALWAYS GOT YOUR HEAD IN THE CLOUDS, EH SQUIRE?
I HOPE YOU HAD FUN, BECAUSE TODAY I NEED YOU ON THE GROUND. LISTEN UP.
AND WHATEVER COMES, YOU MUST NOT FAIL IN THIS TASK.
YES SIR, I'LL--
I TOLD YOU TO LISTEN, NOT TO SPEAK.
KRF

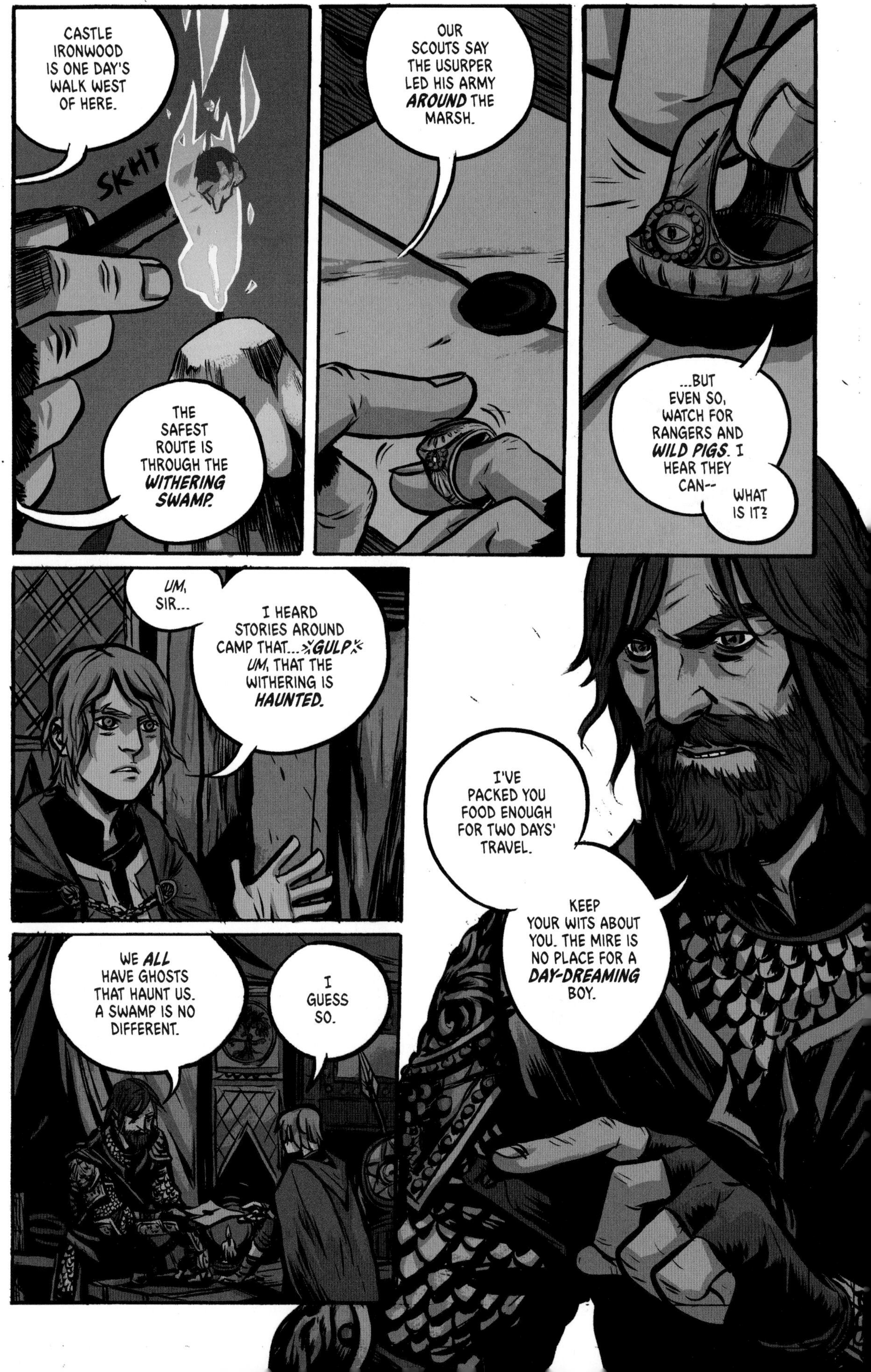
CASTLE IRONWOOD IS ONE DAY'S WALK WEST OF HERE.
SKHT
THE SAFEST ROUTE IS THROUGH THE WITHERING SWAMP.
OUR SCOUTS SAY THE USURPER LED HIS ARMY AROUND THE MARSH.
...BUT EVEN SO, WATCH FOR RANGERS AND WILD PIGS. I HEAR THEY CAN--
WHAT IS IT?
UM, SIR...
I HEARD STORIES AROUND CAMP THAT... *GULP* UM, THAT THE WITHERING IS HAUNTED.
WE ALL HAVE GHOSTS THAT HAUNT US. A SWAMP IS NO DIFFERENT.
I GUESS SO.
I'VE PACKED YOU FOOD ENOUGH FOR TWO DAYS' TRAVEL.
KEEP YOUR WITS ABOUT YOU. THE MIRE IS NO PLACE FOR A DAY-DREAMING BOY.

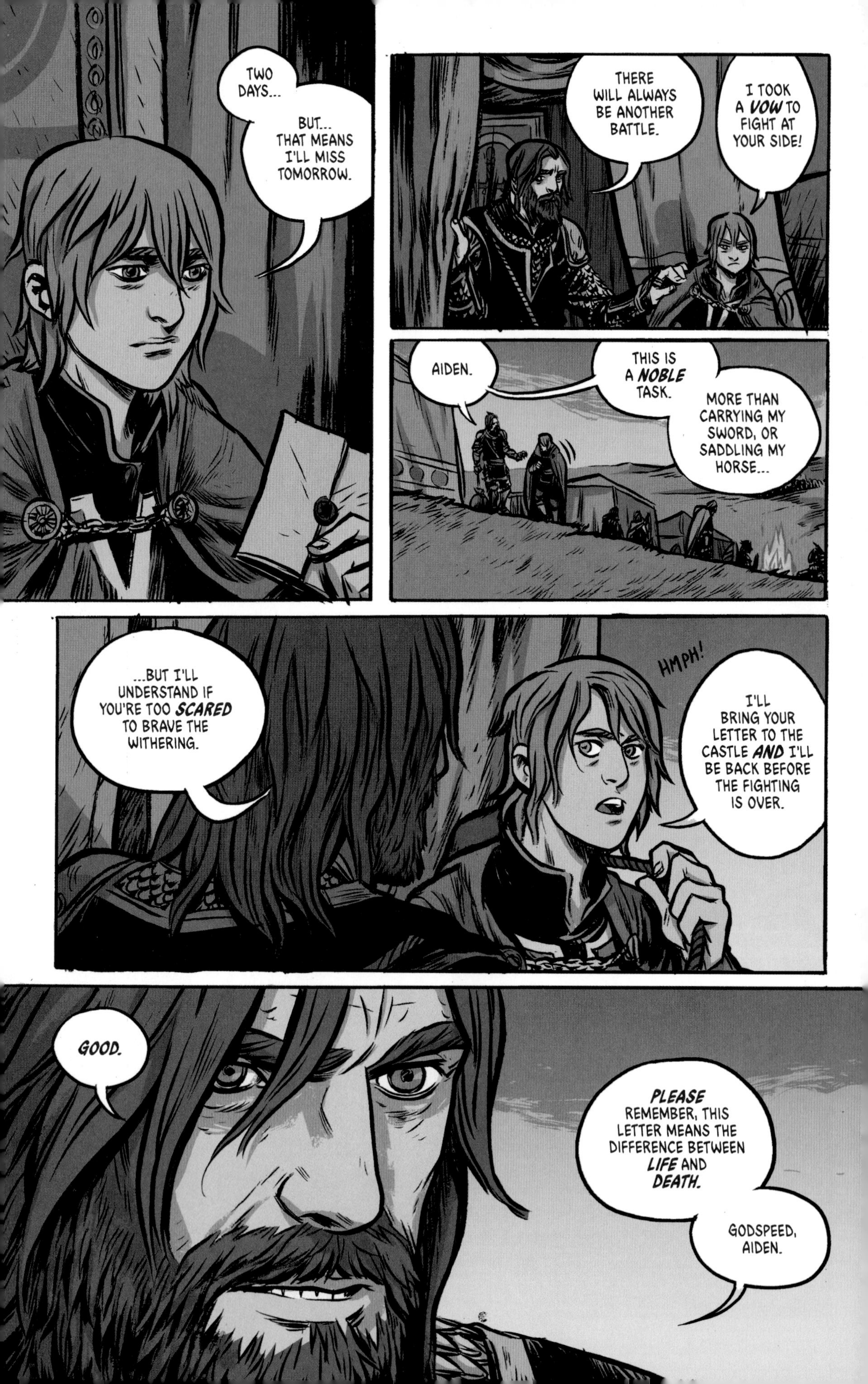
TWO DAYS...
BUT... THAT MEANS I'LL MISS TOMORROW.
THERE WILL ALWAYS BE ANOTHER BATTLE.
I TOOK A VOW TO FIGHT AT YOUR SIDE!
AIDEN.
THIS IS A NOBLE TASK.
MORE THAN CARRYING MY SWORD, OR SADDLING MY HORSE...
...BUT I'LL UNDERSTAND IF YOU'RE TOO SCARED TO BRAVE THE WITHERING.
HMPH!
I'LL BRING YOUR LETTER TO THE CASTLE AND I'LL BE BACK BEFORE THE FIGHTING IS OVER.
GOOD.
PLEASE REMEMBER, THIS LETTER MEANS THE DIFFERENCE BETWEEN LIFE AND DEATH.
GODSPEED, AIDEN.

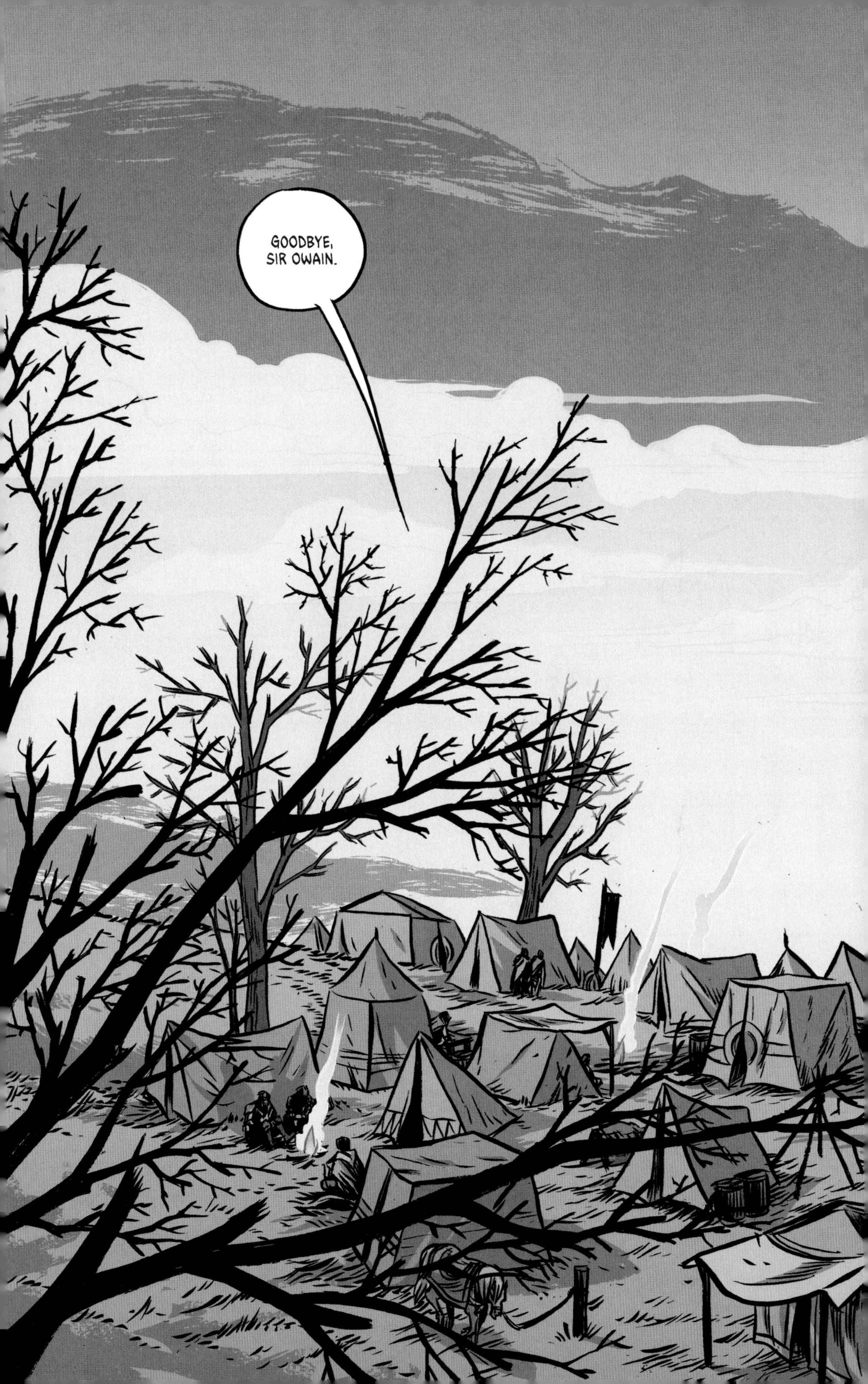
GOODBYE, SIR OWAIN.

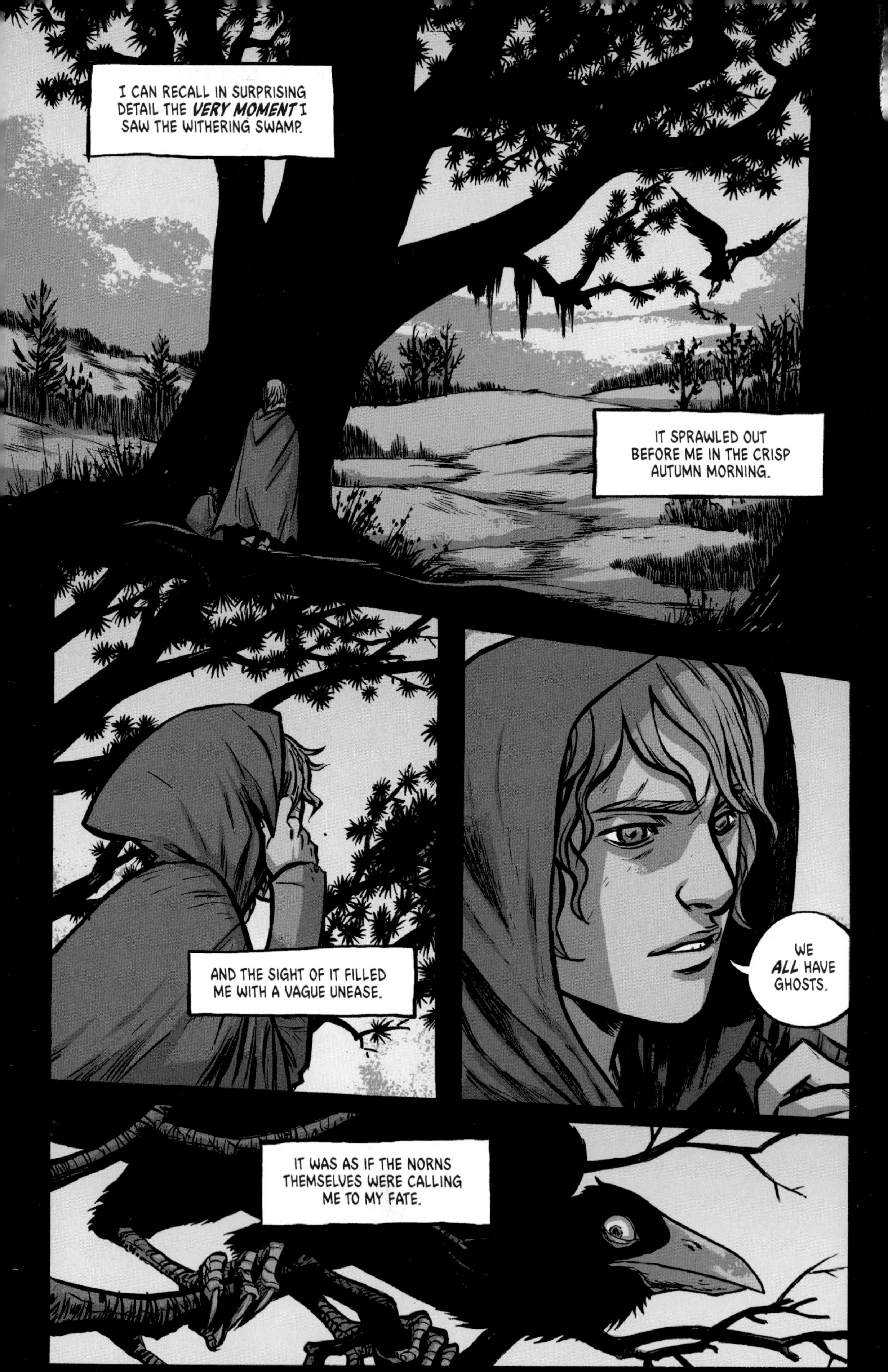
I CAN RECALL IN SURPRISING DETAIL THE VERY MOMENT I SAW THE WITHERING SWAMP.
IT SPRAWLED OUT BEFORE ME IN THE CRISP AUTUMN MORNING.
AND THE SIGHT OF IT FILLED ME WITH A VAGUE UNEASE.
WE ALL HAVE GHOSTS.
IT WAS AS IF THE NORNS THEMSELVES WERE CALLING ME TO MY FATE.

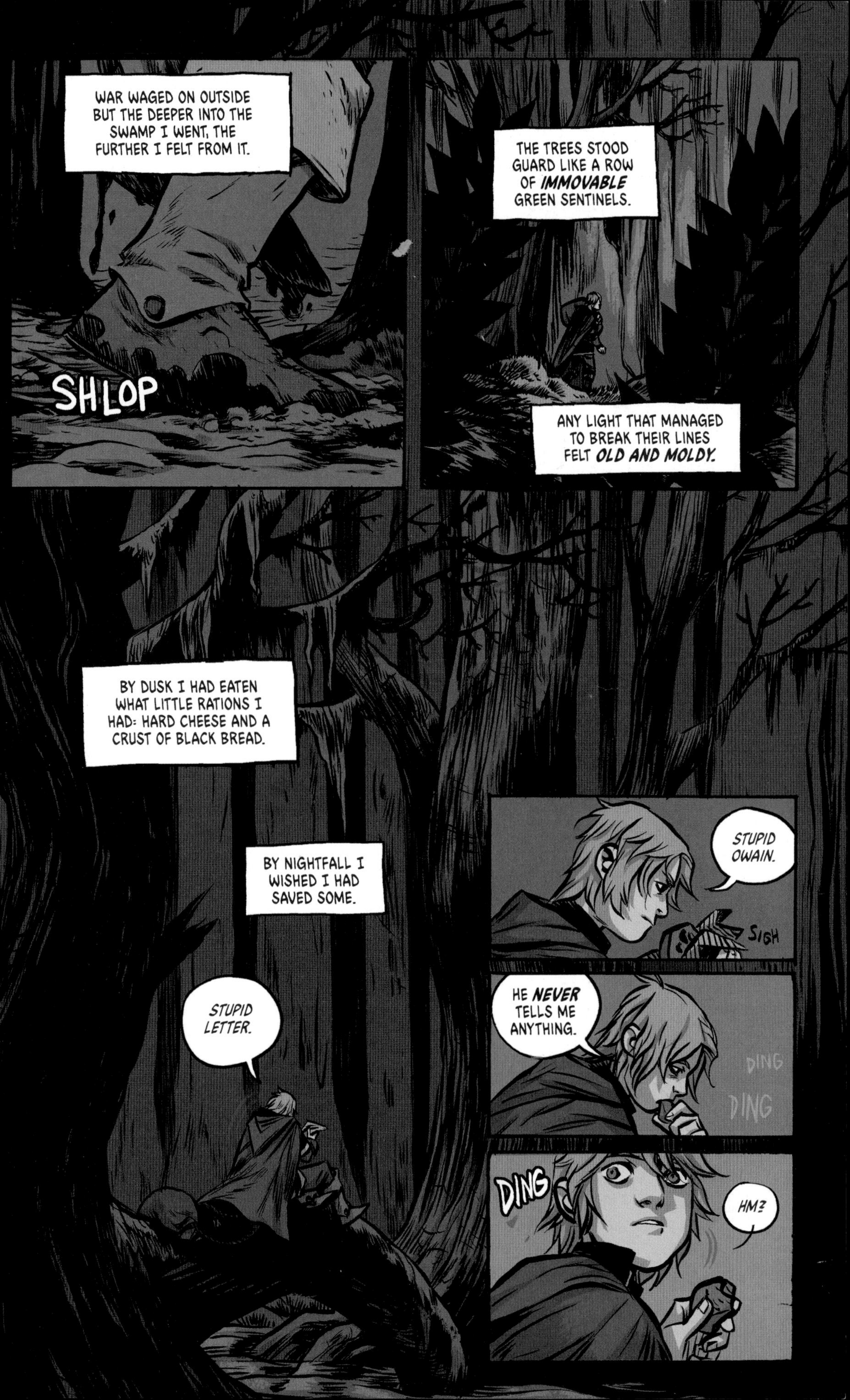
WAR WAGED ON OUTSIDE BUT THE DEEPER INTO THE SWAMP I WENT, THE FURTHER I FELT FROM IT.
SHLOP
THE TREES STOOD GUARD LIKE A ROW OF IMMOVABLE GREEN SENTINELS.
ANY LIGHT THAT MANAGED TO BREAK THEIR LINES FELT OLD AND MOLDY.
BY DUSK I HAD EATEN WHAT LITTLE RATIONS I HAD: HARD CHEESE AND A CRUST OF BLACK BREAD.
BY NIGHTFALL I WISHED I HAD SAVED SOME.
STUPID LETTER.
STUPID OWAIN.
SIGH
HE NEVER TELLS ME ANYTHING.
DING
DING
DING
HM?

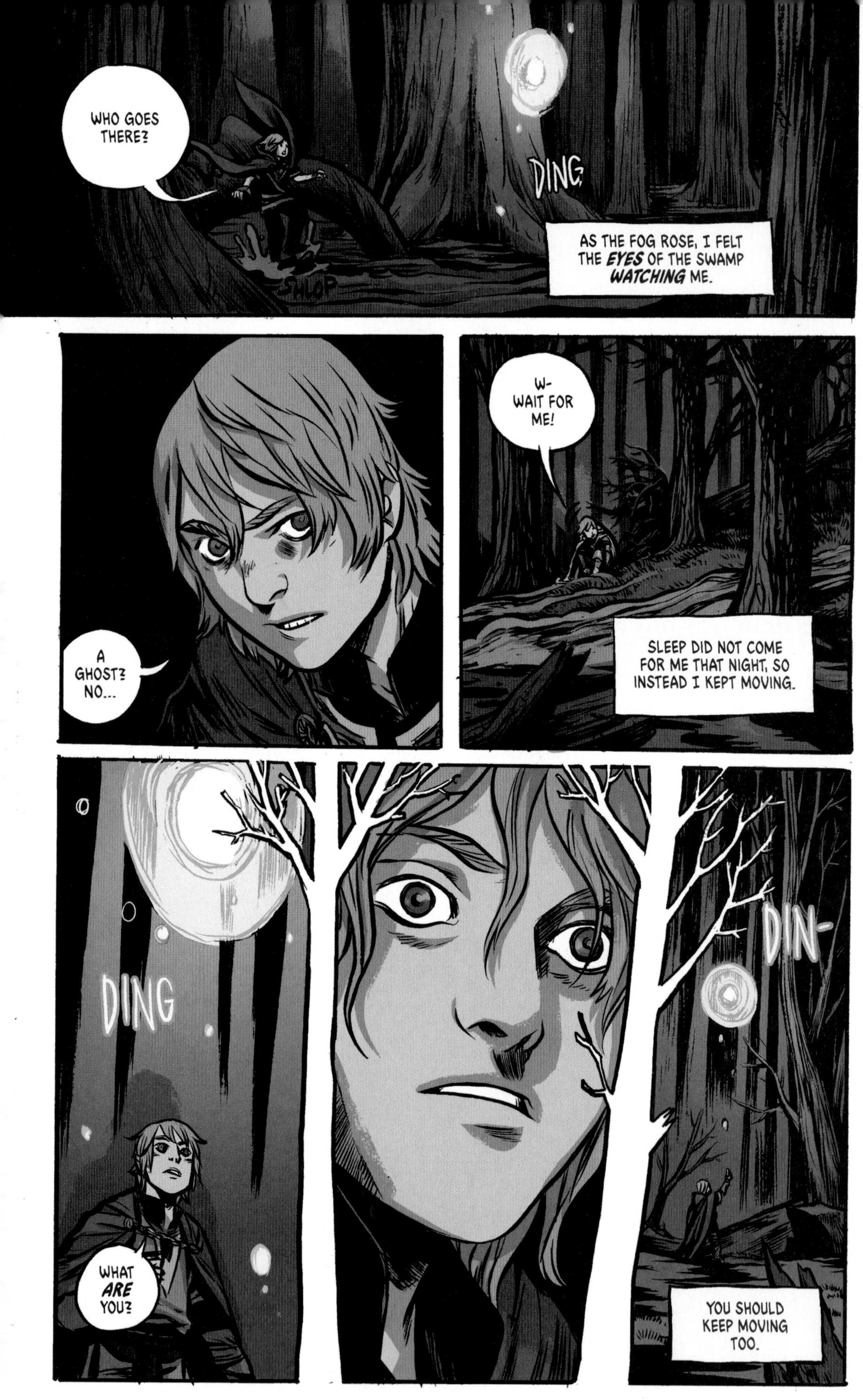
WHO GOES THERE?
DING
AS THE FOG ROSE, I FELT THE *EYES* OF THE SWAMP *WATCHING* ME.
SHLOP
A GHOST? NO...
W- WAIT FOR ME!
SLEEP DID NOT COME FOR ME THAT NIGHT, SO INSTEAD I KEPT MOVING.
DING
WHAT *ARE* YOU?
DIN-
YOU SHOULD KEEP MOVING TOO.

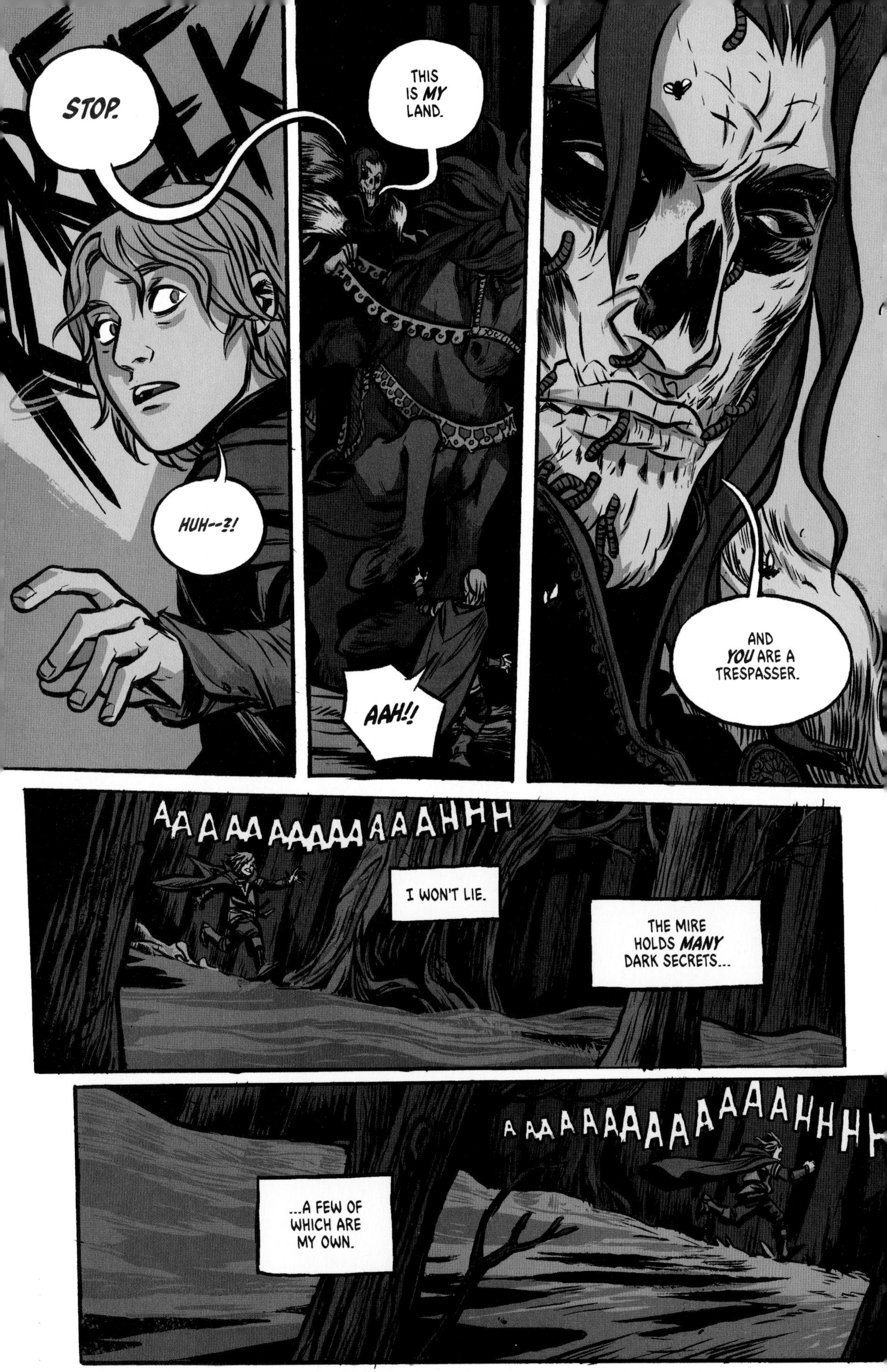
STOP.
HUH--?!
THIS IS MY LAND.
AAH!!
AND YOU ARE A TRESPASSER.
AAAAAAAAAAAAAHHHH
I WON'T LIE.
THE MIRE HOLDS MANY DARK SECRETS...
AAAAAAAAAAAAAAAHHHH
...A FEW OF WHICH ARE MY OWN.

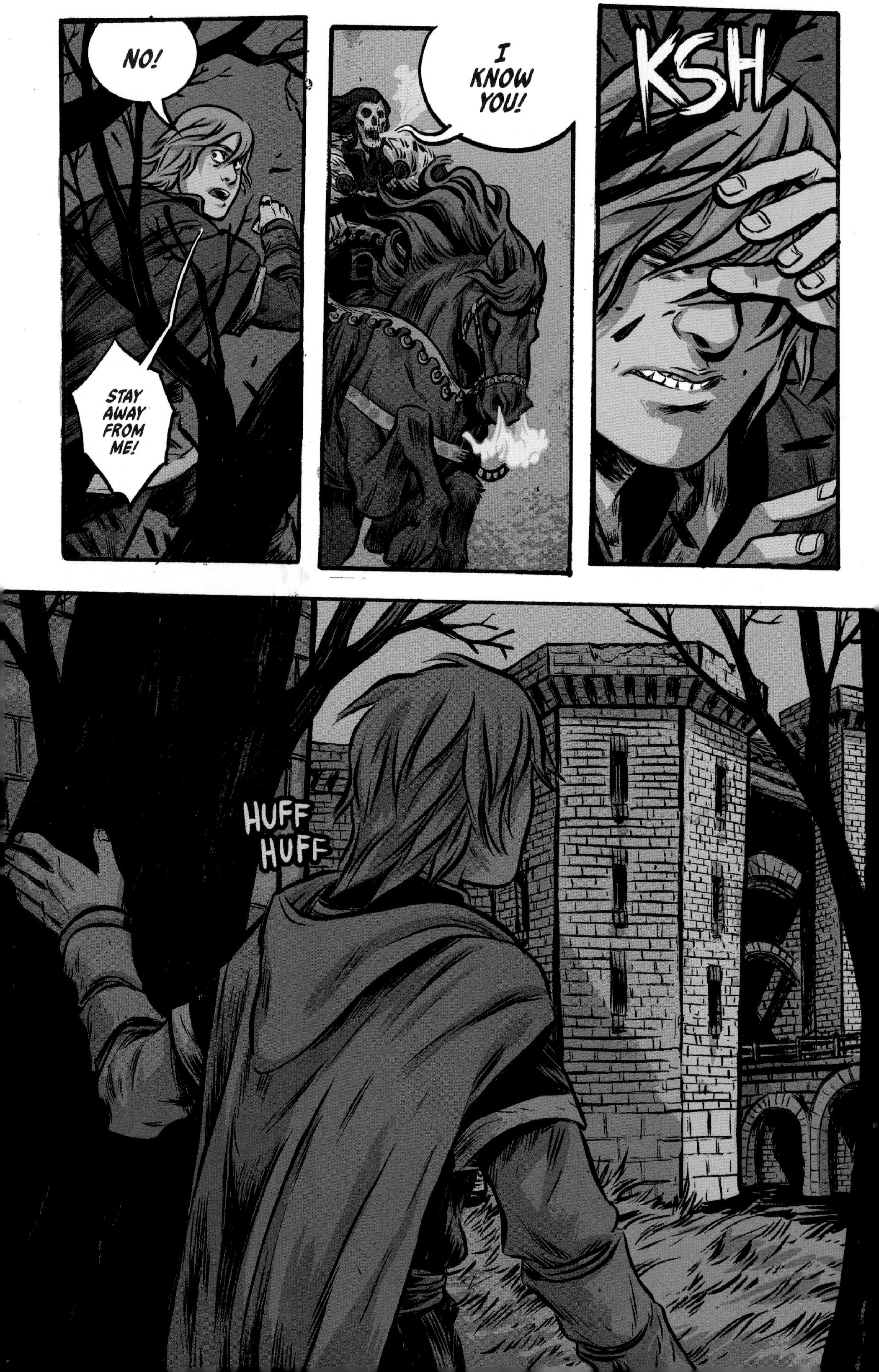
NO!
STAY AWAY FROM ME!
I KNOW YOU!
KSH
HUFF HUFF

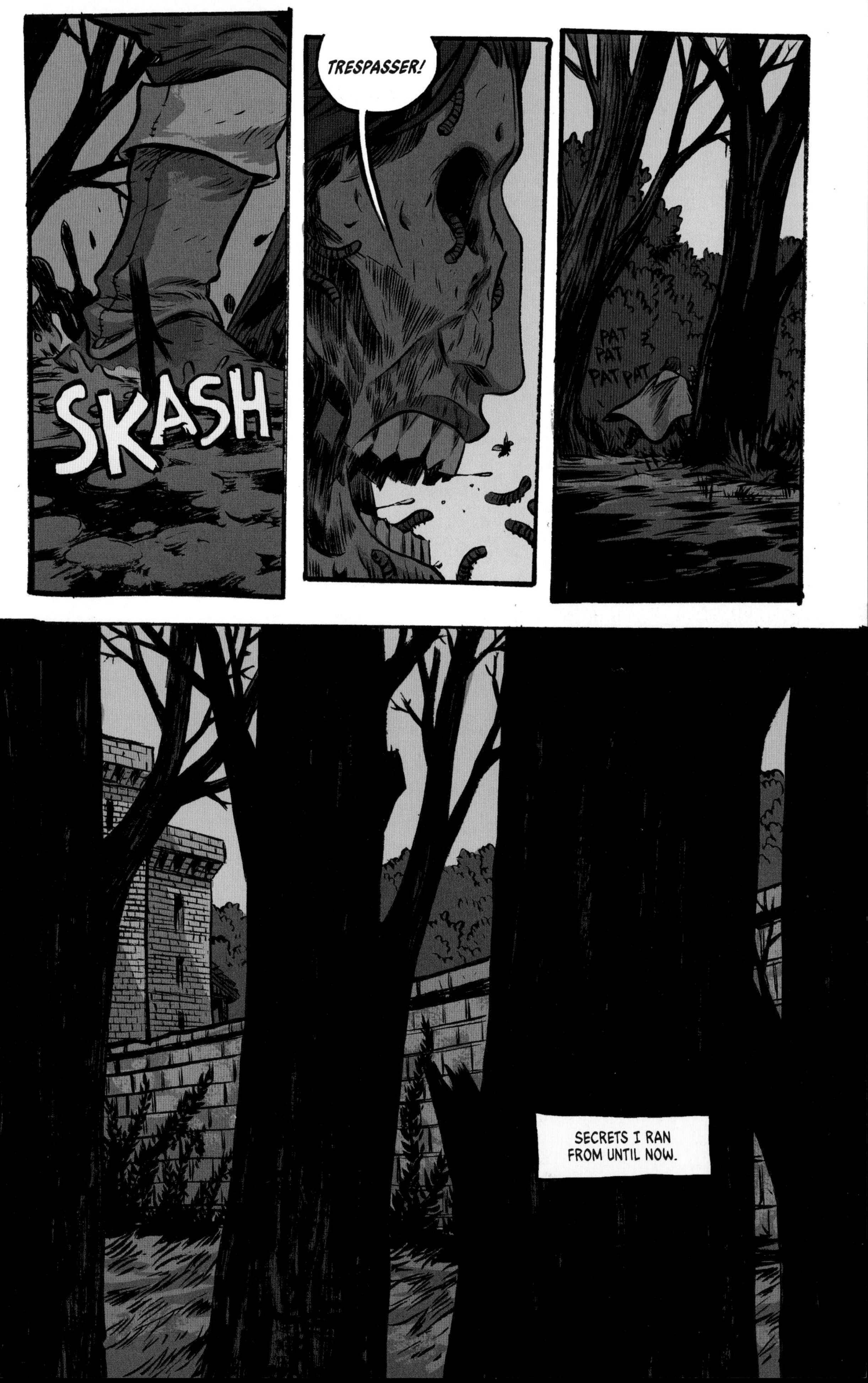
SKASH
TRESPASSER!
PAT PAT PAT PAT
SECRETS I RAN FROM UNTIL NOW.

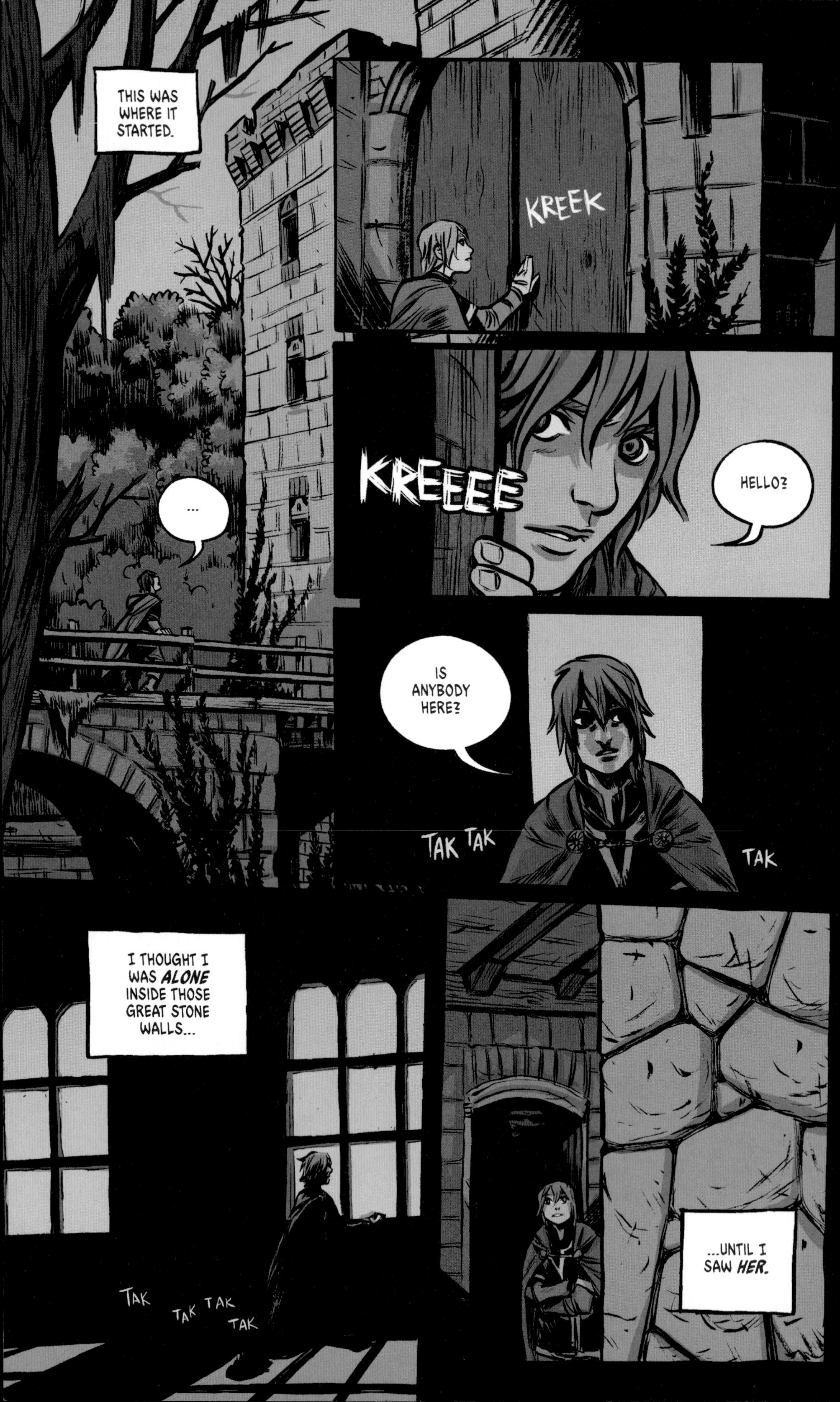
THIS WAS WHERE IT STARTED.
KREEK
KREEEEE
...
HELLO?
IS ANYBODY HERE?
TAK TAK
TAK
I THOUGHT I WAS *ALONE* INSIDE THOSE GREAT STONE WALLS...
TAK
TAK TAK
TAK
...UNTIL I SAW *HER*.

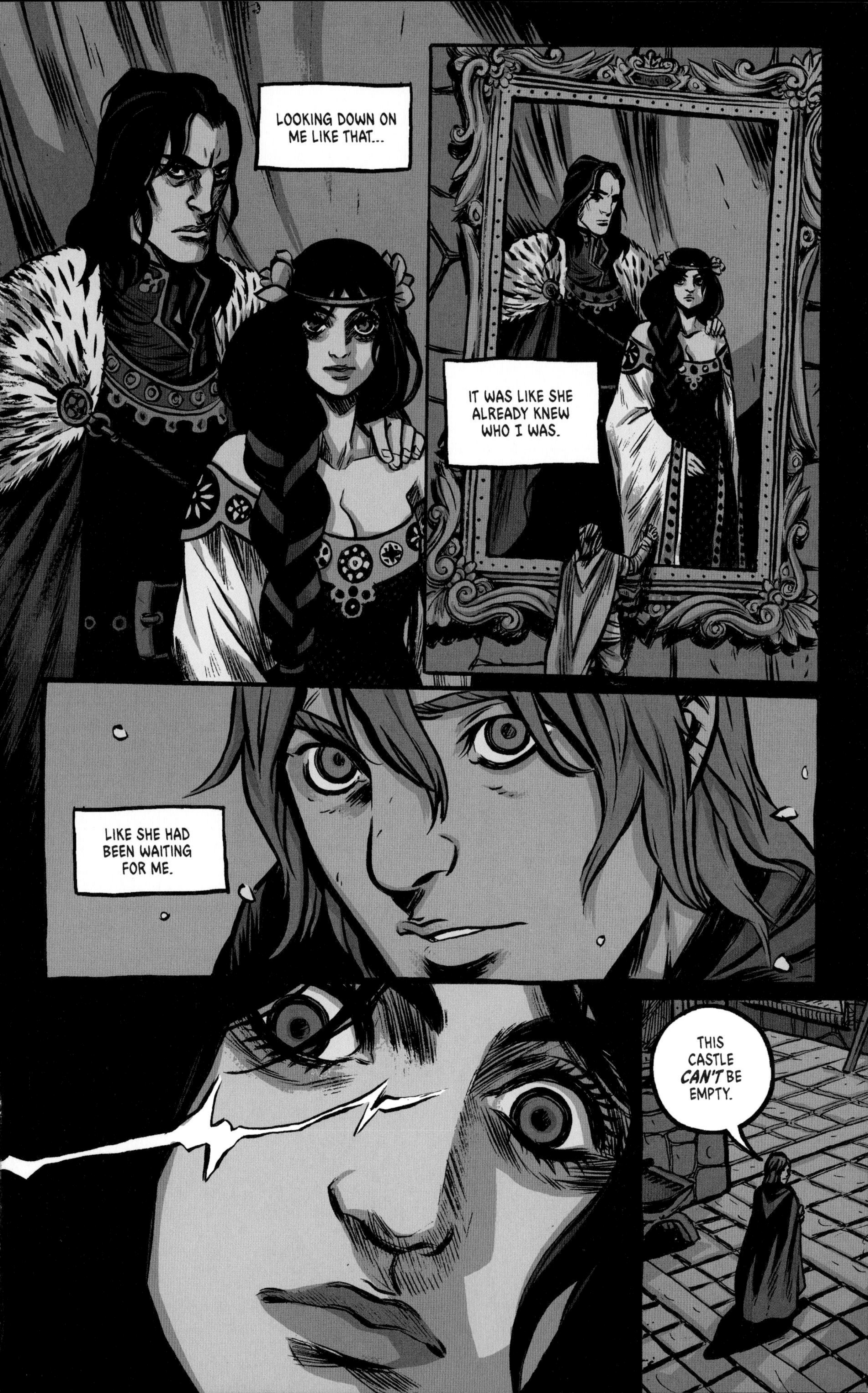
LOOKING DOWN ON ME LIKE THAT...
IT WAS LIKE SHE ALREADY KNEW WHO I WAS.
LIKE SHE HAD BEEN WAITING FOR ME.
THIS CASTLE *CAN'T* BE EMPTY.

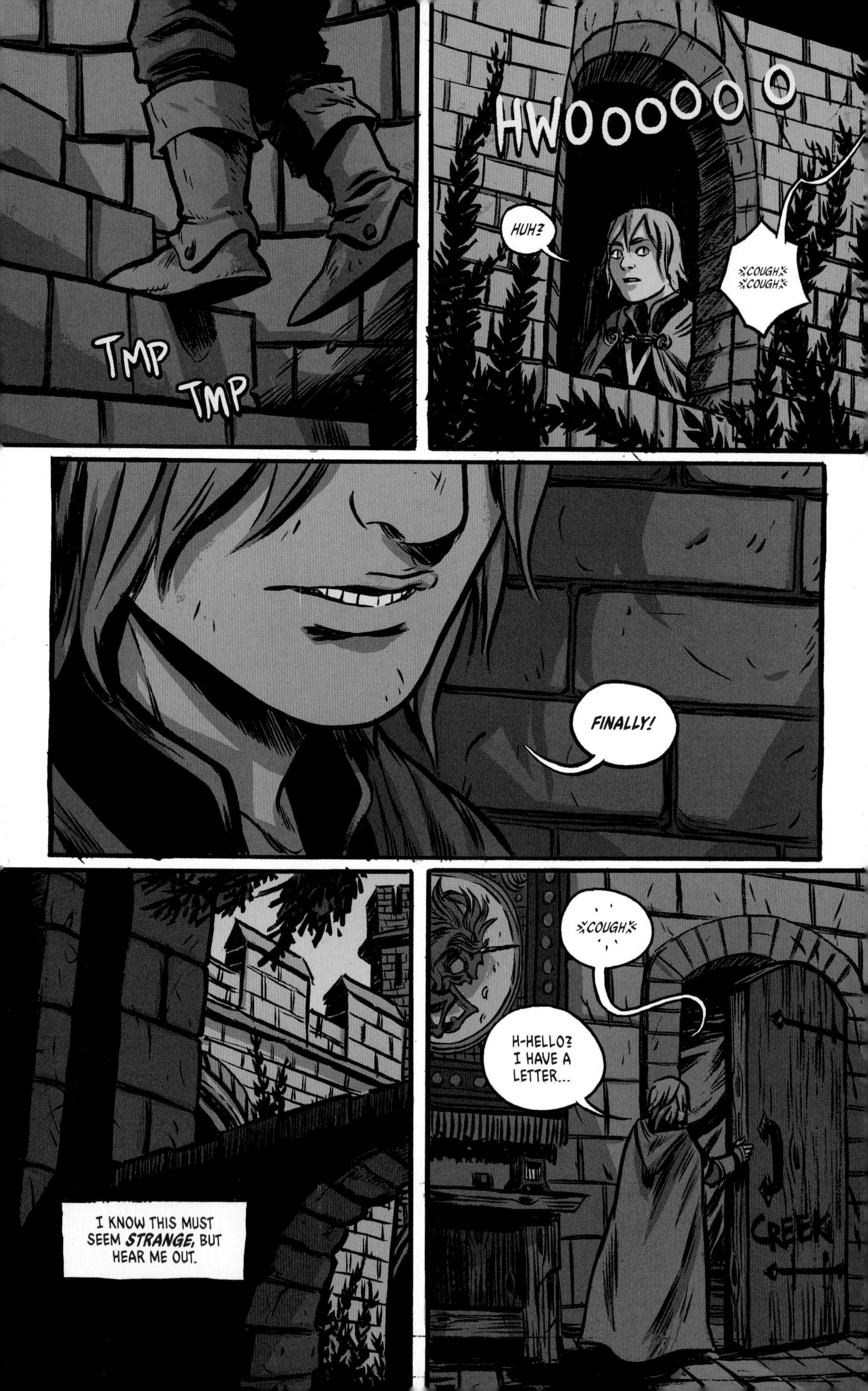
TMP
TMP
HWOOOOOO
HUH?
COUGH COUGH
FINALLY!
I KNOW THIS MUST SEEM STRANGE, BUT HEAR ME OUT.
COUGH
H-HELLO? I HAVE A LETTER...
CREEK

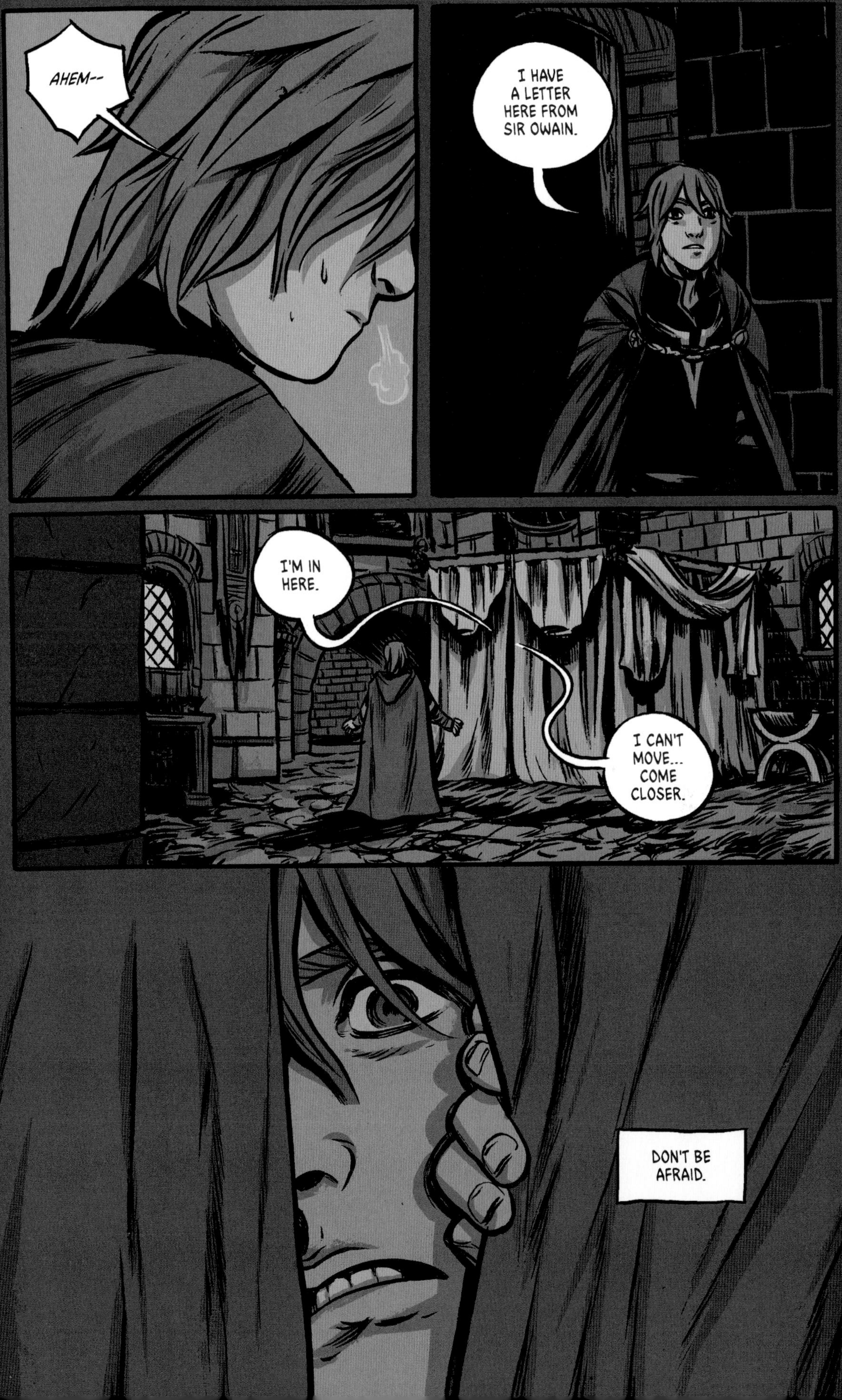
AHEM--
I HAVE A LETTER HERE FROM SIR OWAIN.
I'M IN HERE.
I CAN'T MOVE... COME CLOSER.
DON'T BE AFRAID.

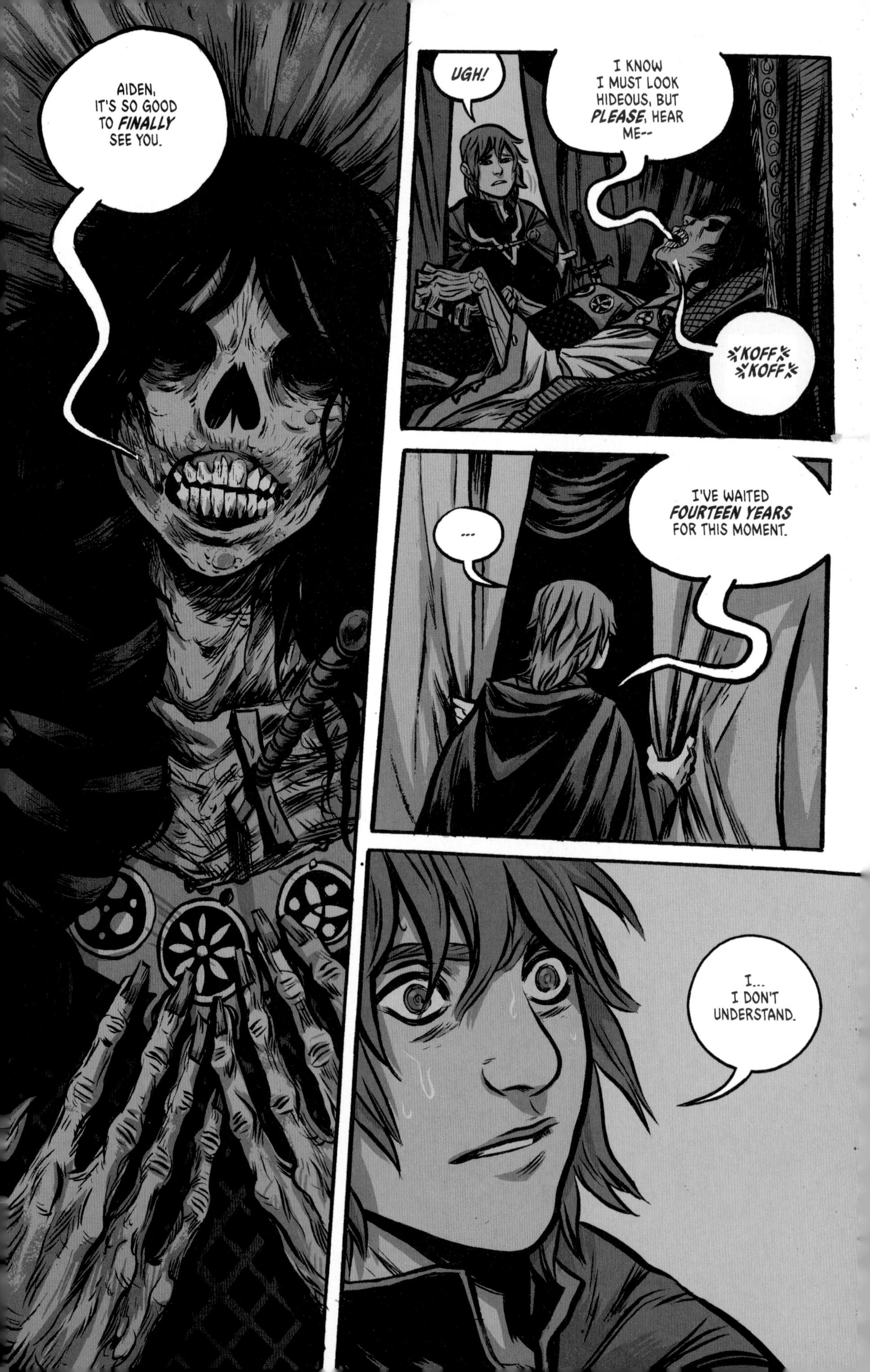
AIDEN, IT'S SO GOOD TO *FINALLY* SEE YOU.
*UGH!*
I KNOW I MUST LOOK HIDEOUS, BUT *PLEASE*, HEAR ME--
KOFF KOFF
...
I'VE WAITED *FOURTEEN YEARS* FOR THIS MOMENT.
I... I DON'T UNDERSTAND.

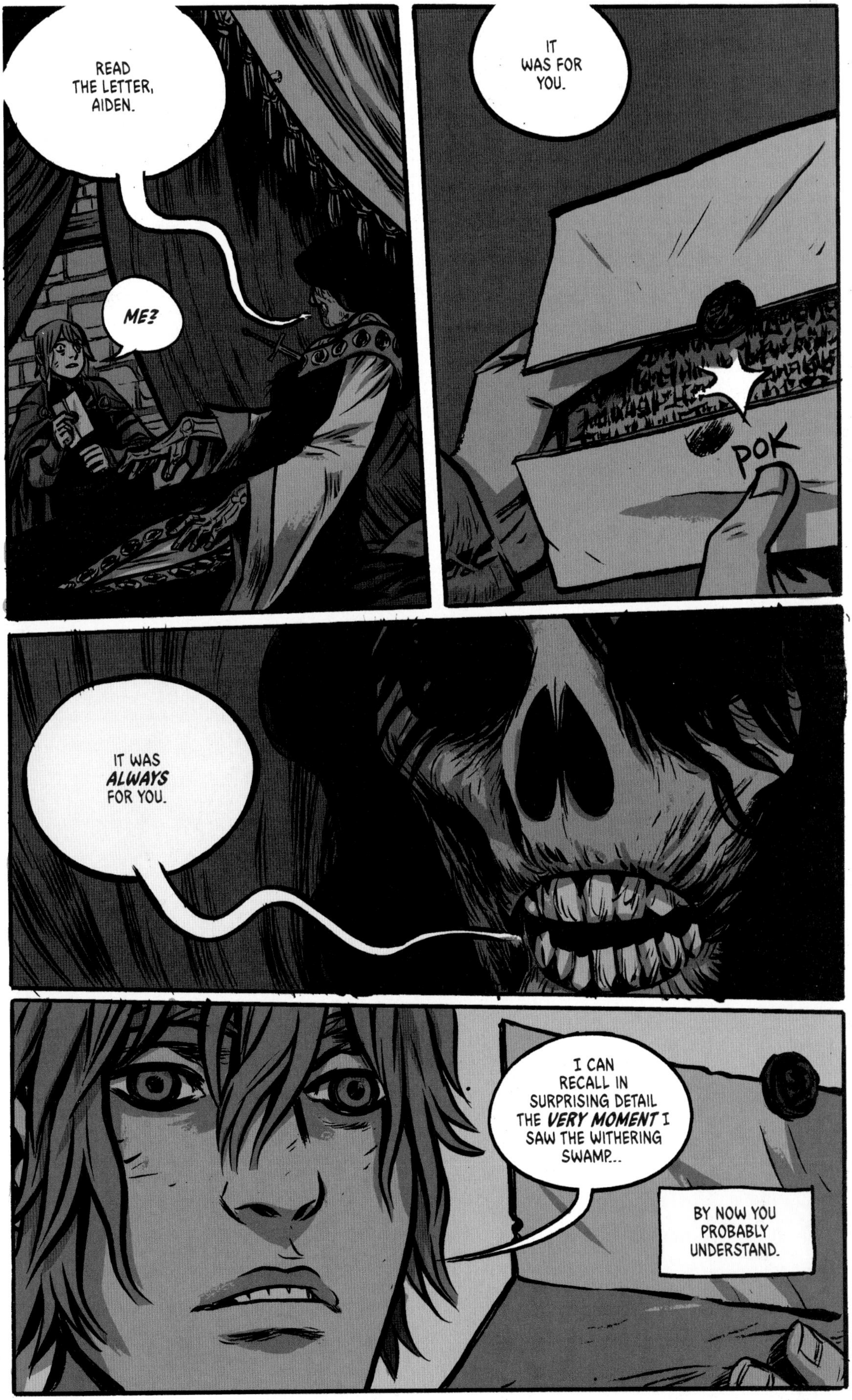
READ THE LETTER, AIDEN.
ME?
IT WAS FOR YOU.
POK
IT WAS ALWAYS FOR YOU.
I CAN RECALL IN SURPRISING DETAIL THE VERY MOMENT I SAW THE WITHERING SWAMP...
BY NOW YOU PROBABLY UNDERSTAND.

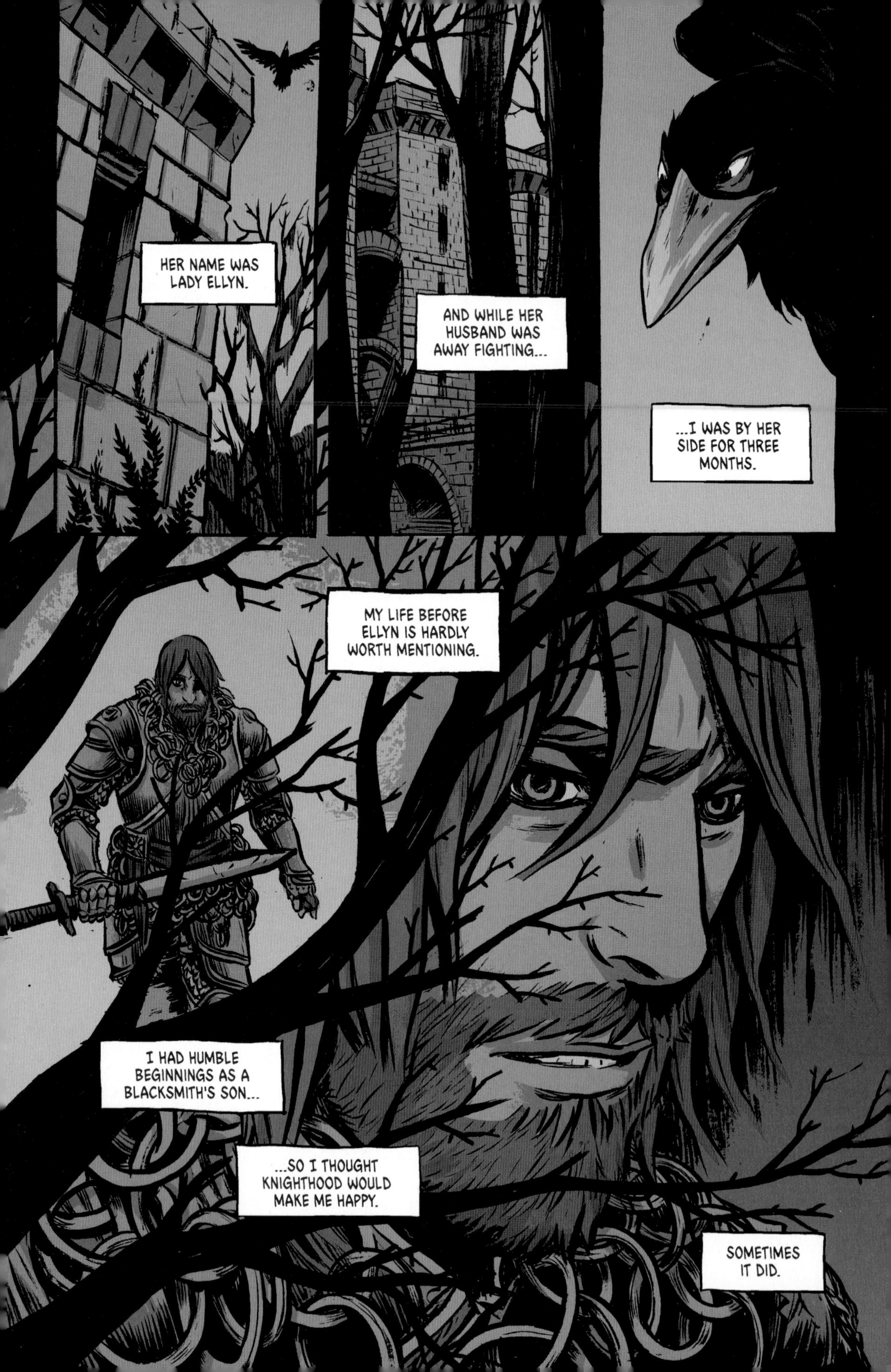

HER NAME WAS LADY ELLYN.
AND WHILE HER HUSBAND WAS AWAY FIGHTING...
...I WAS BY HER SIDE FOR THREE MONTHS.
MY LIFE BEFORE ELLYN IS HARDLY WORTH MENTIONING.
I HAD HUMBLE BEGINNINGS AS A BLACKSMITH'S SON...
...SO I THOUGHT KNIGHTHOOD WOULD MAKE ME HAPPY.
SOMETIMES IT DID.

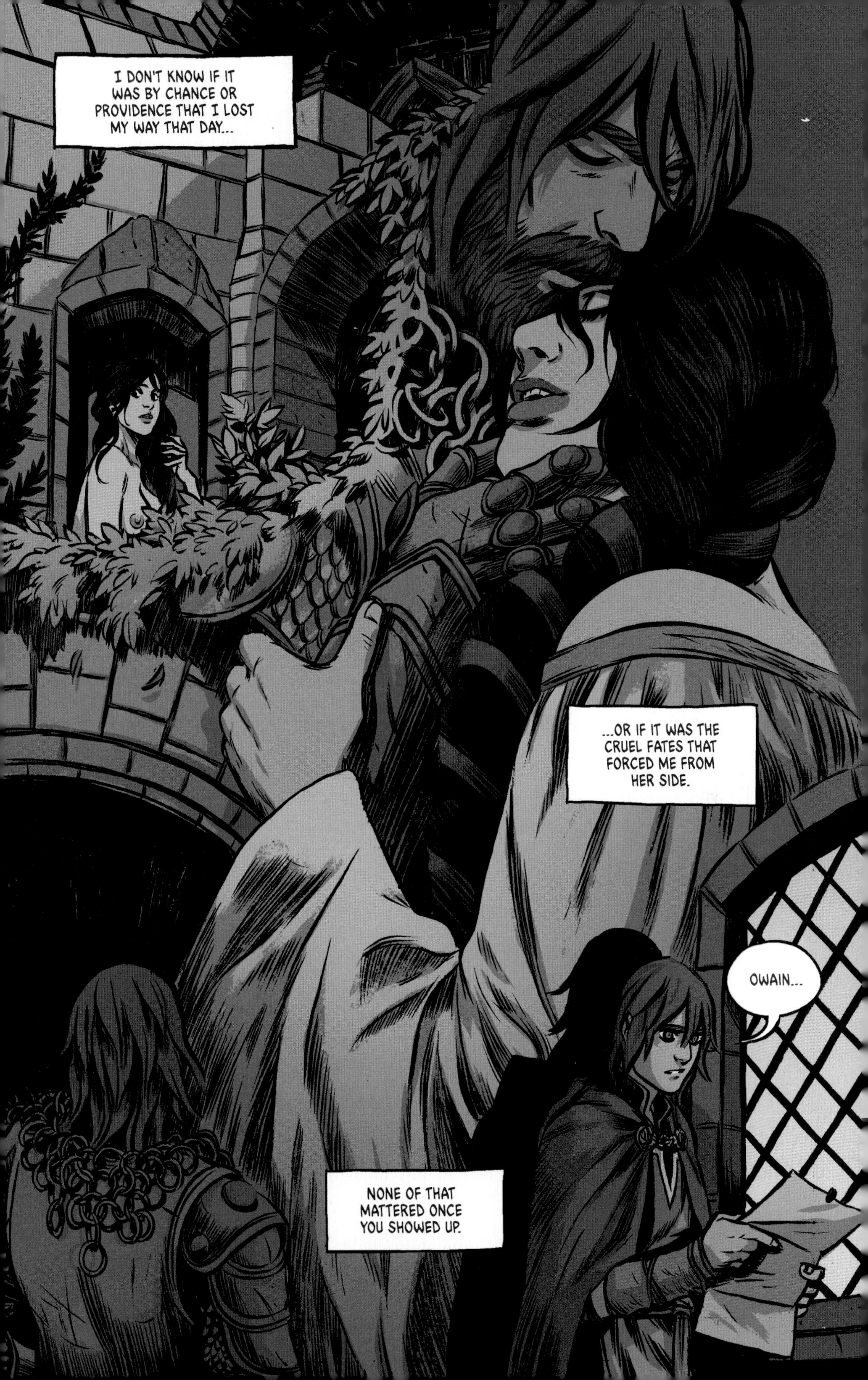
I DON'T KNOW IF IT WAS BY CHANCE OR PROVIDENCE THAT I LOST MY WAY THAT DAY...
...OR IF IT WAS THE CRUEL FATES THAT FORCED ME FROM HER SIDE.
OWAIN...
NONE OF THAT MATTERED ONCE YOU SHOWED UP.

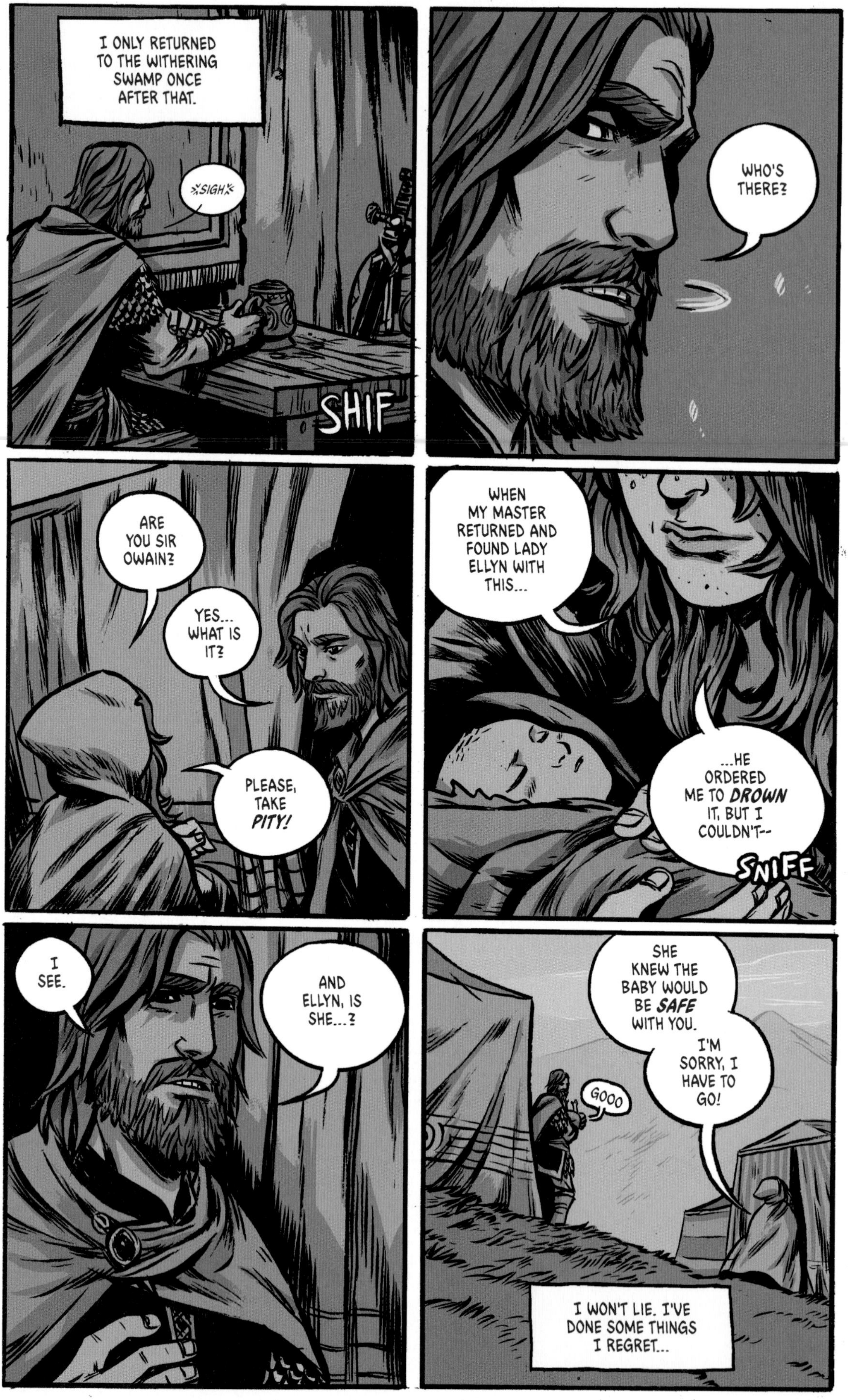
I ONLY RETURNED TO THE WITHERING SWAMP ONCE AFTER THAT.
*SIGH*
SHIF
WHO'S THERE?
ARE YOU SIR OWAIN?
YES... WHAT IS IT?
PLEASE, TAKE *PITY!*
WHEN MY MASTER RETURNED AND FOUND LADY ELLYN WITH THIS...
...HE ORDERED ME TO *DROWN* IT, BUT I COULDN'T--
SNIFF
I SEE.
AND ELLYN, IS SHE...?
SHE KNEW THE BABY WOULD BE *SAFE* WITH YOU.
I'M SORRY, I HAVE TO GO!
GOOO
I WON'T LIE. I'VE DONE SOME THINGS I REGRET...

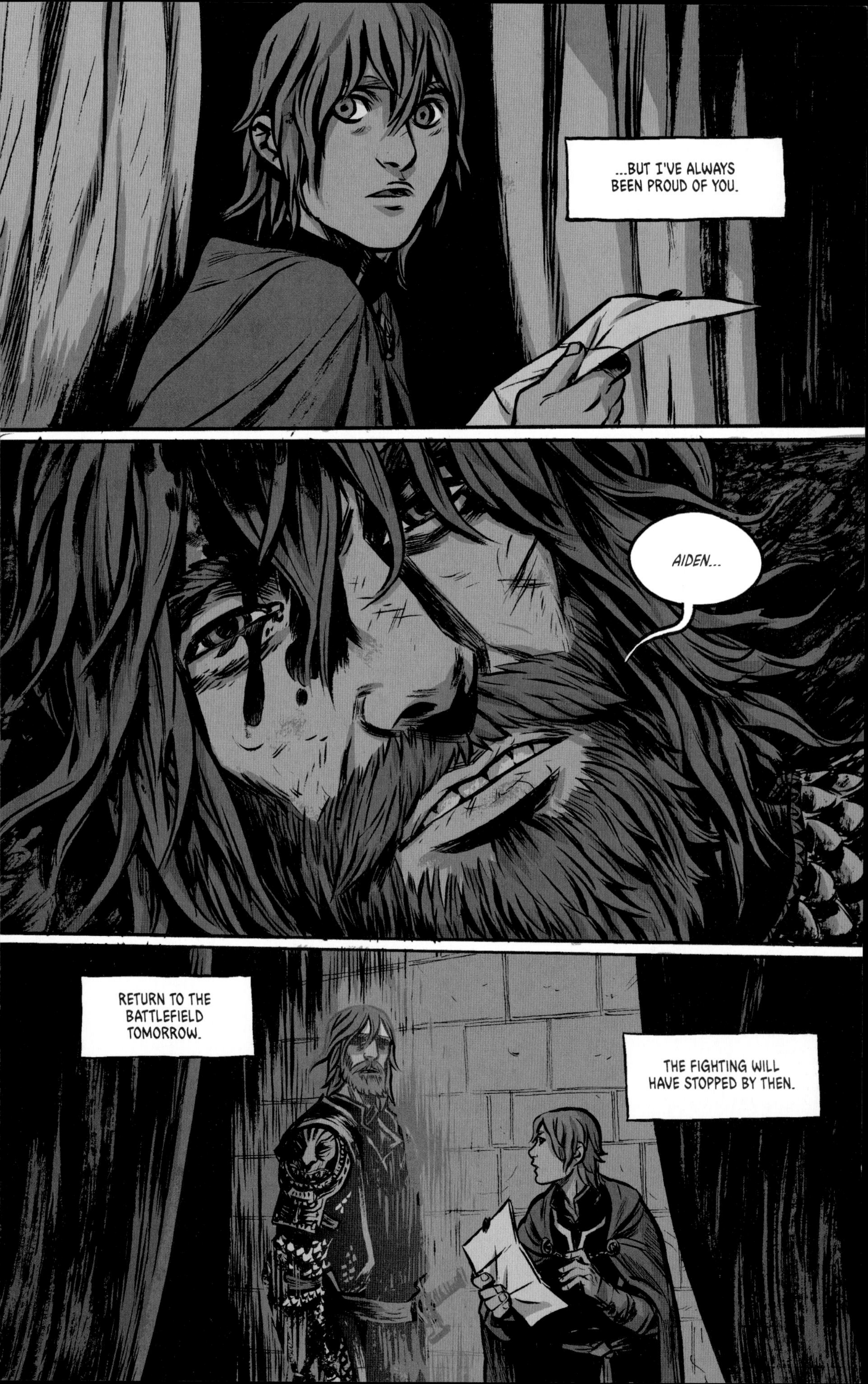
...BUT I'VE ALWAYS BEEN PROUD OF YOU.
AIDEN...
RETURN TO THE BATTLEFIELD TOMORROW.
THE FIGHTING WILL HAVE STOPPED BY THEN.

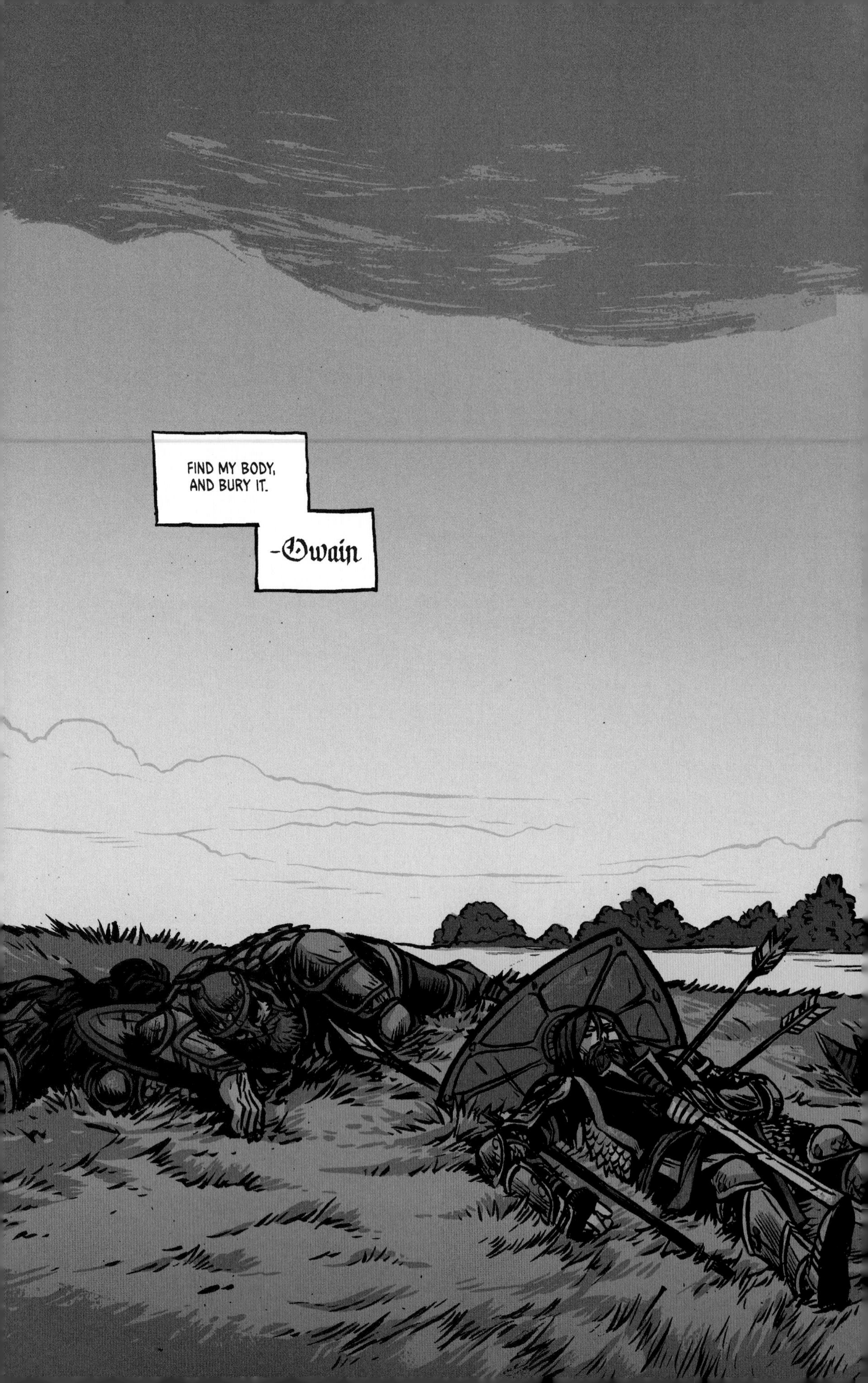
FIND MY BODY, AND BURY IT.
-Owain

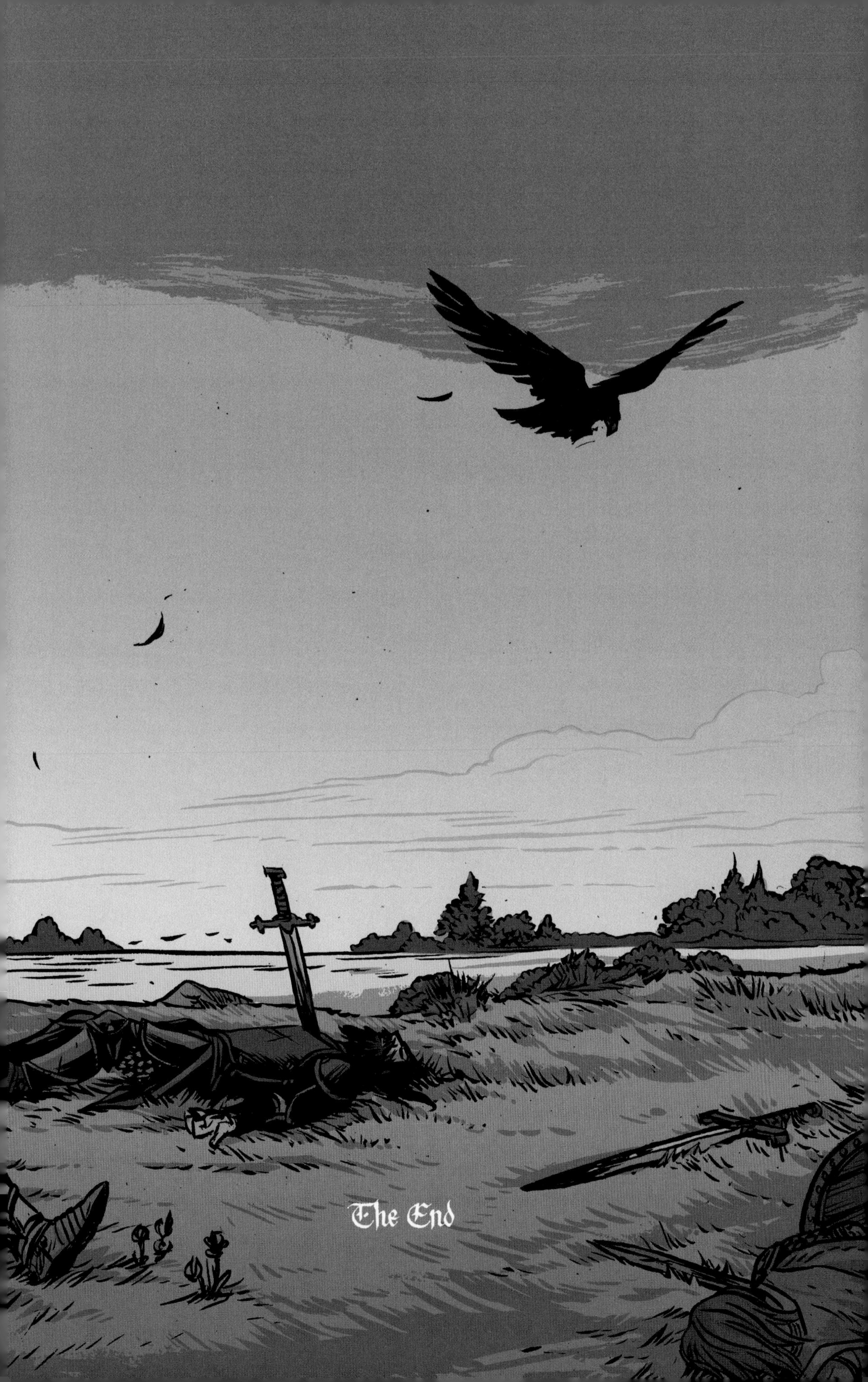
The End

# III.

# Demeter

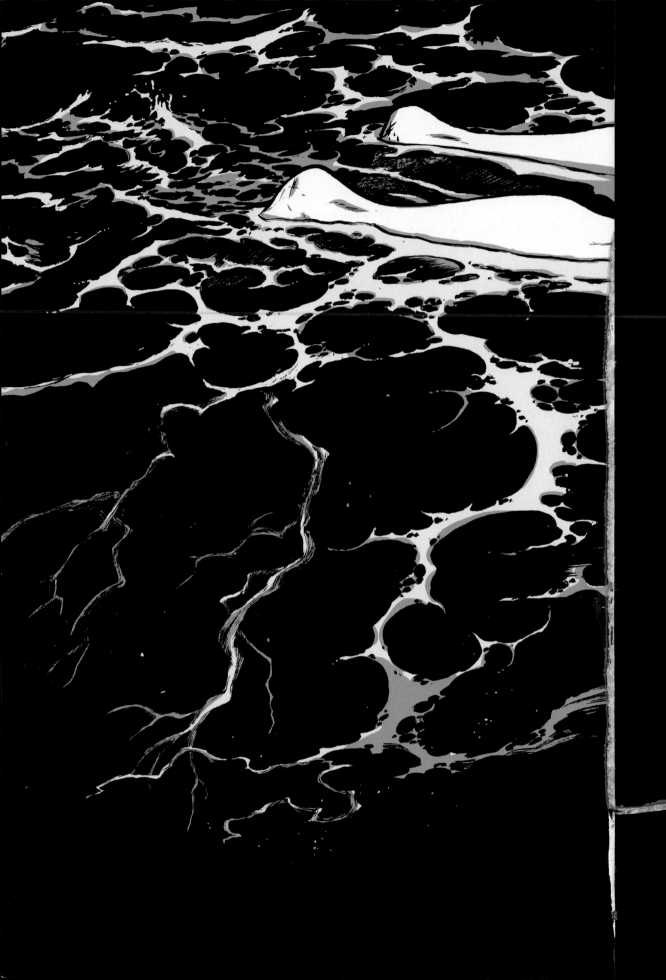

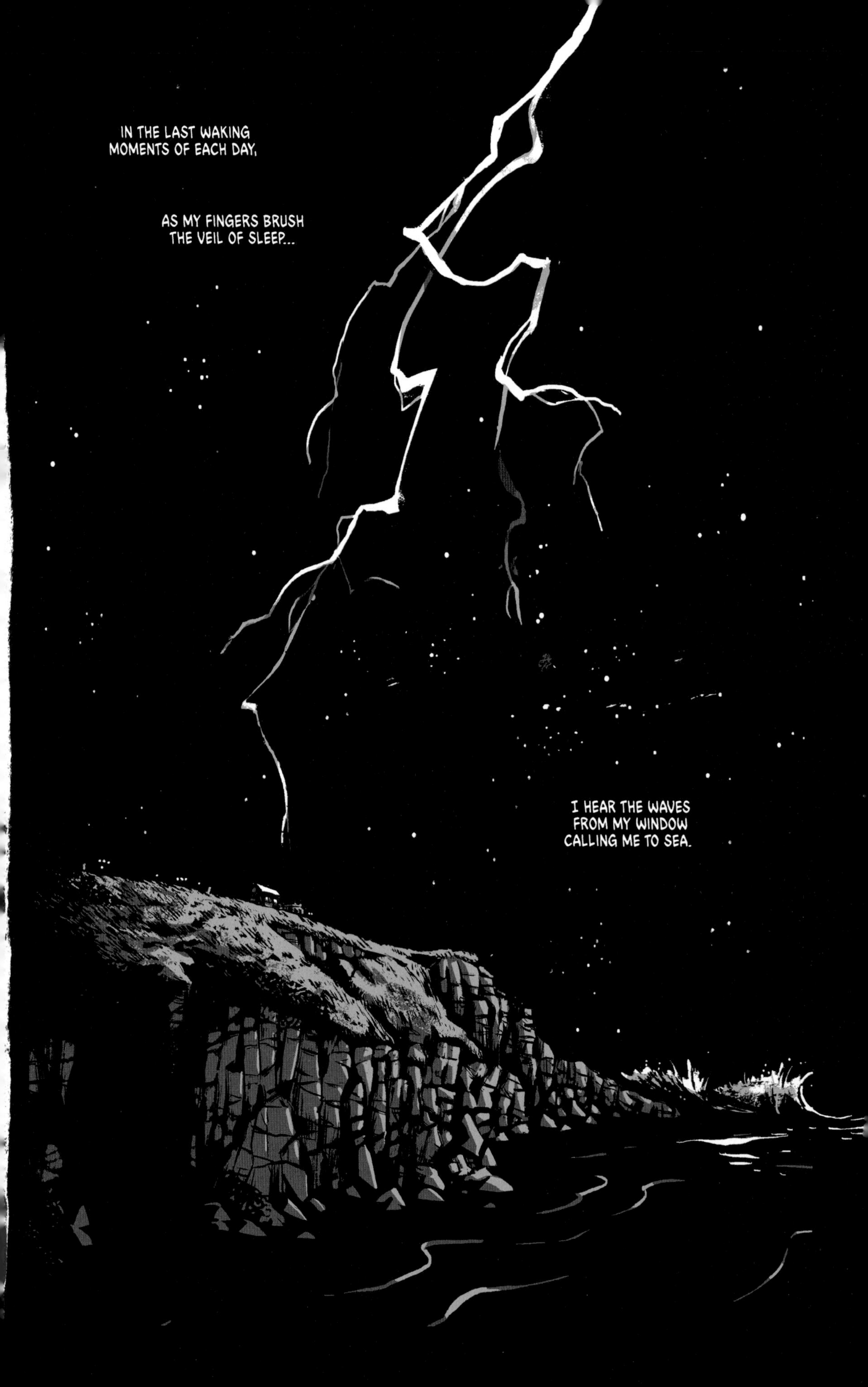
IN THE LAST WAKING MOMENTS OF EACH DAY,
AS MY FINGERS BRUSH THE VEIL OF SLEEP...
I HEAR THE WAVES FROM MY WINDOW CALLING ME TO SEA.

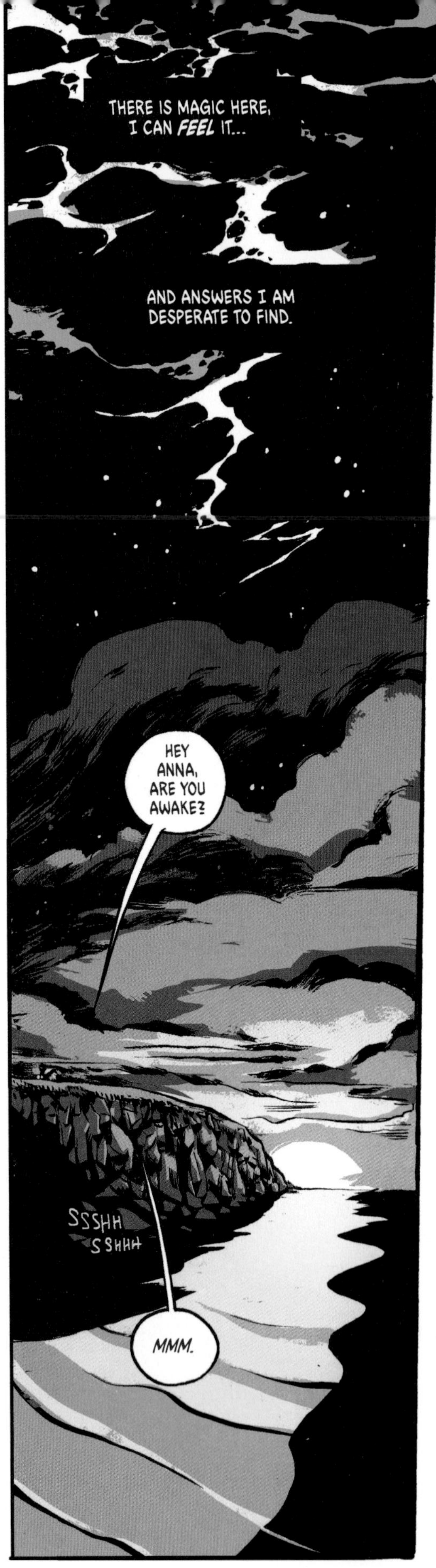
THERE IS MAGIC HERE, I CAN *FEEL* IT...
AND ANSWERS I AM DESPERATE TO FIND.
HEY ANNA, ARE YOU AWAKE?
SSSHH
SSHHH
MMM.

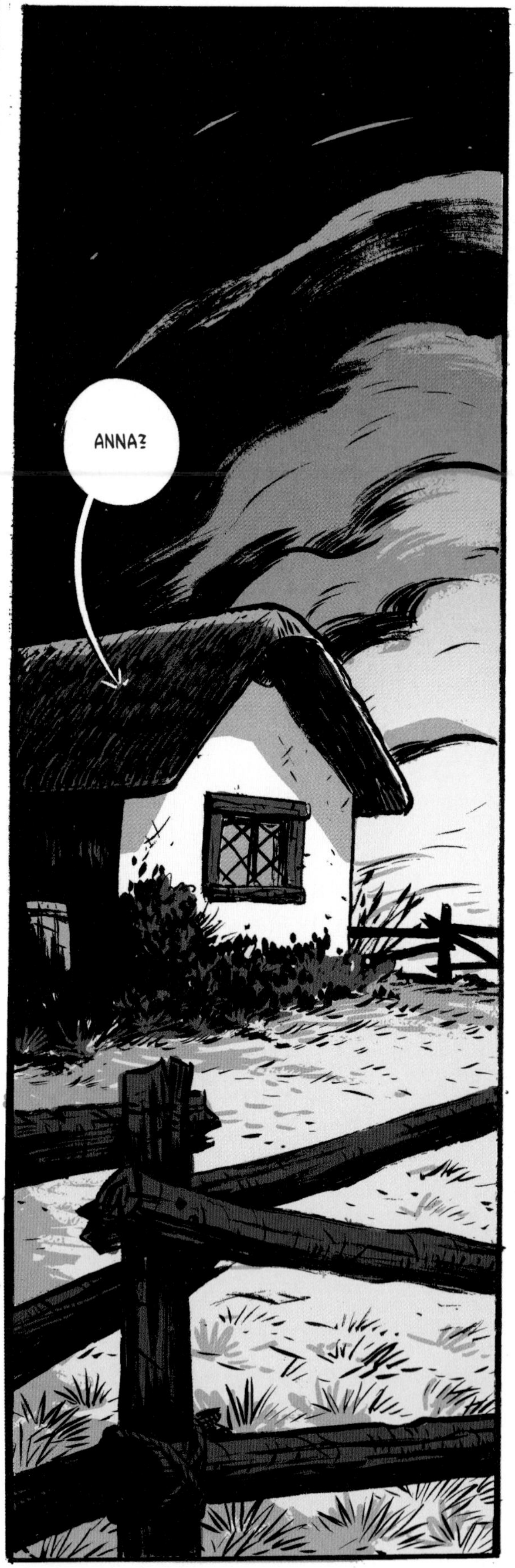
ANNA?

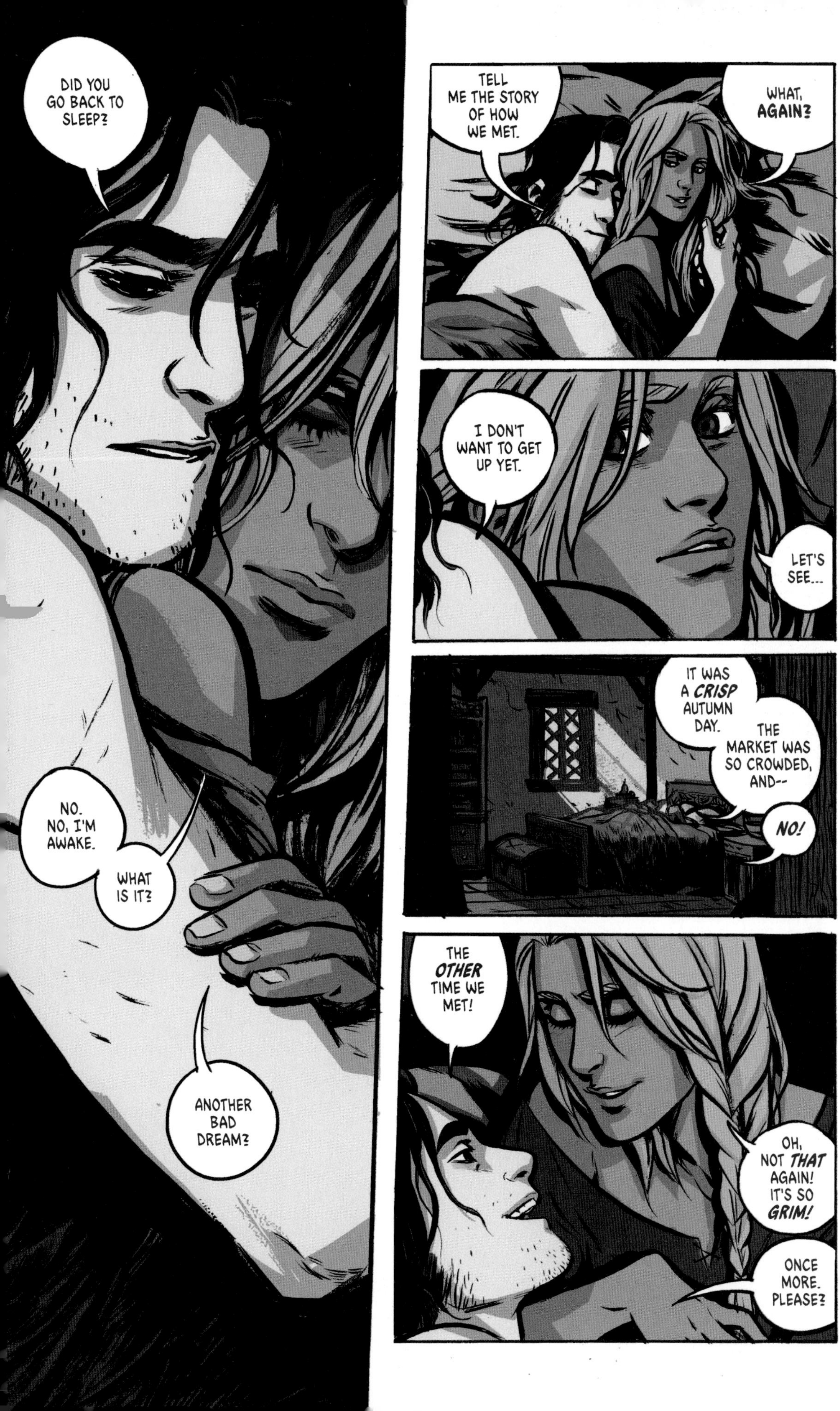

DID YOU GO BACK TO SLEEP?
NO. NO, I'M AWAKE.
WHAT IS IT?
ANOTHER BAD DREAM?
TELL ME THE STORY OF HOW WE MET.
WHAT, **AGAIN?**
I DON'T WANT TO GET UP YET.
LET'S SEE...
IT WAS A ***CRISP*** AUTUMN DAY.
THE MARKET WAS SO CROWDED, AND--
***NO!***
THE ***OTHER*** TIME WE MET!
OH, NOT ***THAT*** AGAIN! IT'S SO ***GRIM!***
ONCE MORE. PLEASE?

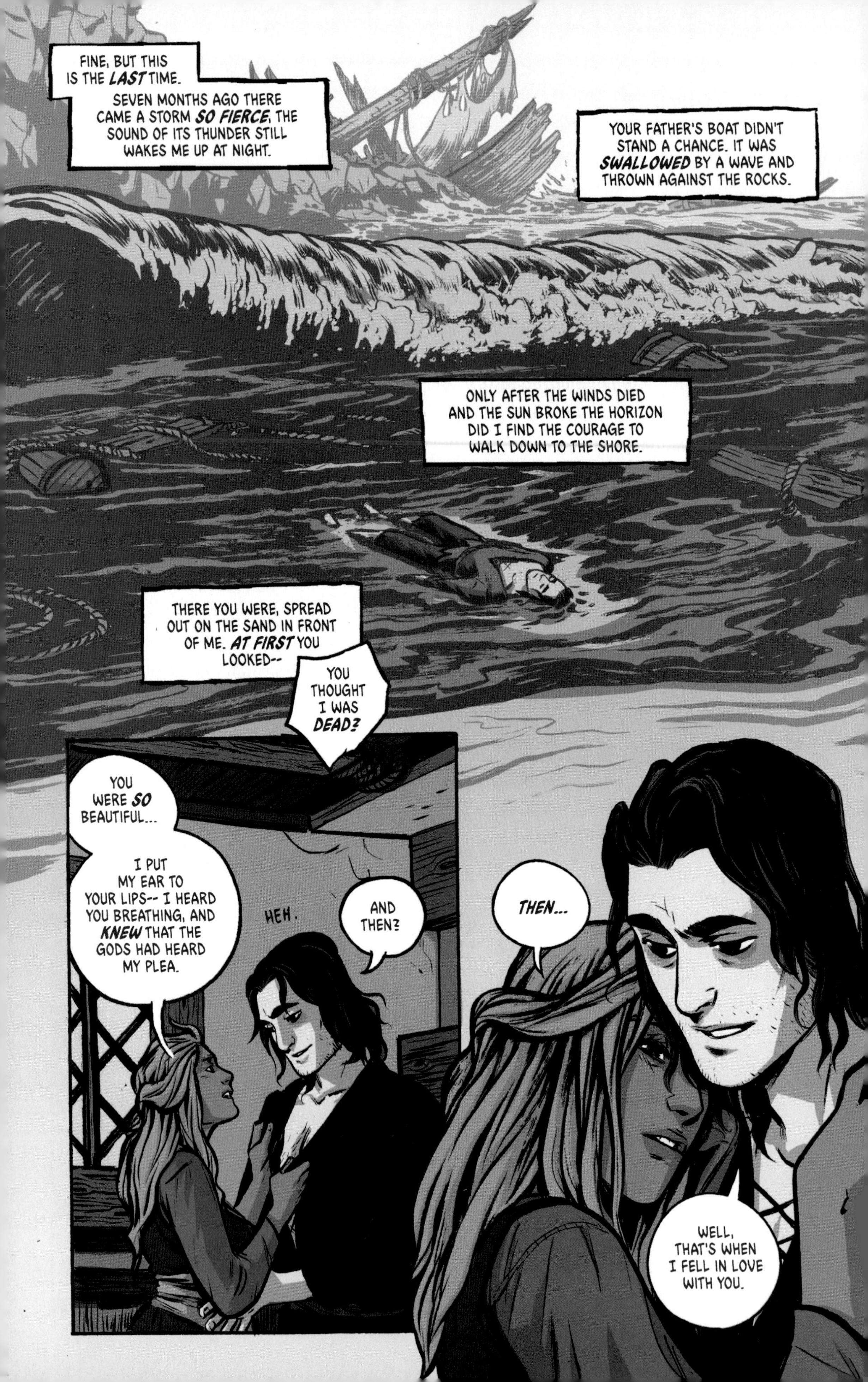
FINE, BUT THIS IS THE LAST TIME.
SEVEN MONTHS AGO THERE CAME A STORM SO FIERCE, THE SOUND OF ITS THUNDER STILL WAKES ME UP AT NIGHT.
YOUR FATHER'S BOAT DIDN'T STAND A CHANCE. IT WAS SWALLOWED BY A WAVE AND THROWN AGAINST THE ROCKS.
ONLY AFTER THE WINDS DIED AND THE SUN BROKE THE HORIZON DID I FIND THE COURAGE TO WALK DOWN TO THE SHORE.
THERE YOU WERE, SPREAD OUT ON THE SAND IN FRONT OF ME. AT FIRST YOU LOOKED--
YOU THOUGHT I WAS DEAD?
YOU WERE SO BEAUTIFUL...
I PUT MY EAR TO YOUR LIPS-- I HEARD YOU BREATHING, AND KNEW THAT THE GODS HAD HEARD MY PLEA.
HEH.
AND THEN?
THEN...
WELL, THAT'S WHEN I FELL IN LOVE WITH YOU.

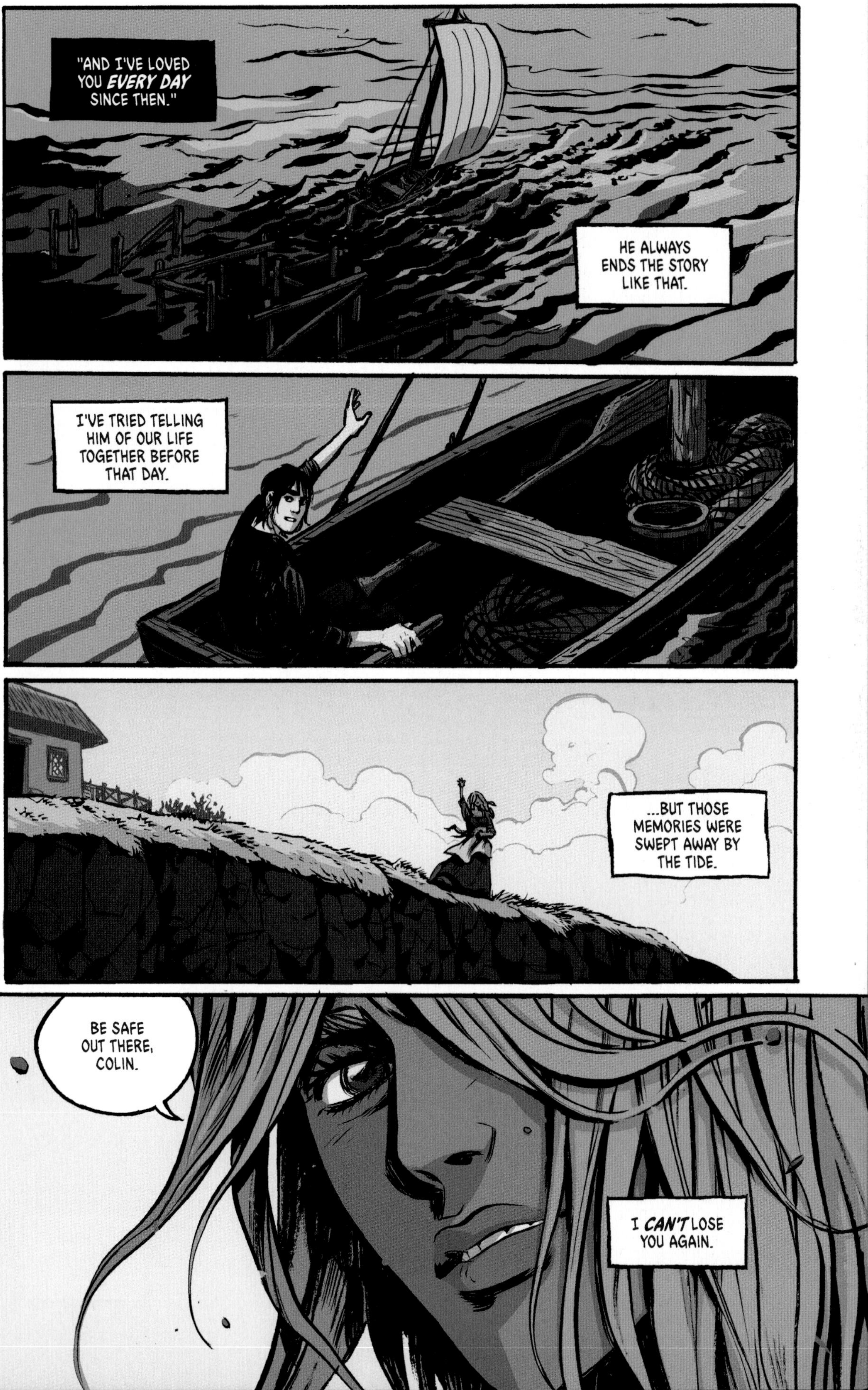
"AND I'VE LOVED YOU *EVERY DAY* SINCE THEN."
HE ALWAYS ENDS THE STORY LIKE THAT.
I'VE TRIED TELLING HIM OF OUR LIFE TOGETHER BEFORE THAT DAY.
...BUT THOSE MEMORIES WERE SWEPT AWAY BY THE TIDE.
BE SAFE OUT THERE, COLIN.
I *CAN'T* LOSE YOU AGAIN.

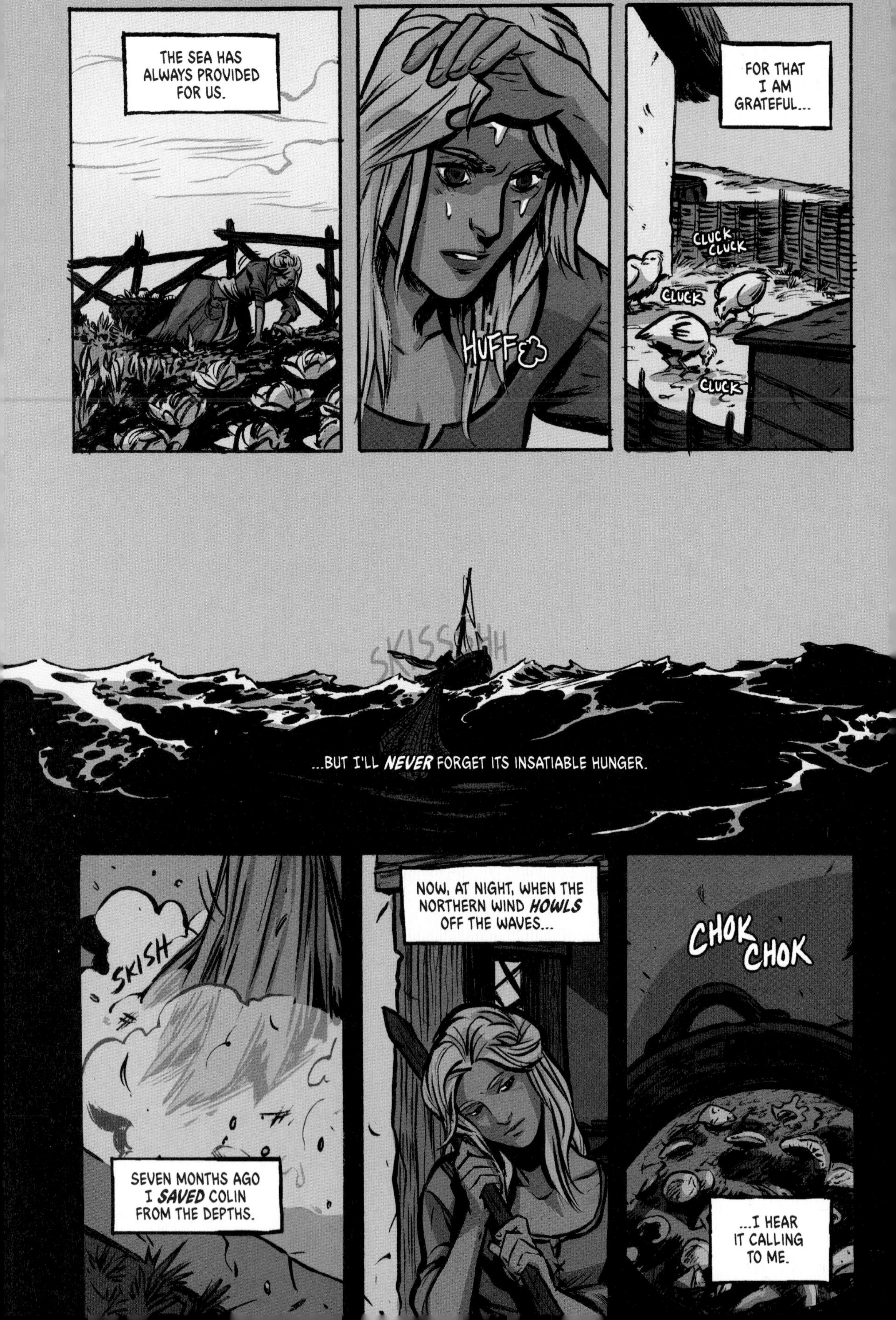
THE SEA HAS ALWAYS PROVIDED FOR US.
HUFF
FOR THAT I AM GRATEFUL...
CLUCK CLUCK
CLUCK
CLUCK
SKISSHH
...BUT I'LL NEVER FORGET ITS INSATIABLE HUNGER.
SKISH
SEVEN MONTHS AGO I SAVED COLIN FROM THE DEPTHS.
NOW, AT NIGHT, WHEN THE NORTHERN WIND HOWLS OFF THE WAVES...
CHOK CHOK
...I HEAR IT CALLING TO ME.

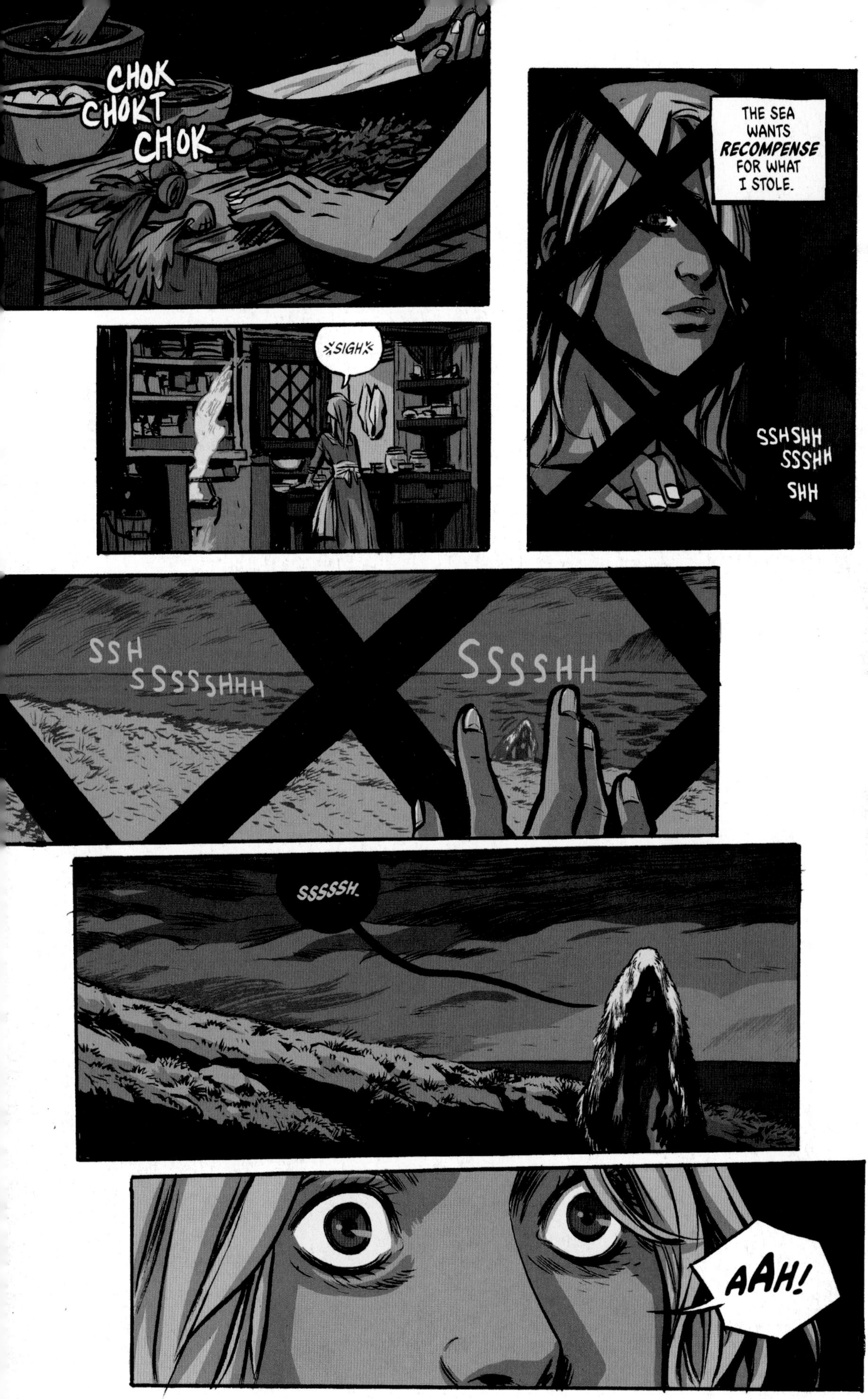
CHOK
CHOKT
CHOK
THE SEA WANTS RECOMPENSE FOR WHAT I STOLE.
SIGH
SSHSHH SSSHH SHH
SSH SSSSSHHH
SSSSHH
SSSSSH.
AAH!

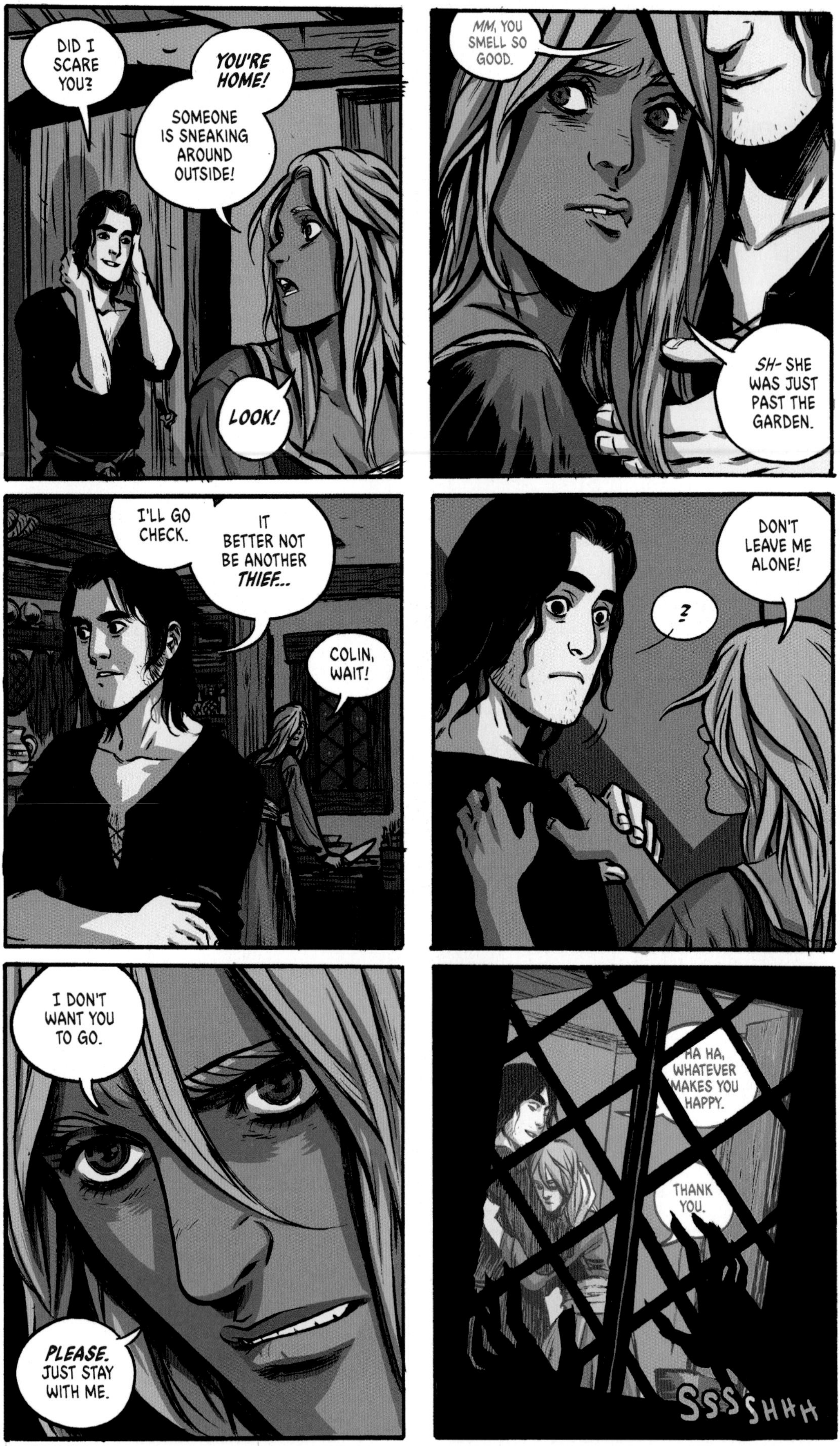
DID I SCARE YOU?
YOU'RE HOME!
SOMEONE IS SNEAKING AROUND OUTSIDE!
LOOK!
MM, YOU SMELL SO GOOD.
SH- SHE WAS JUST PAST THE GARDEN.
I'LL GO CHECK.
IT BETTER NOT BE ANOTHER THIEF...
COLIN, WAIT!
DON'T LEAVE ME ALONE!
?
I DON'T WANT YOU TO GO.
PLEASE. JUST STAY WITH ME.
HA HA, WHATEVER MAKES YOU HAPPY.
THANK YOU.
SSSSHHH

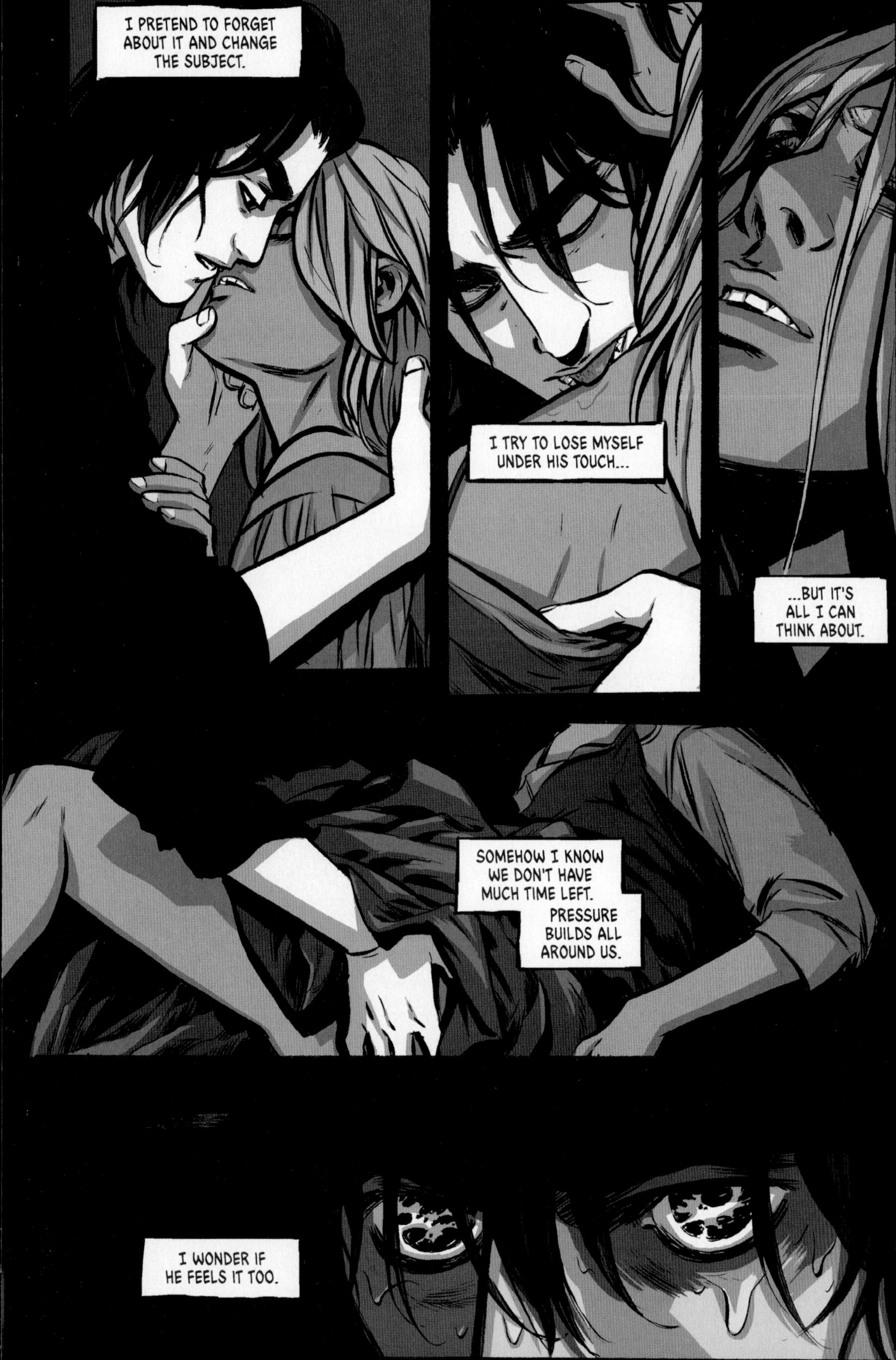
I PRETEND TO FORGET ABOUT IT AND CHANGE THE SUBJECT.
I TRY TO LOSE MYSELF UNDER HIS TOUCH...
...BUT IT'S ALL I CAN THINK ABOUT.
SOMEHOW I KNOW WE DON'T HAVE MUCH TIME LEFT.
PRESSURE BUILDS ALL AROUND US.
I WONDER IF HE FEELS IT TOO.

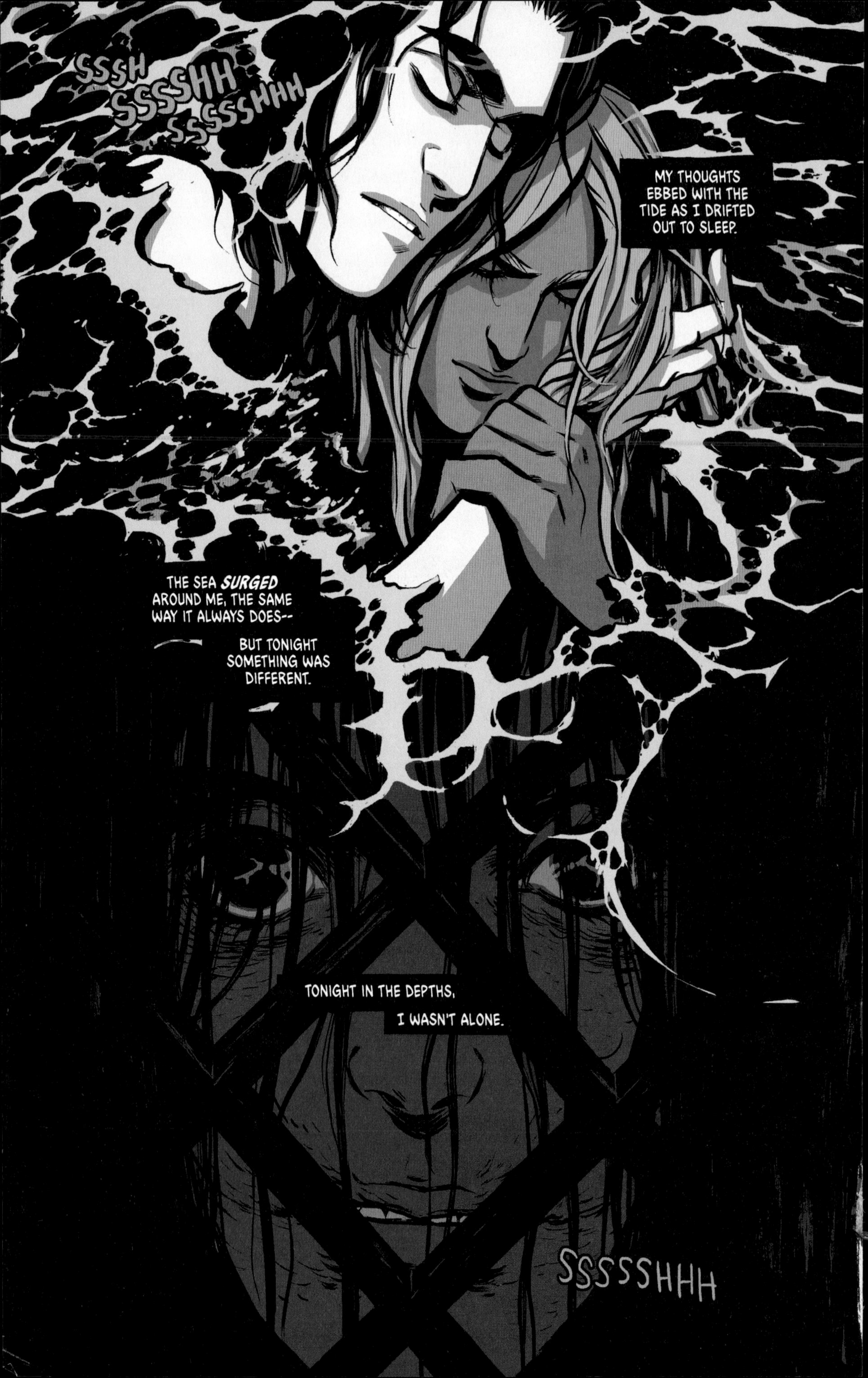
SSSH
SSSSHH
SSSSSSHHH
MY THOUGHTS EBBED WITH THE TIDE AS I DRIFTED OUT TO SLEEP.
THE SEA SURGED AROUND ME, THE SAME WAY IT ALWAYS DOES--
BUT TONIGHT SOMETHING WAS DIFFERENT.
TONIGHT IN THE DEPTHS,
I WASN'T ALONE.
SSSSSHHH

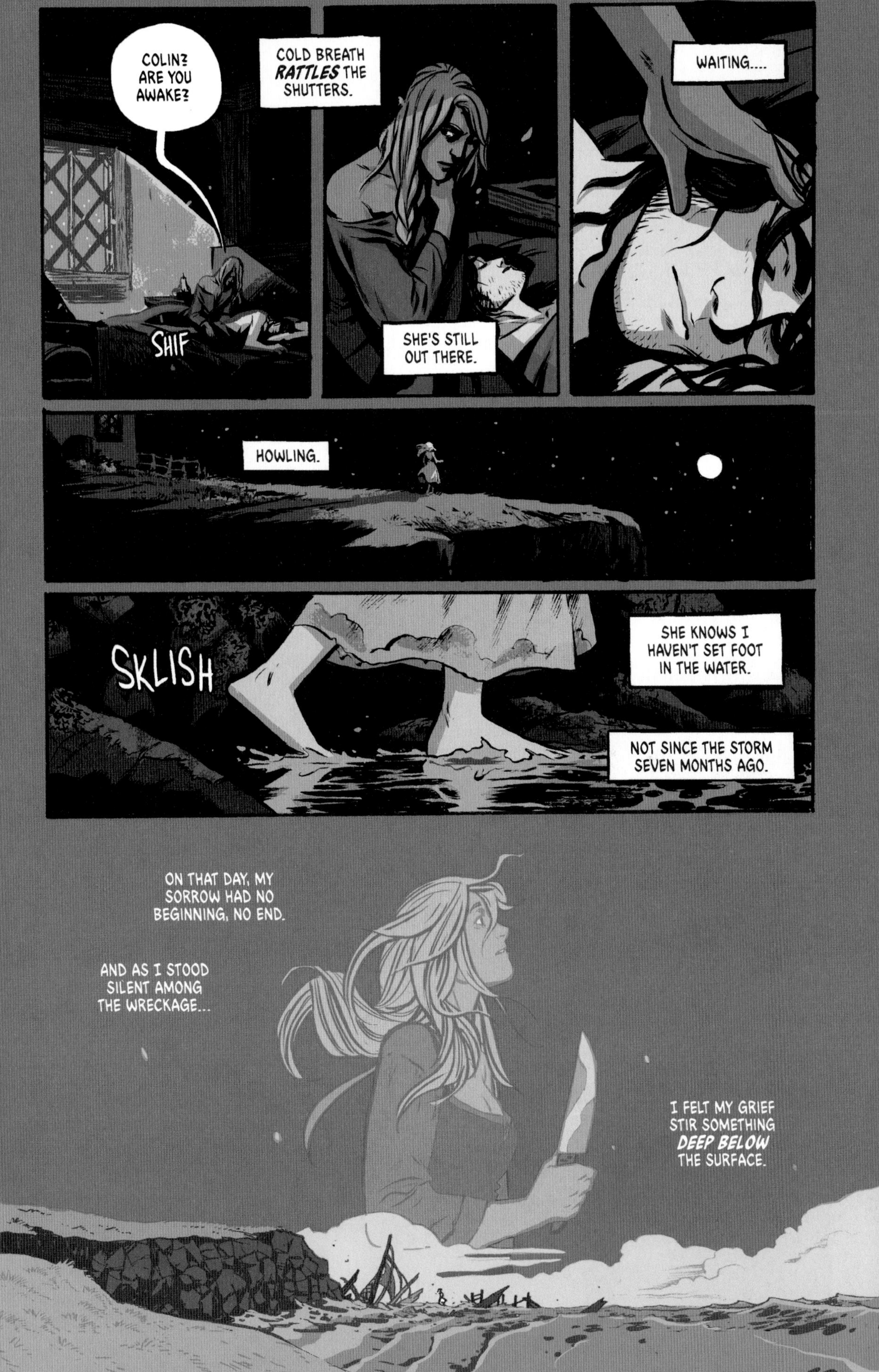
COLIN? ARE YOU AWAKE?
SHIF
COLD BREATH *RATTLES* THE SHUTTERS.
SHE'S STILL OUT THERE.
WAITING....
HOWLING.
SKLISH
SHE KNOWS I HAVEN'T SET FOOT IN THE WATER.
NOT SINCE THE STORM SEVEN MONTHS AGO.
ON THAT DAY, MY SORROW HAD NO BEGINNING, NO END.
AND AS I STOOD SILENT AMONG THE WRECKAGE...
I FELT MY GRIEF STIR SOMETHING *DEEP BELOW* THE SURFACE.

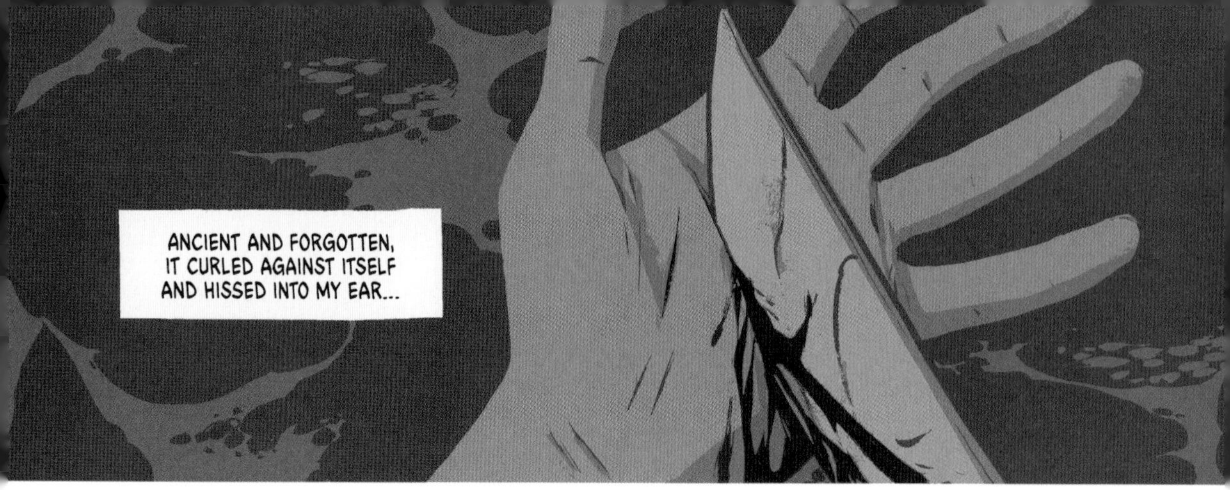
ANCIENT AND FORGOTTEN, IT CURLED AGAINST ITSELF AND HISSED INTO MY EAR...

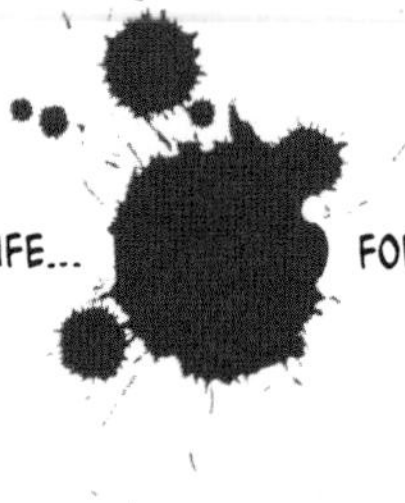
SEVEN MONTHS OF LIFE...
FOR SEVEN DROPS OF BLOOD...

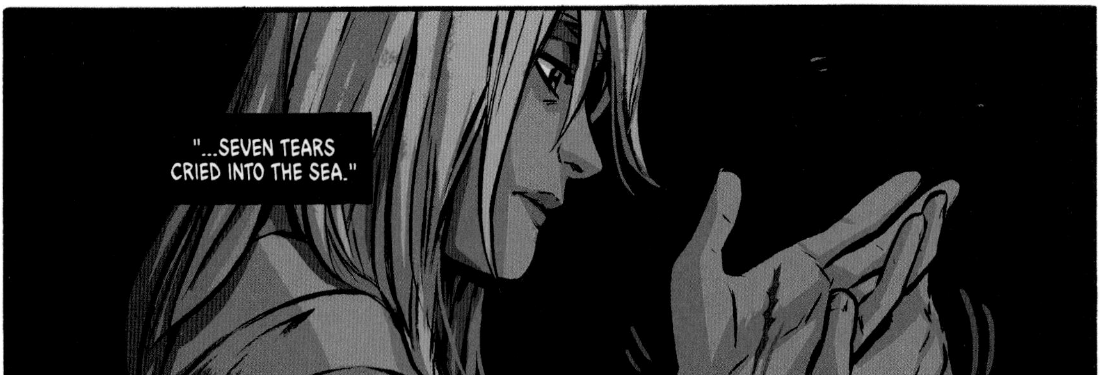
"...SEVEN TEARS CRIED INTO THE SEA."

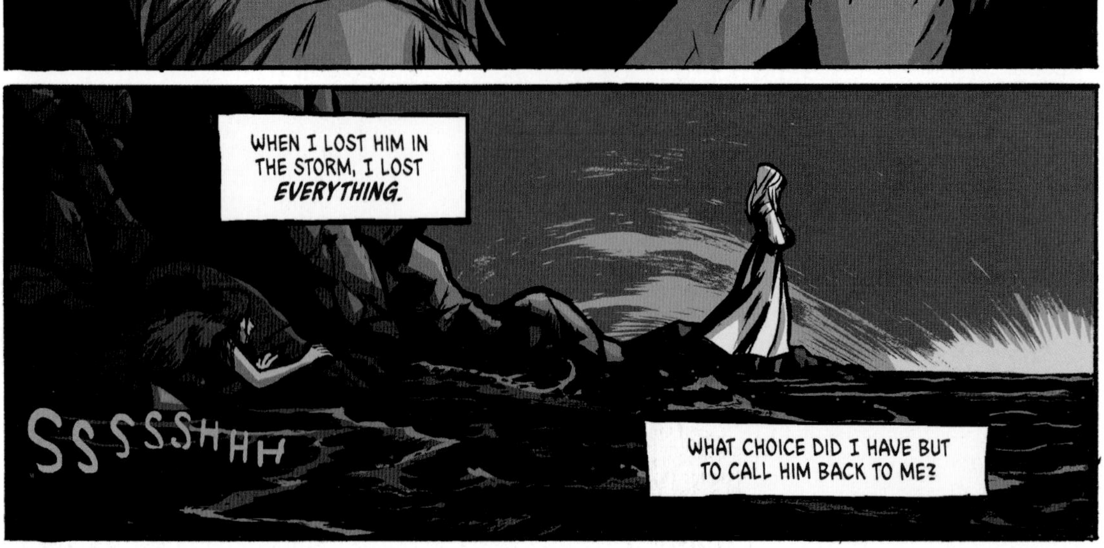
WHEN I LOST HIM IN THE STORM, I LOST *EVERYTHING.*
SSSSSHHH
WHAT CHOICE DID I HAVE BUT TO CALL HIM BACK TO ME?

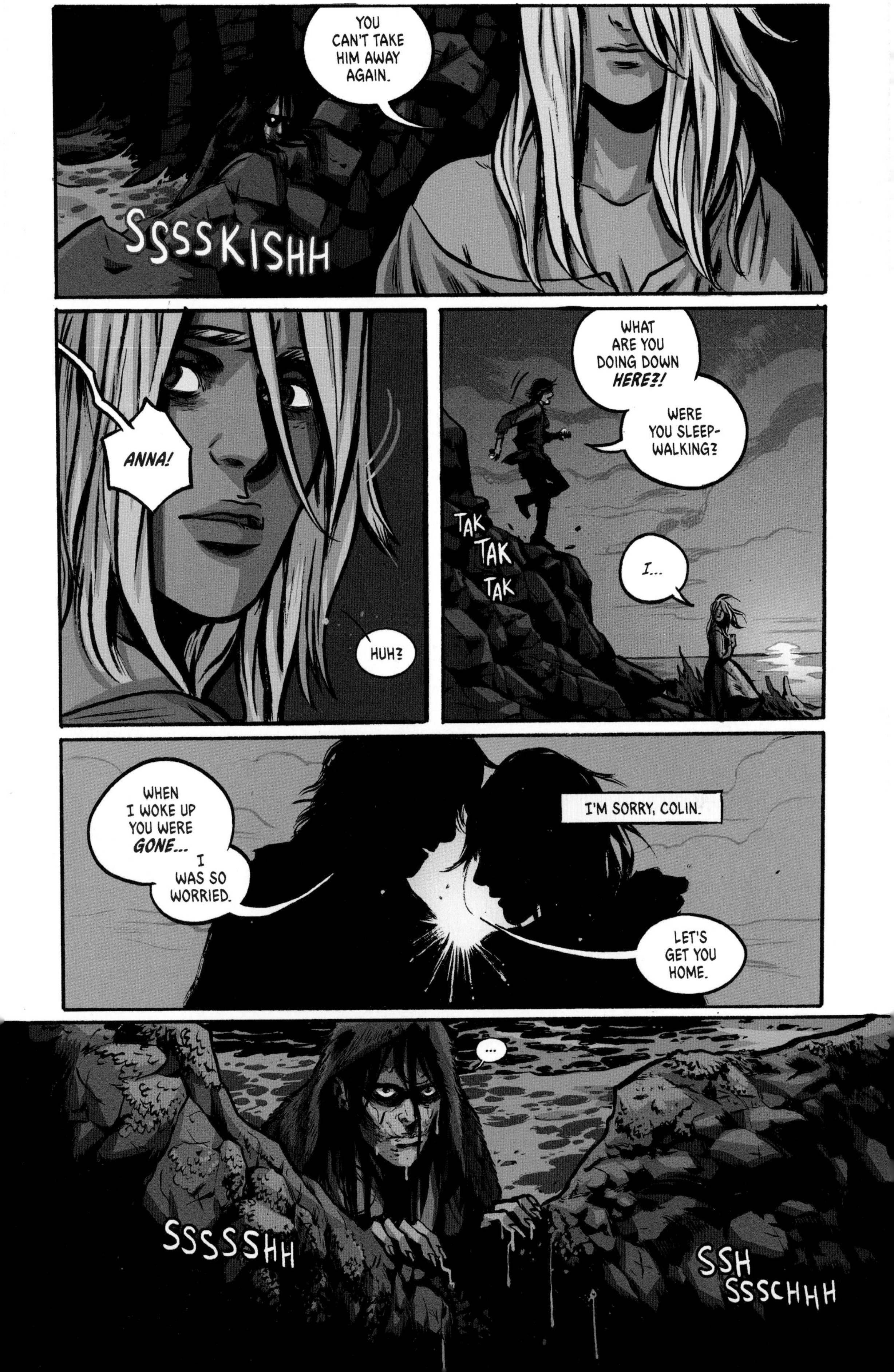
YOU CAN'T TAKE HIM AWAY AGAIN.
SSSSKISHH
ANNA!
HUH?
WHAT ARE YOU DOING DOWN HERE?!
WERE YOU SLEEP-WALKING?
TAK TAK TAK
I...
WHEN I WOKE UP YOU WERE GONE... I WAS SO WORRIED.
I'M SORRY, COLIN.
LET'S GET YOU HOME.
...
SSSSSHH
SSH SSSCHHH

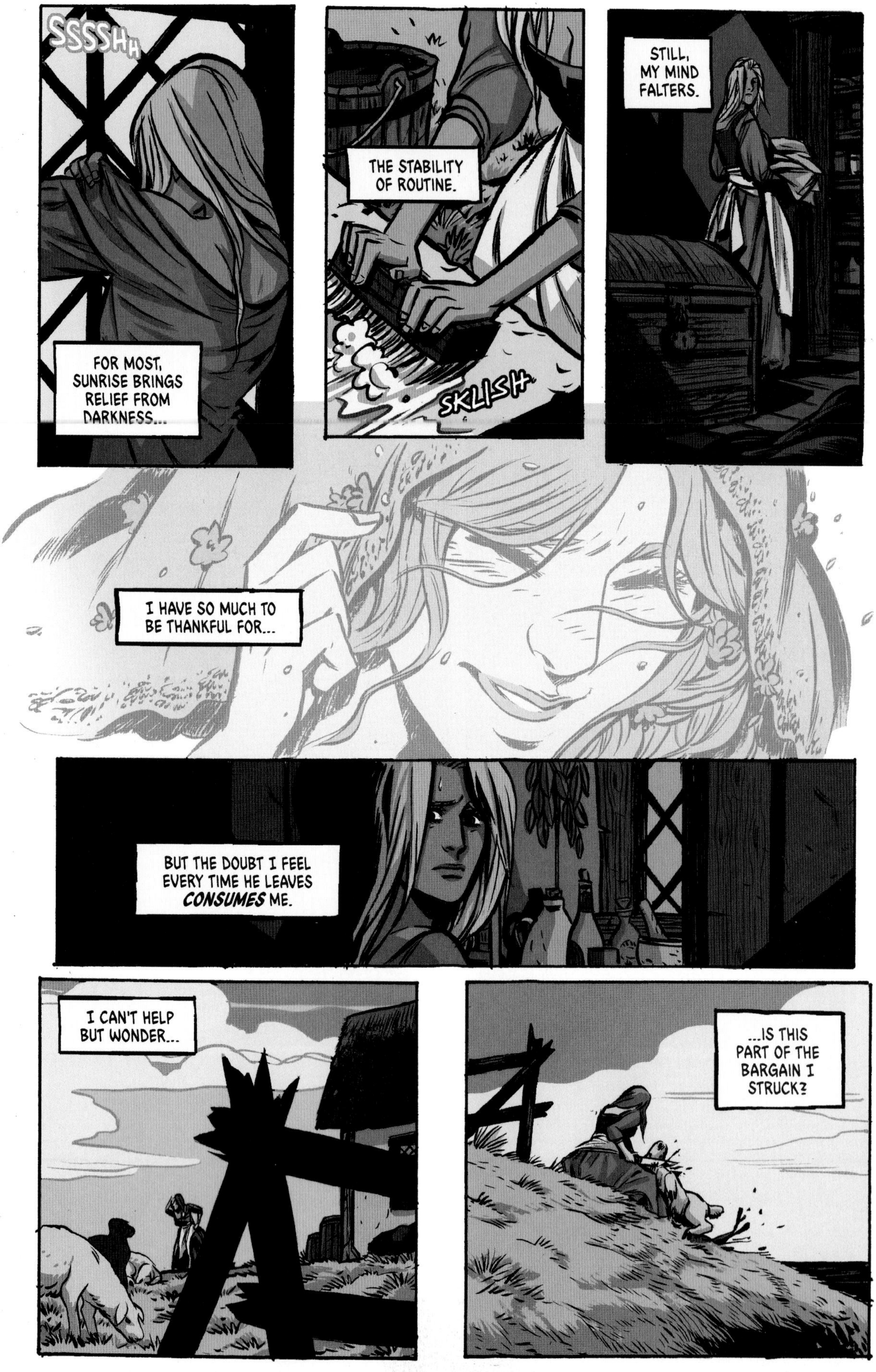
SSSSHH
FOR MOST, SUNRISE BRINGS RELIEF FROM DARKNESS...
THE STABILITY OF ROUTINE.
SKLISH
STILL, MY MIND FALTERS.
I HAVE SO MUCH TO BE THANKFUL FOR...
BUT THE DOUBT I FEEL EVERY TIME HE LEAVES *CONSUMES* ME.
I CAN'T HELP BUT WONDER...
...IS THIS PART OF THE BARGAIN I STRUCK?

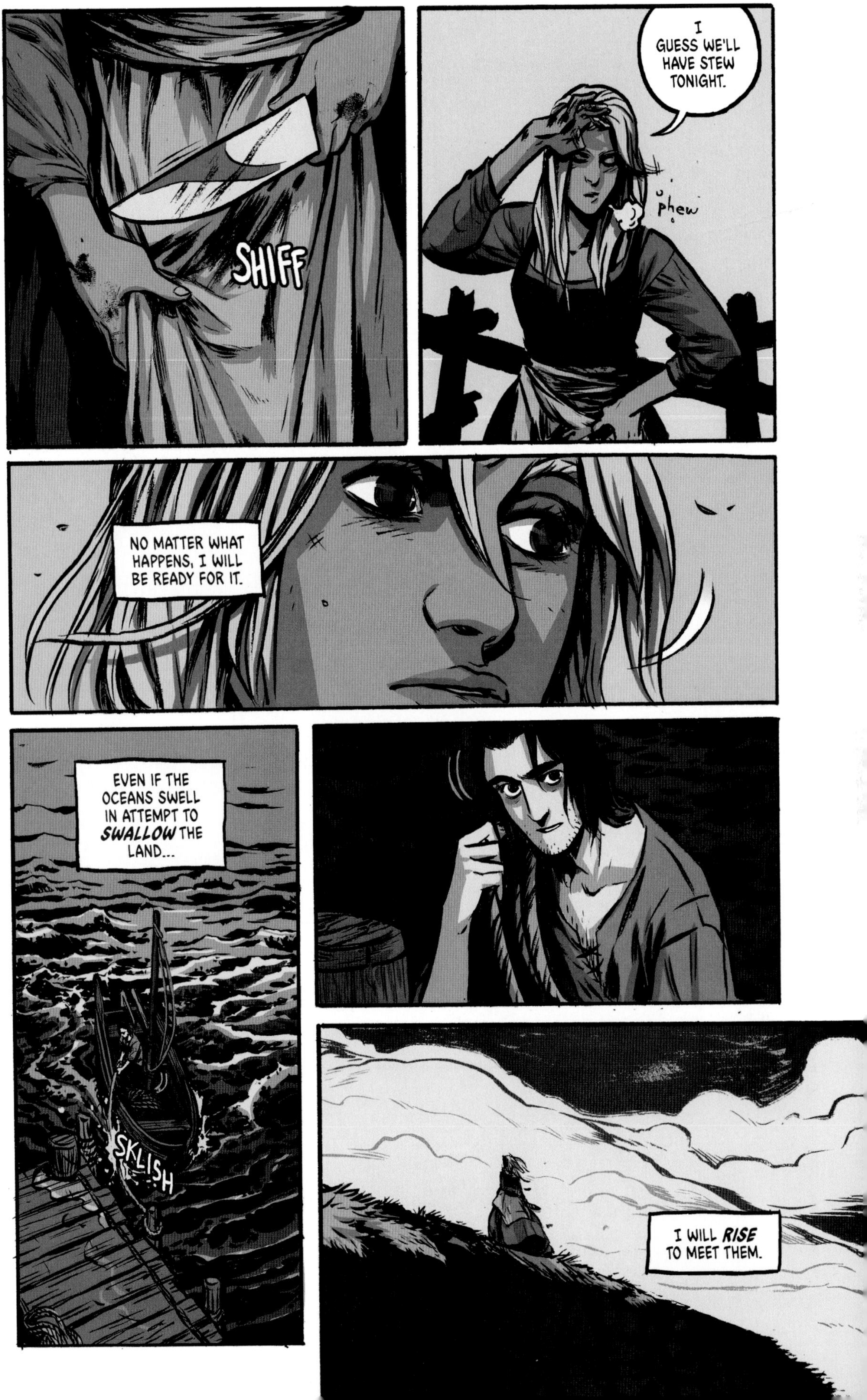

SHIFF
I GUESS WE'LL HAVE STEW TONIGHT.
phew
NO MATTER WHAT HAPPENS, I WILL BE READY FOR IT.
EVEN IF THE OCEANS SWELL IN ATTEMPT TO SWALLOW THE LAND...
SKLISH
I WILL RISE TO MEET THEM.

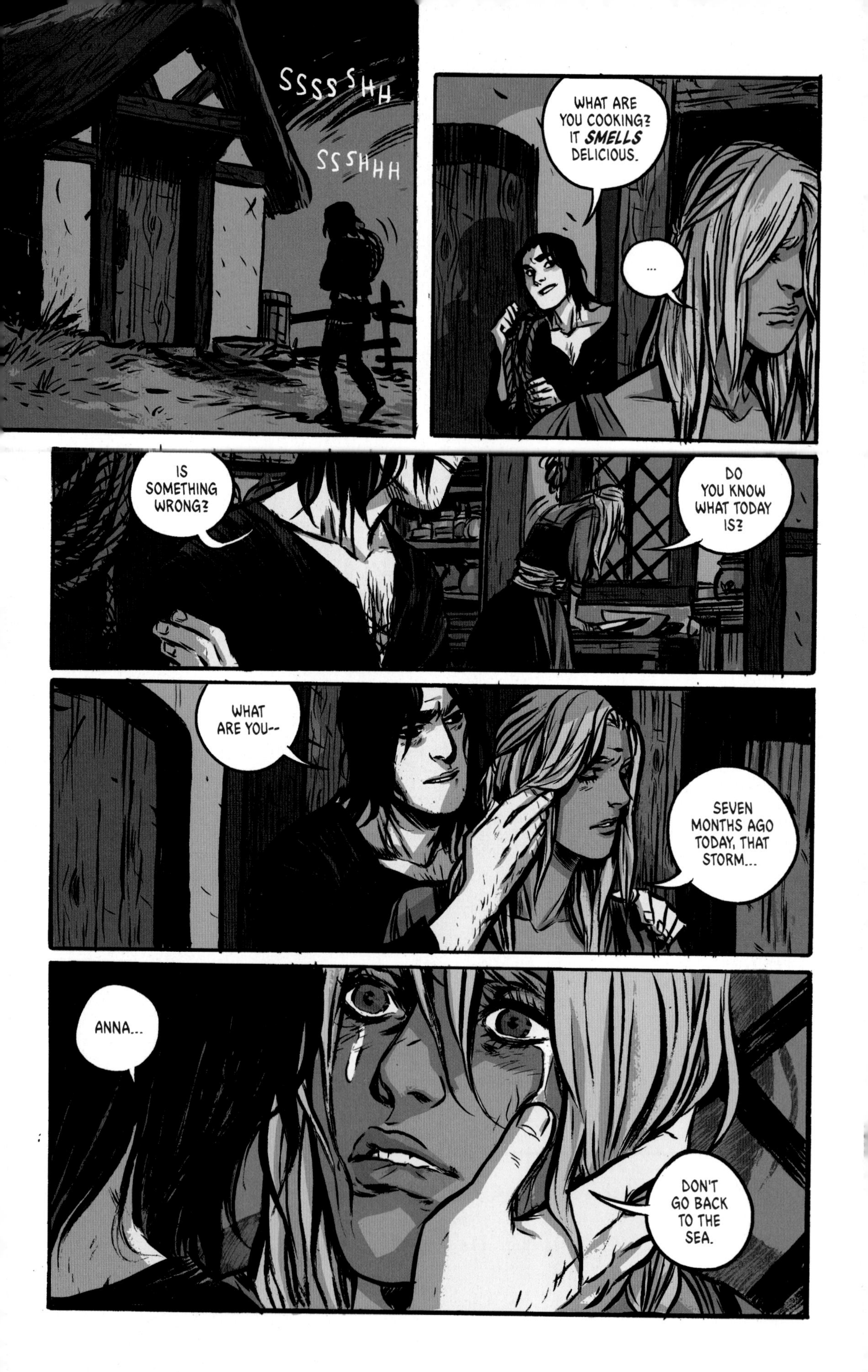
SSSSSHH
SSSHHH
WHAT ARE YOU COOKING? IT SMELLS DELICIOUS.
...
IS SOMETHING WRONG?
DO YOU KNOW WHAT TODAY IS?
WHAT ARE YOU--
SEVEN MONTHS AGO TODAY, THAT STORM...
ANNA...
DON'T GO BACK TO THE SEA.

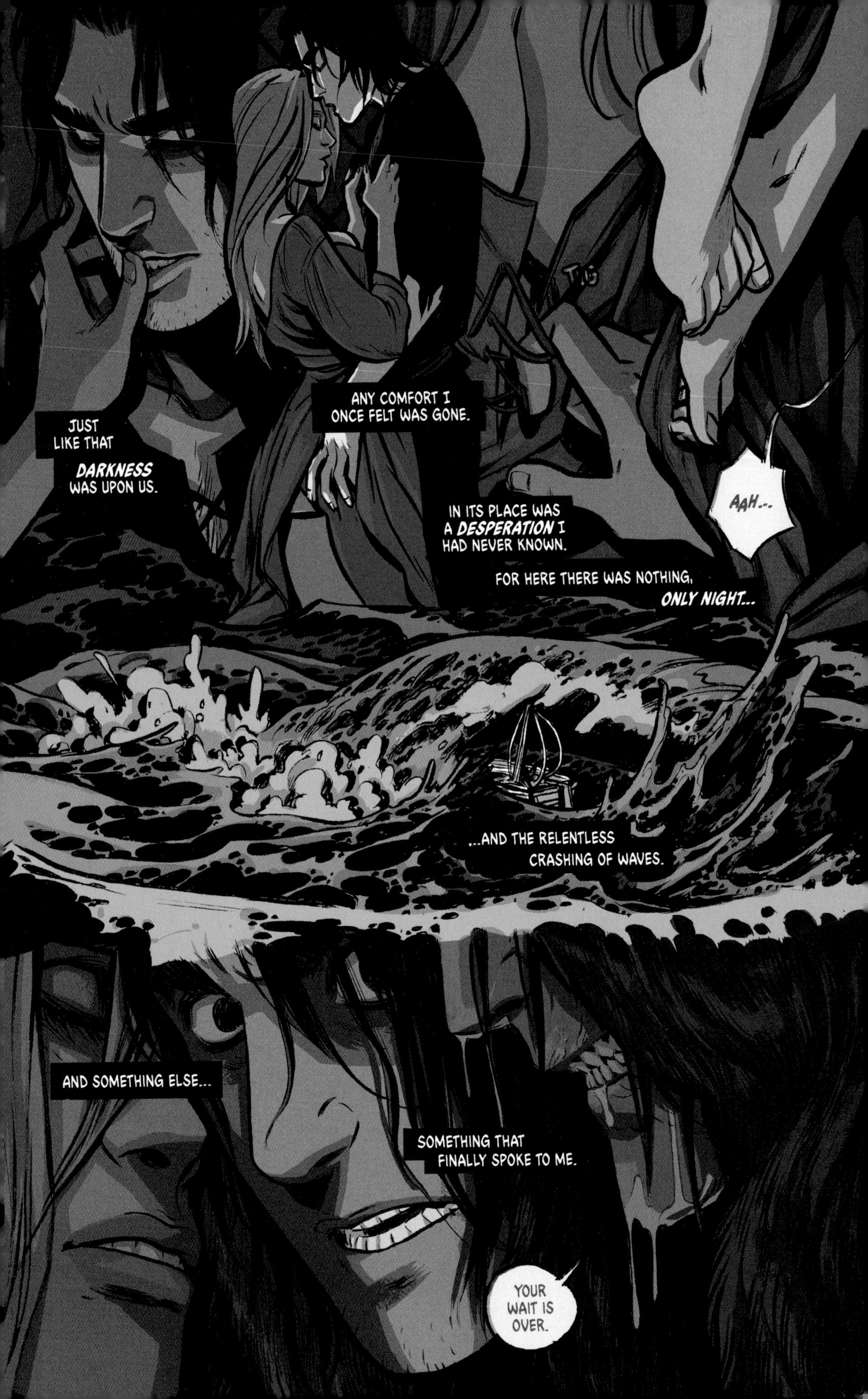
JUST LIKE THAT DARKNESS WAS UPON US.
ANY COMFORT I ONCE FELT WAS GONE.
IN ITS PLACE WAS A DESPERATION I HAD NEVER KNOWN.
AAH...
FOR HERE THERE WAS NOTHING, ONLY NIGHT...
...AND THE RELENTLESS CRASHING OF WAVES.
AND SOMETHING ELSE...
SOMETHING THAT FINALLY SPOKE TO ME.
YOUR WAIT IS OVER.

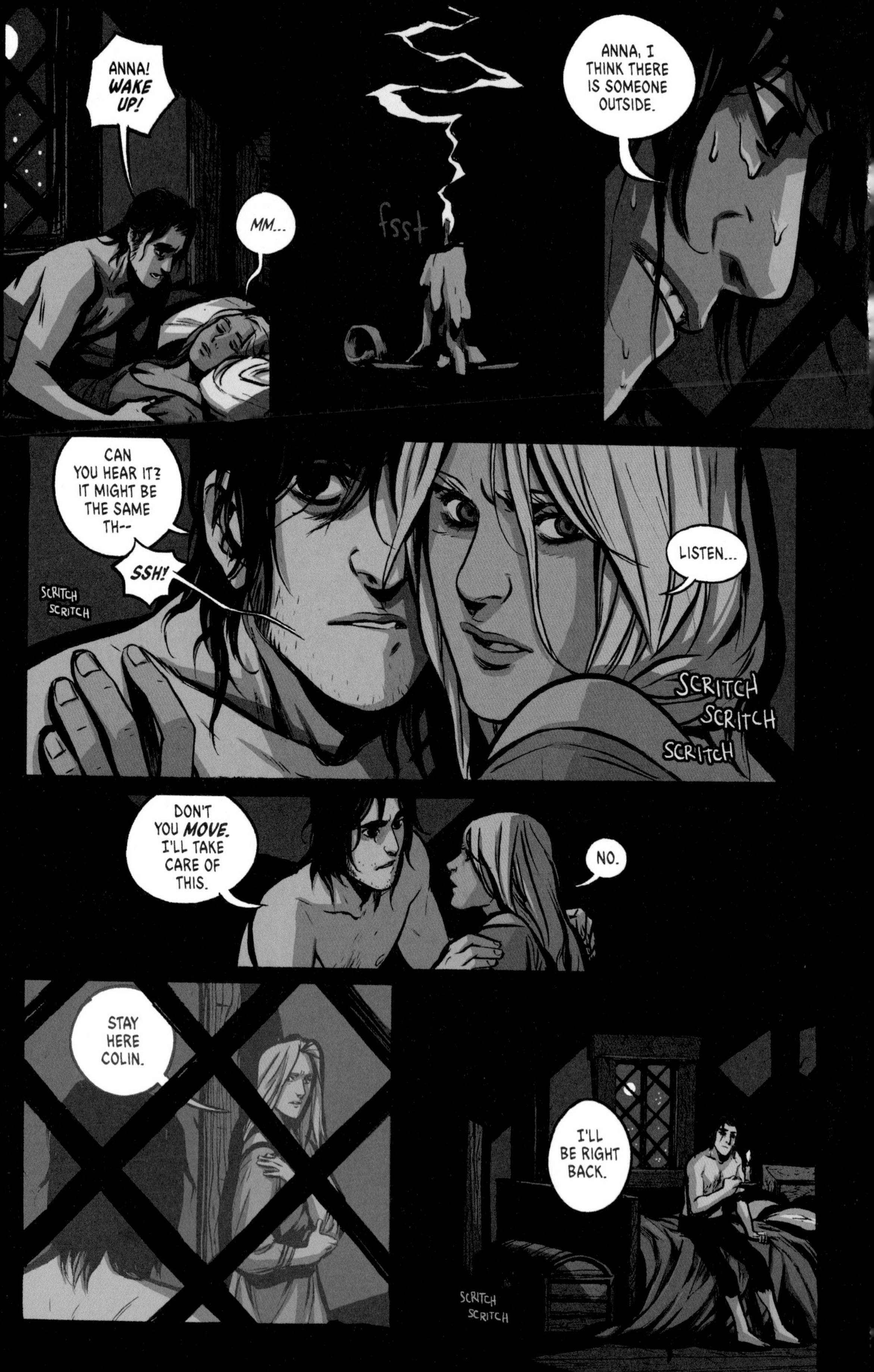

ANNA! WAKE UP!
MM...
fsst
ANNA, I THINK THERE IS SOMEONE OUTSIDE.
CAN YOU HEAR IT? IT MIGHT BE THE SAME TH--
SSH!
SCRITCH SCRITCH
LISTEN...
SCRITCH SCRITCH SCRITCH
DON'T YOU MOVE. I'LL TAKE CARE OF THIS.
NO.
STAY HERE COLIN.
I'LL BE RIGHT BACK.
SCRITCH SCRITCH

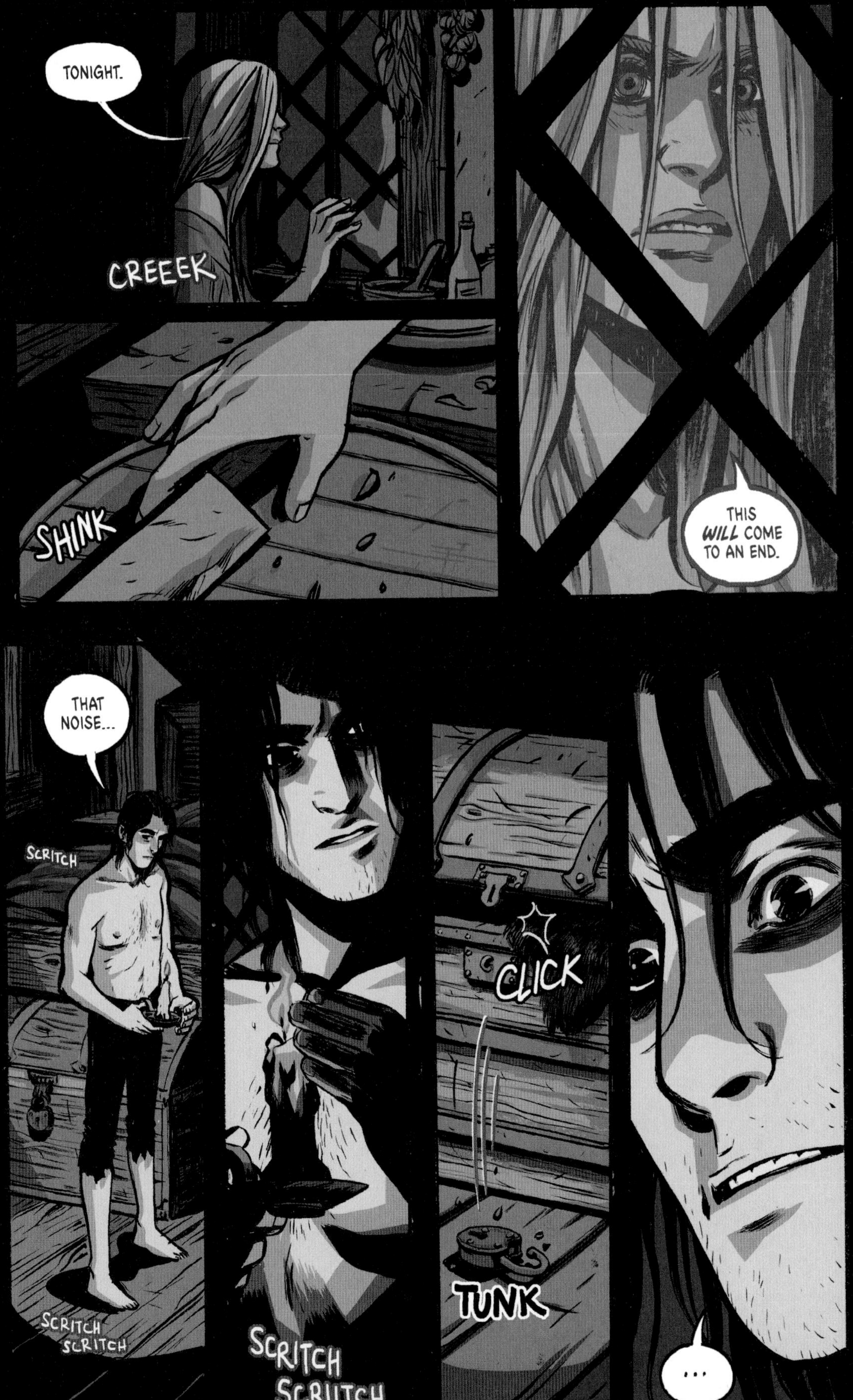
TONIGHT.
CREEEK
SHINK
THIS *WILL* COME TO AN END.
THAT NOISE...
SCRITCH
SCRITCH SCRITCH
SCRITCH SCRIITCH
CLICK
TUNK
...

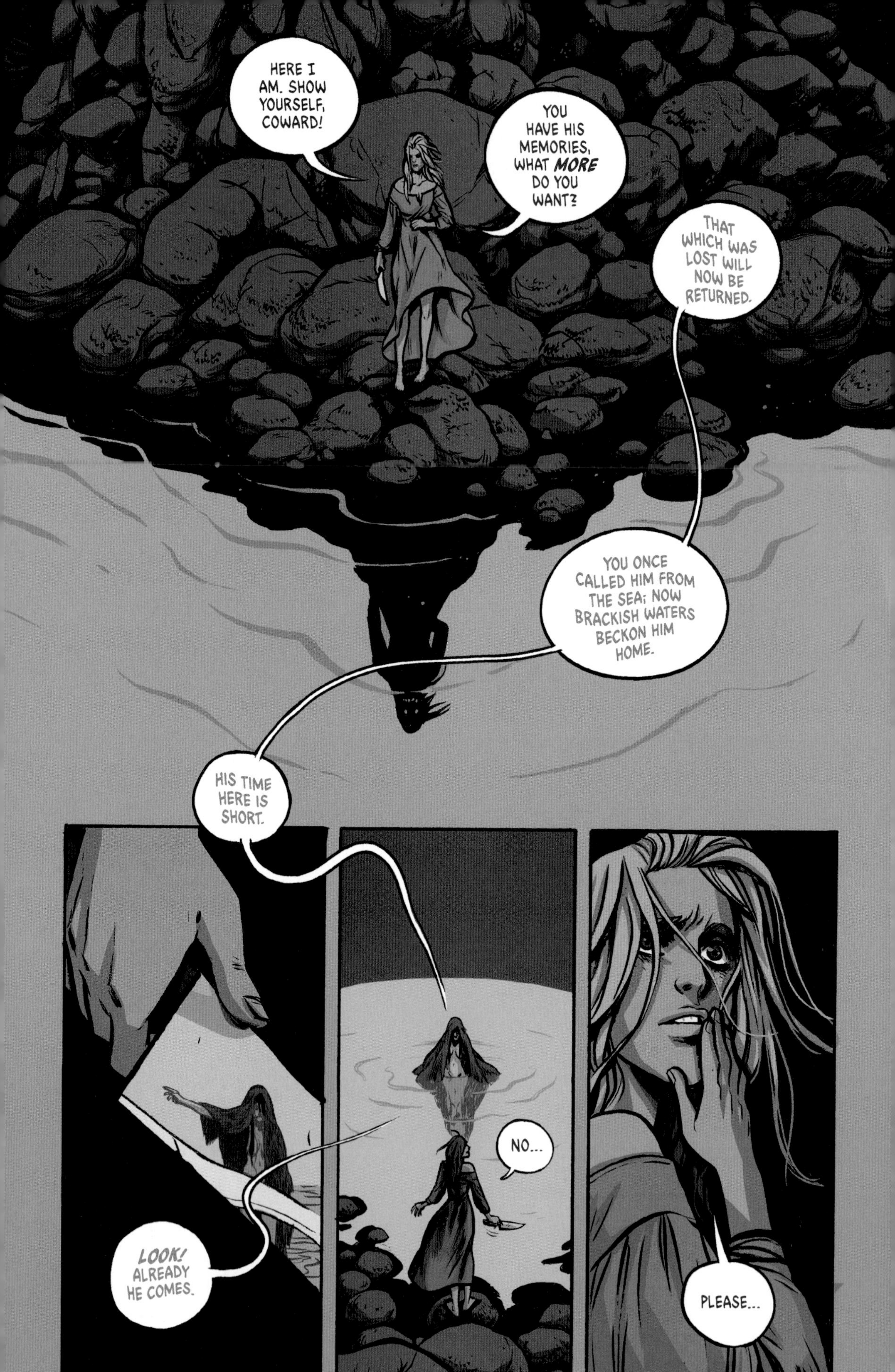
HERE I AM. SHOW YOURSELF, COWARD!
YOU HAVE HIS MEMORIES, WHAT MORE DO YOU WANT?
THAT WHICH WAS LOST WILL NOW BE RETURNED.
YOU ONCE CALLED HIM FROM THE SEA; NOW BRACKISH WATERS BECKON HIM HOME.
HIS TIME HERE IS SHORT.
LOOK! ALREADY HE COMES.
NO...
PLEASE...

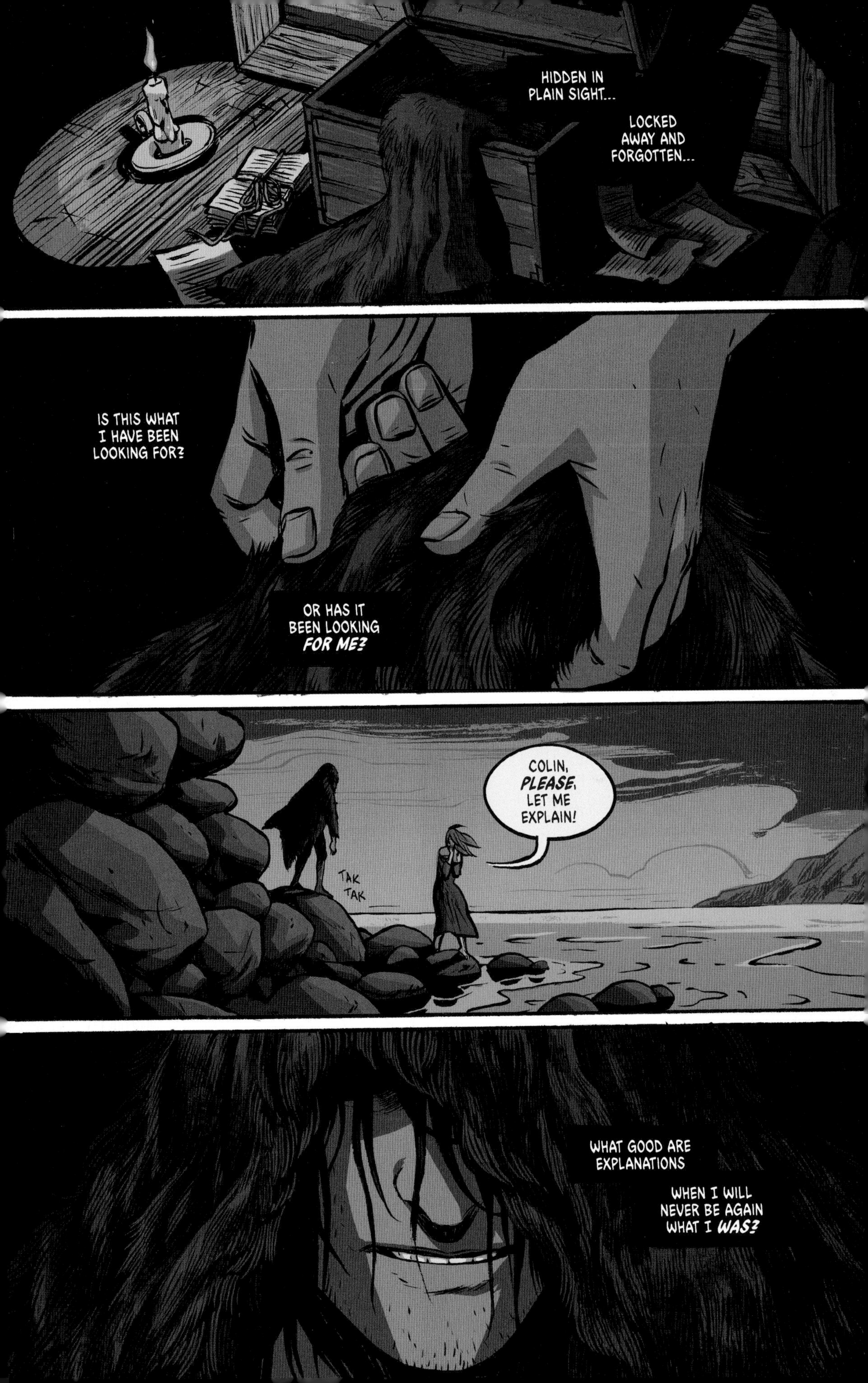
HIDDEN IN PLAIN SIGHT...
LOCKED AWAY AND FORGOTTEN...
IS THIS WHAT I HAVE BEEN LOOKING FOR?
OR HAS IT BEEN LOOKING *FOR ME?*
TAK TAK
COLIN, *PLEASE*, LET ME EXPLAIN!
WHAT GOOD ARE EXPLANATIONS
WHEN I WILL NEVER BE AGAIN WHAT I *WAS?*

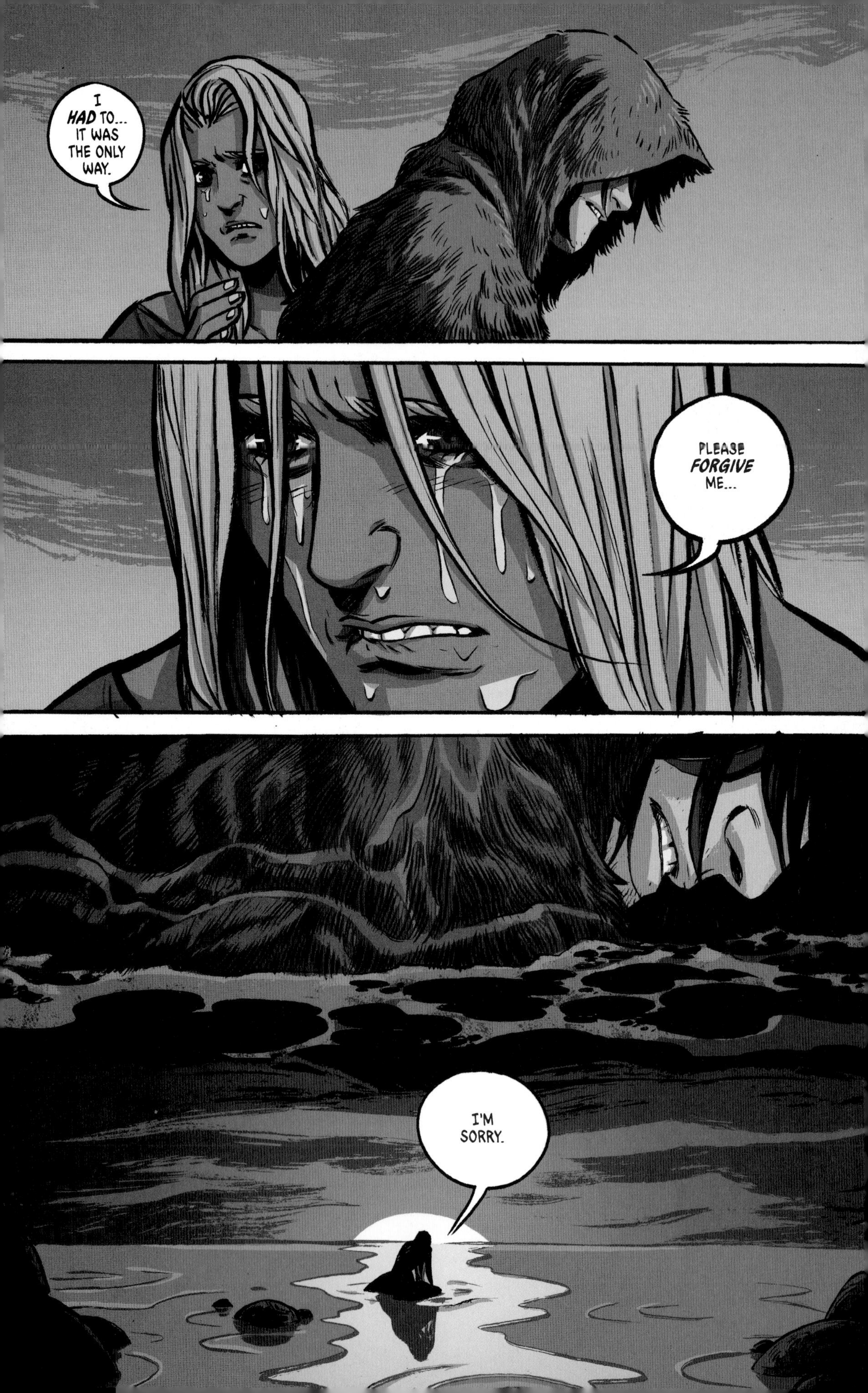
I HAD TO... IT WAS THE ONLY WAY.
PLEASE FORGIVE ME...
I'M SORRY.

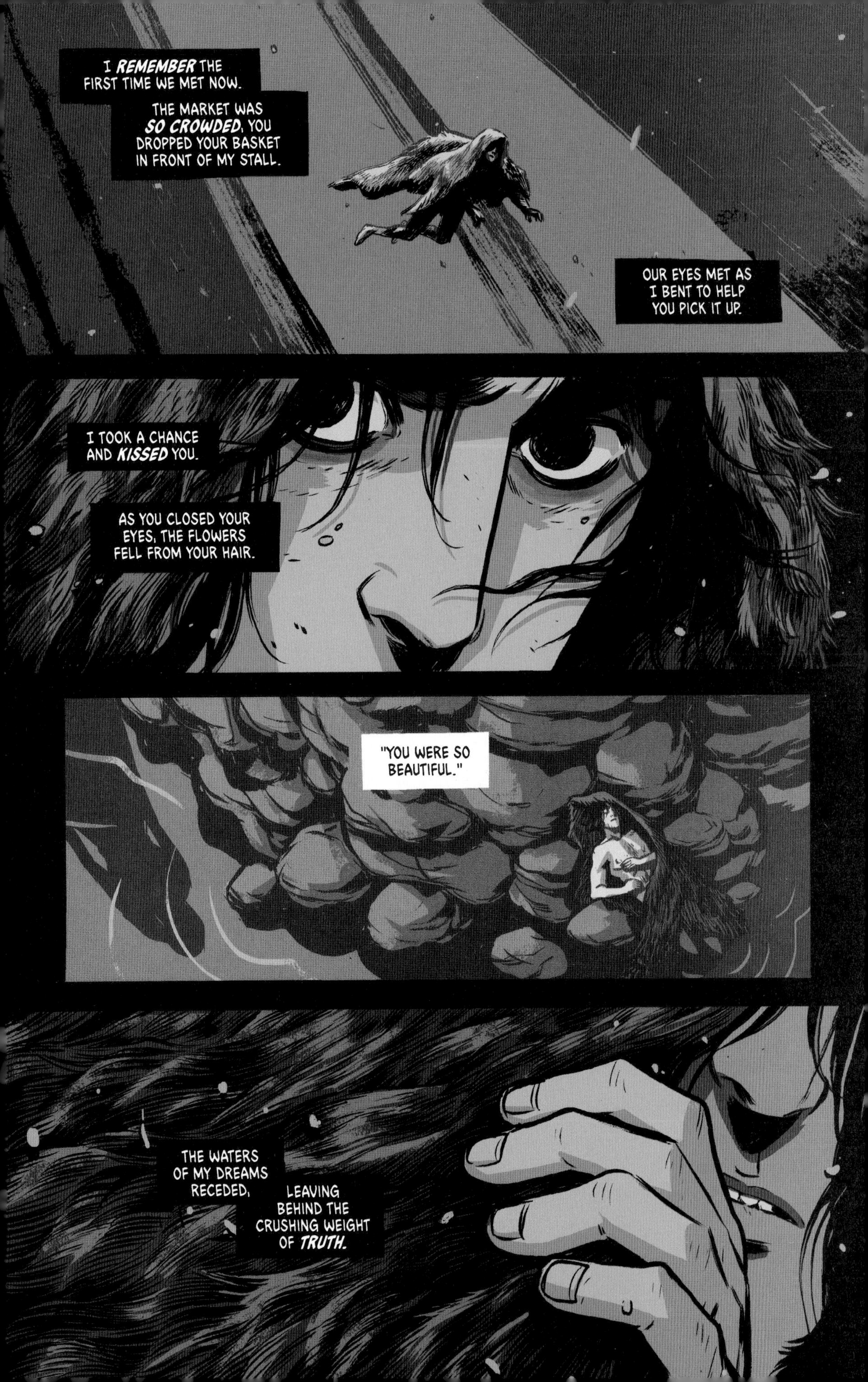
I *REMEMBER* THE FIRST TIME WE MET NOW.
THE MARKET WAS *SO CROWDED*, YOU DROPPED YOUR BASKET IN FRONT OF MY STALL.
OUR EYES MET AS I BENT TO HELP YOU PICK IT UP.
I TOOK A CHANCE AND *KISSED* YOU.
AS YOU CLOSED YOUR EYES, THE FLOWERS FELL FROM YOUR HAIR.
"YOU WERE SO BEAUTIFUL."
THE WATERS OF MY DREAMS RECEDED,
LEAVING BEHIND THE CRUSHING WEIGHT OF *TRUTH*.

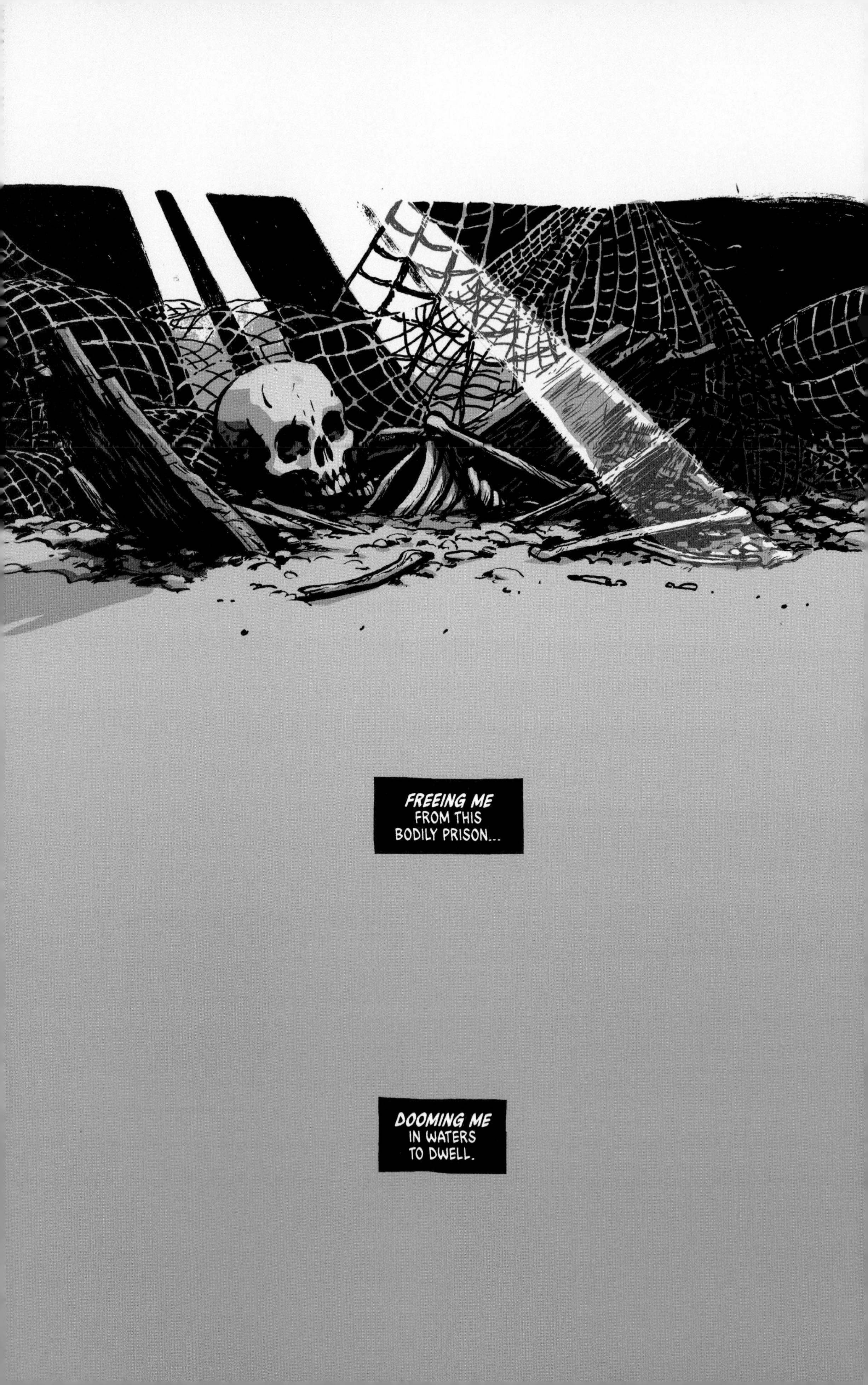
FREEING ME FROM THIS BODILY PRISON...
DOOMING ME IN WATERS TO DWELL.

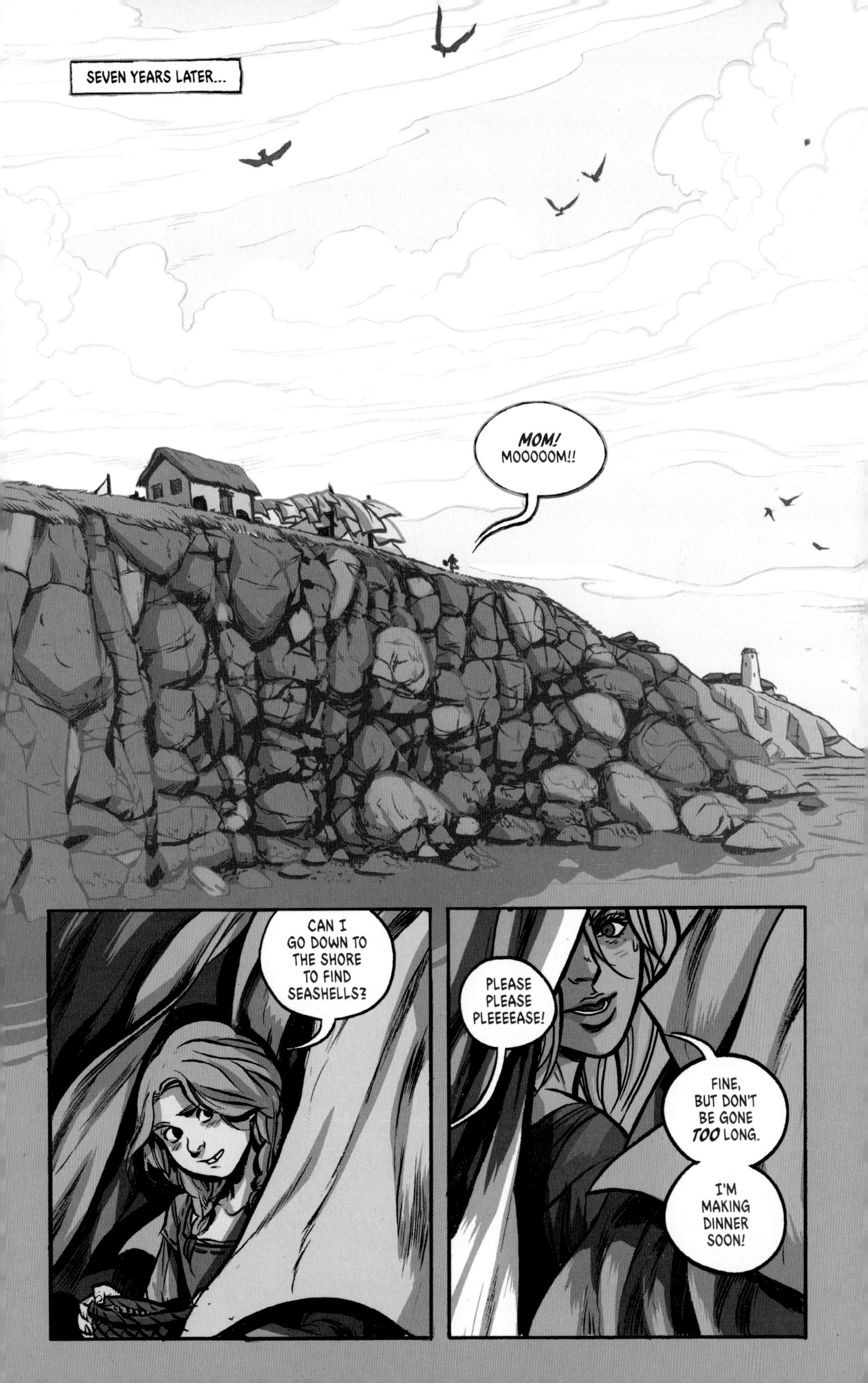
SEVEN YEARS LATER...
MOM! MOOOOOM!!
CAN I GO DOWN TO THE SHORE TO FIND SEASHELLS?
PLEASE PLEASE PLEEEEASE!
FINE, BUT DON'T BE GONE TOO LONG.
I'M MAKING DINNER SOON!

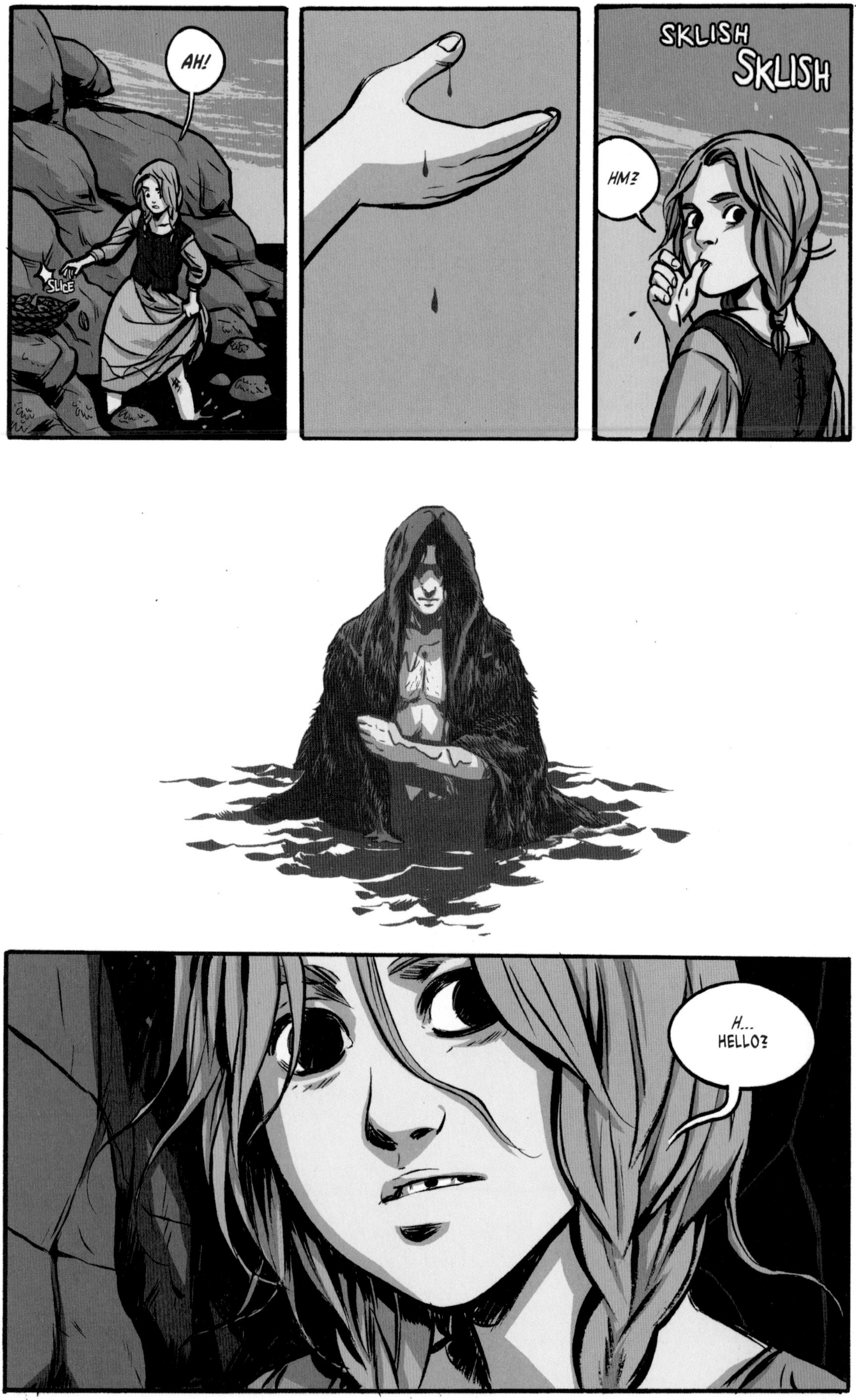
AH!
SLICE
SKLISH
SKLISH
HM?
H...
HELLO?

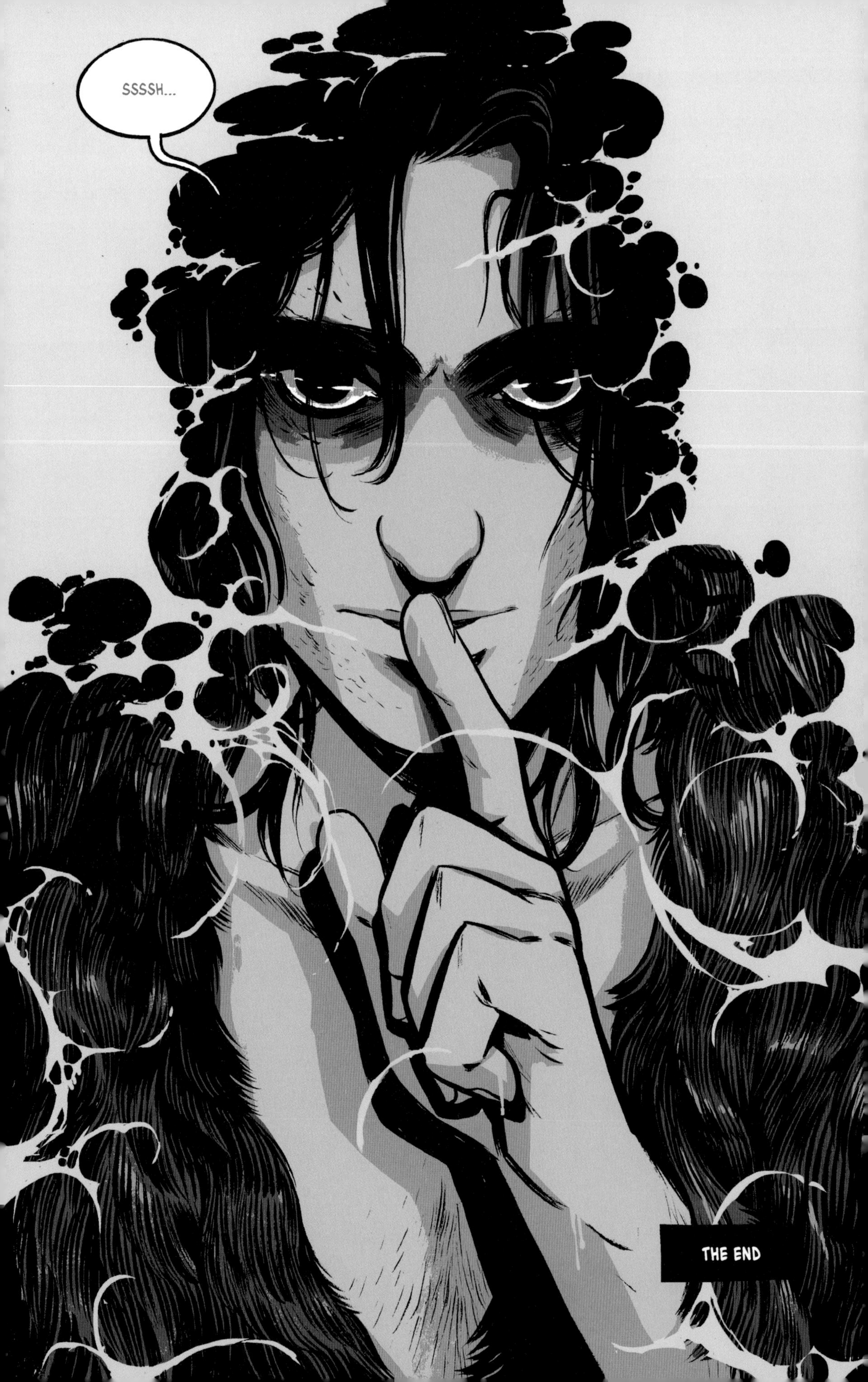
SSSSH...
THE END

# IV.

Concept Sketches
& Illustrations

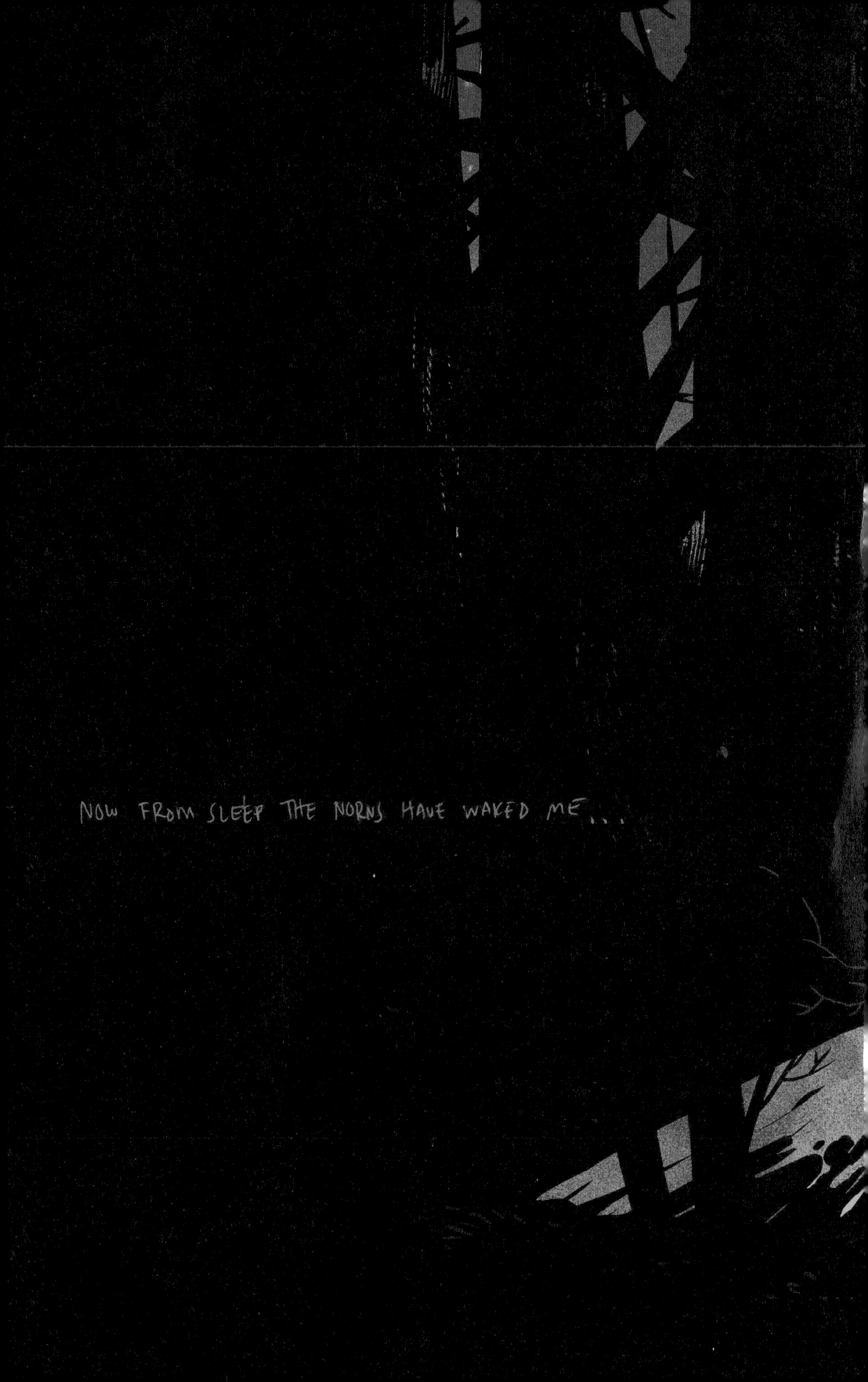
NOW FROM SLEEP THE NORNS HAVE WAKED ME...

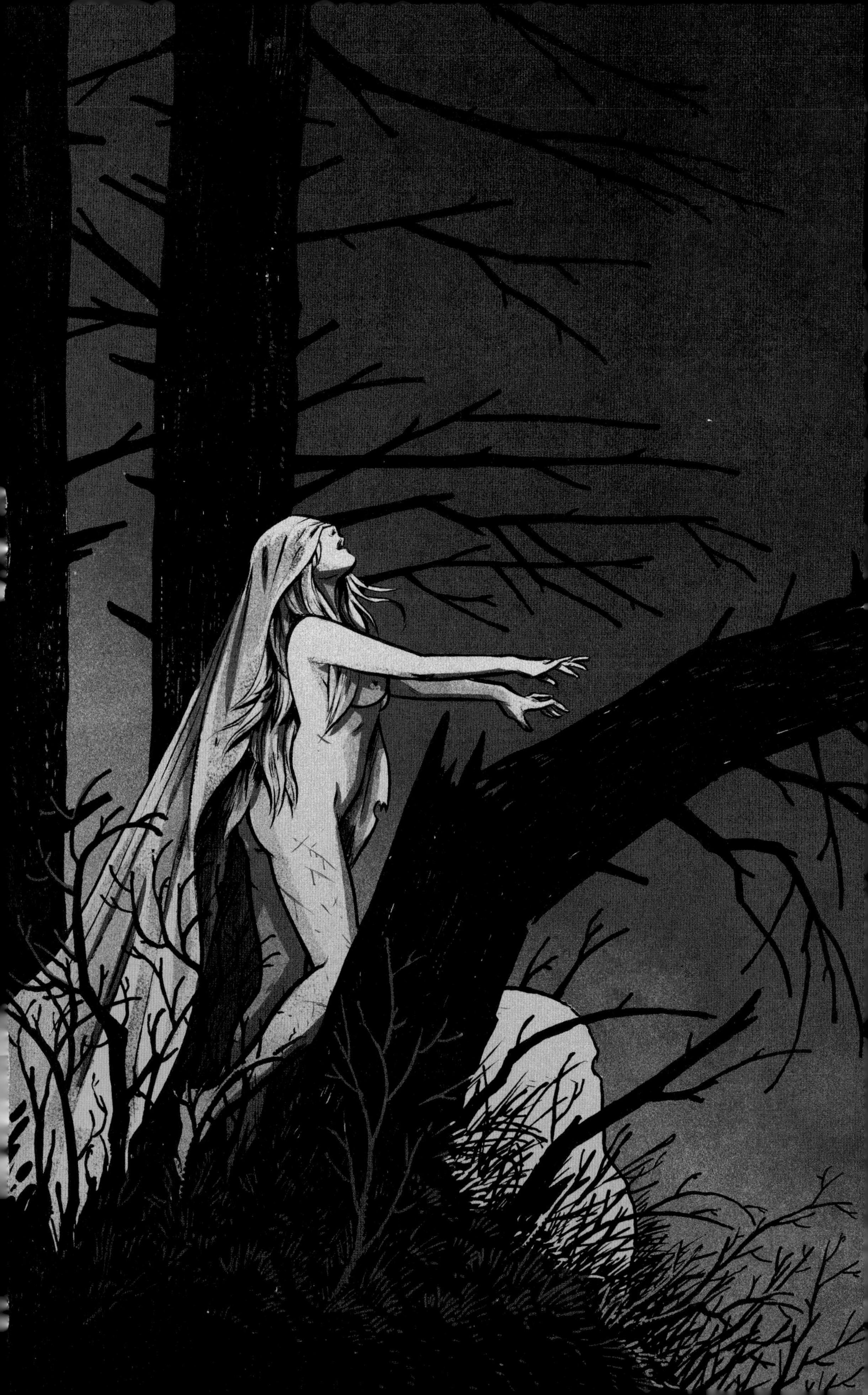

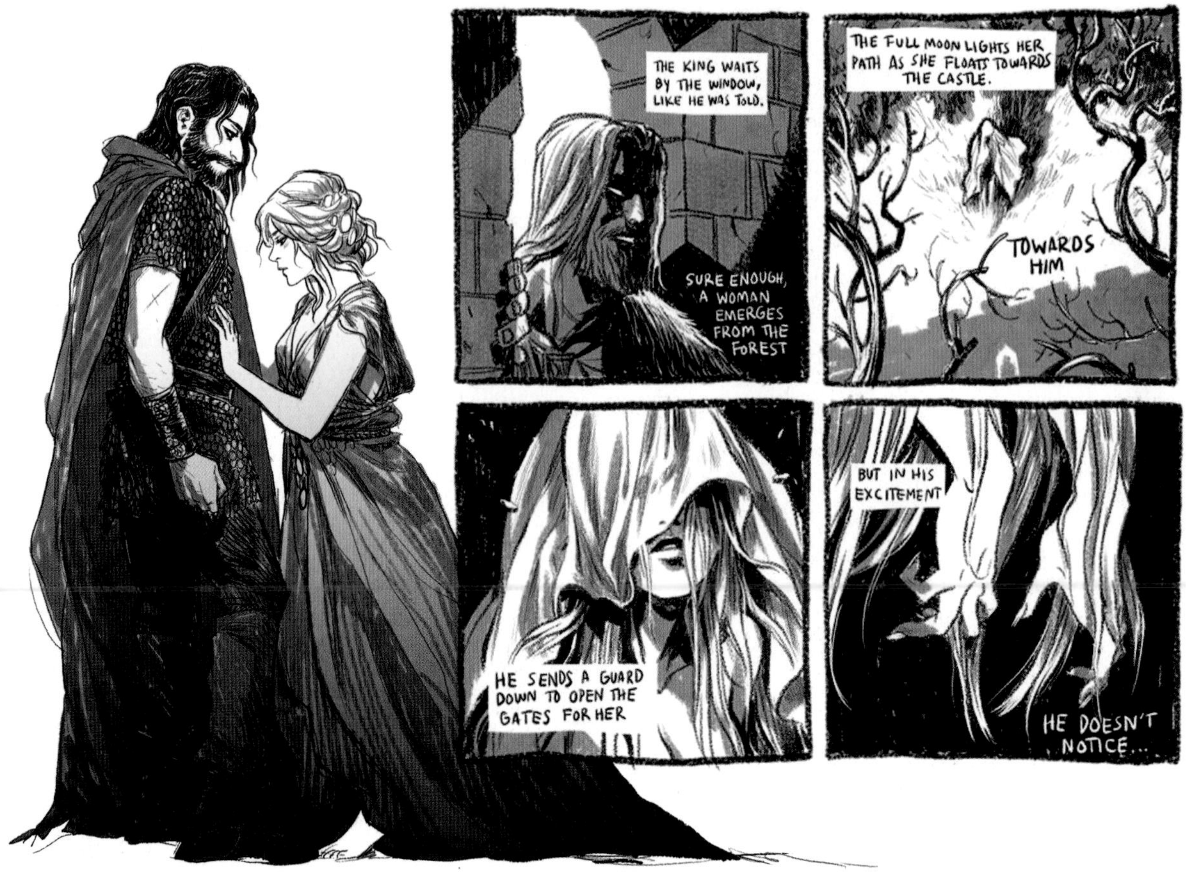
THE KING WAITS BY THE WINDOW, LIKE HE WAS TOLD.
SURE ENOUGH, A WOMAN EMERGES FROM THE FOREST
THE FULL MOON LIGHTS HER PATH AS SHE FLOATS TOWARDS THE CASTLE.
TOWARDS HIM
HE SENDS A GUARD DOWN TO OPEN THE GATES FOR HER
BUT IN HIS EXCITEMENT
HE DOESN'T NOTICE...

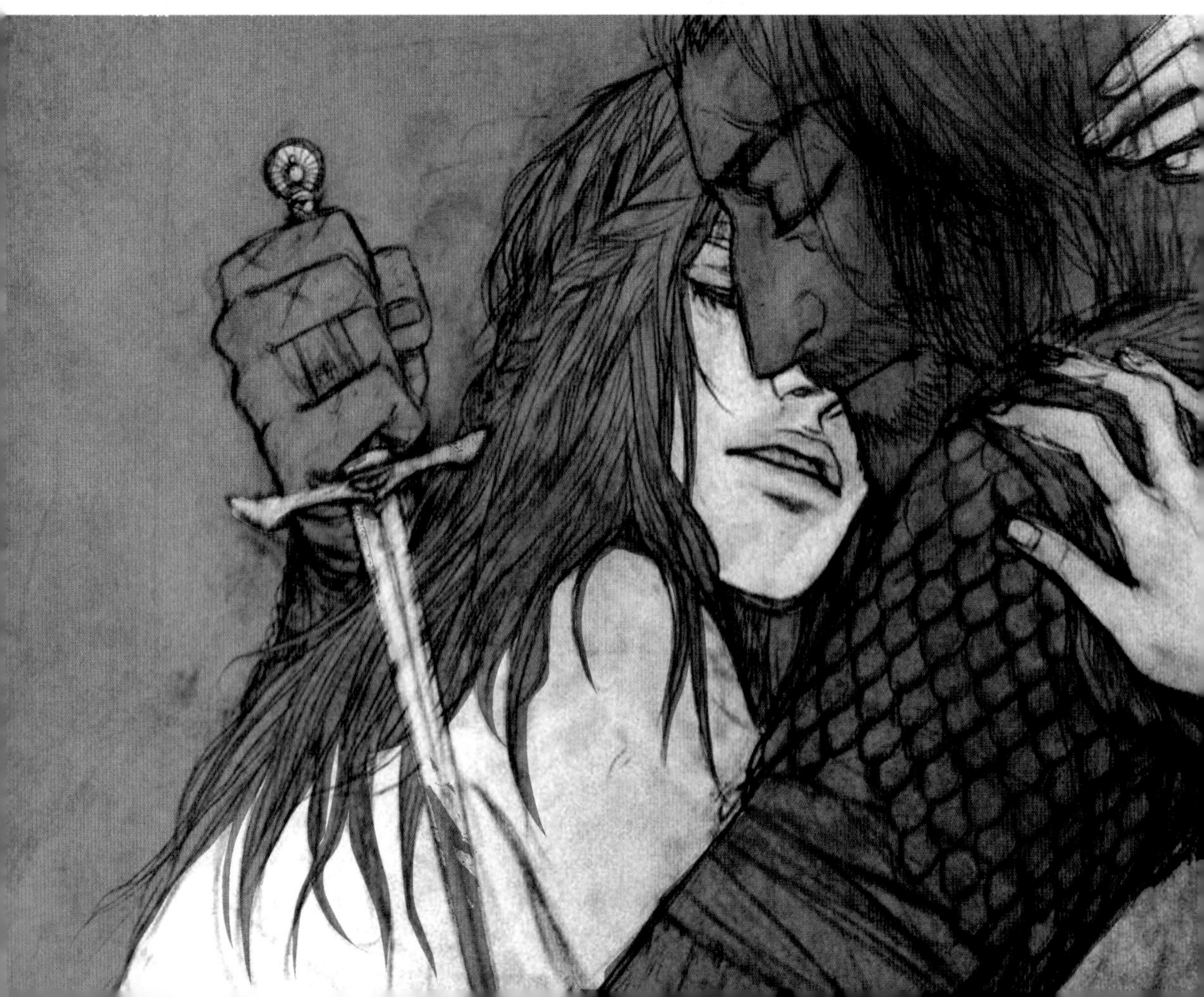

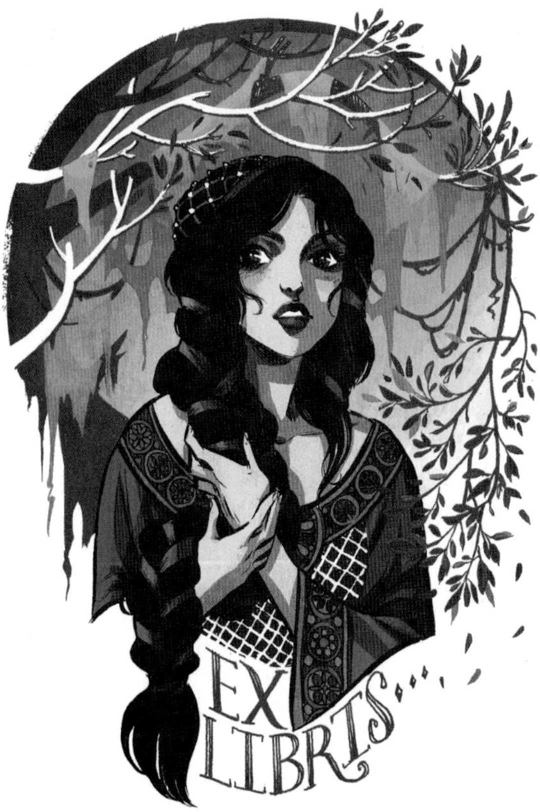
EX
LIBRIS
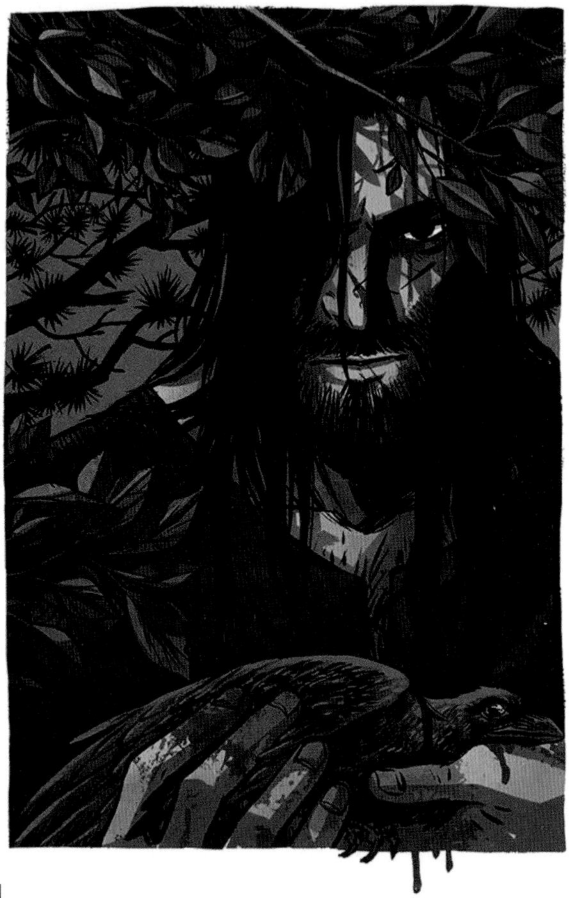
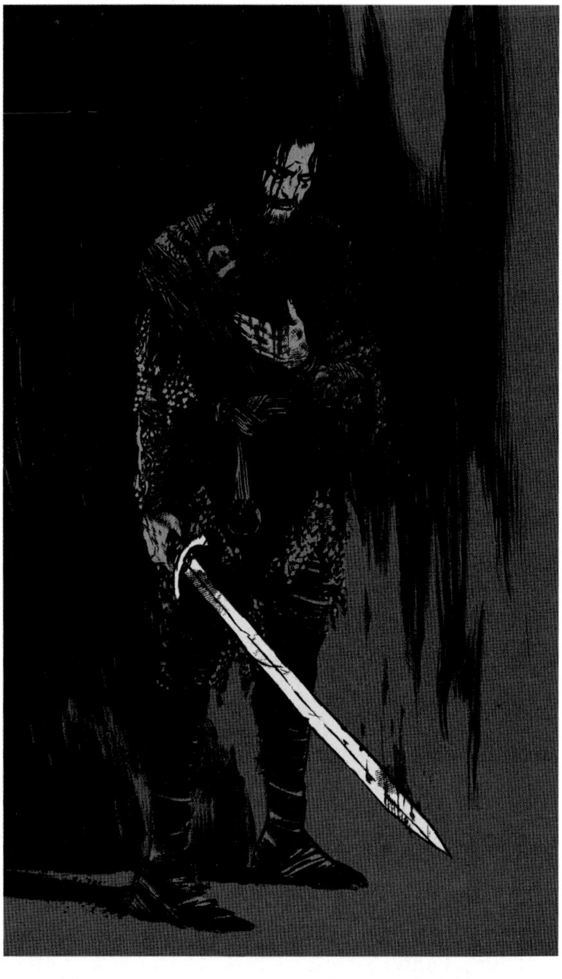
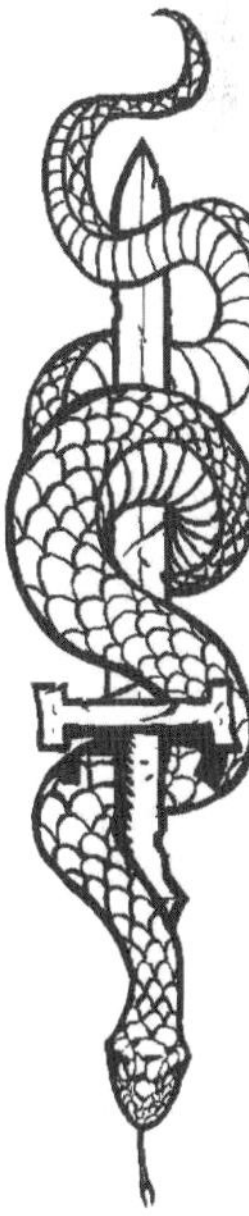

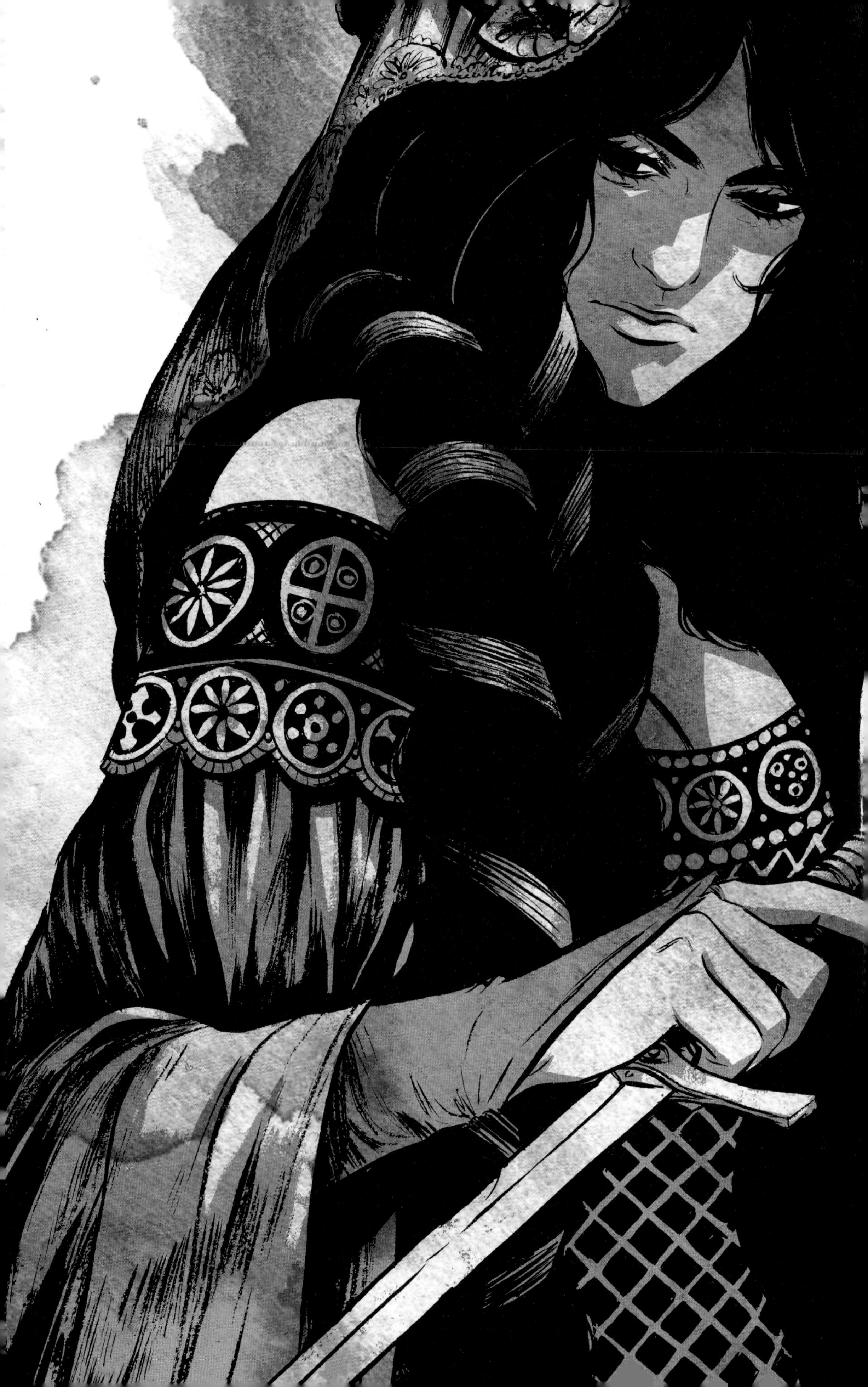

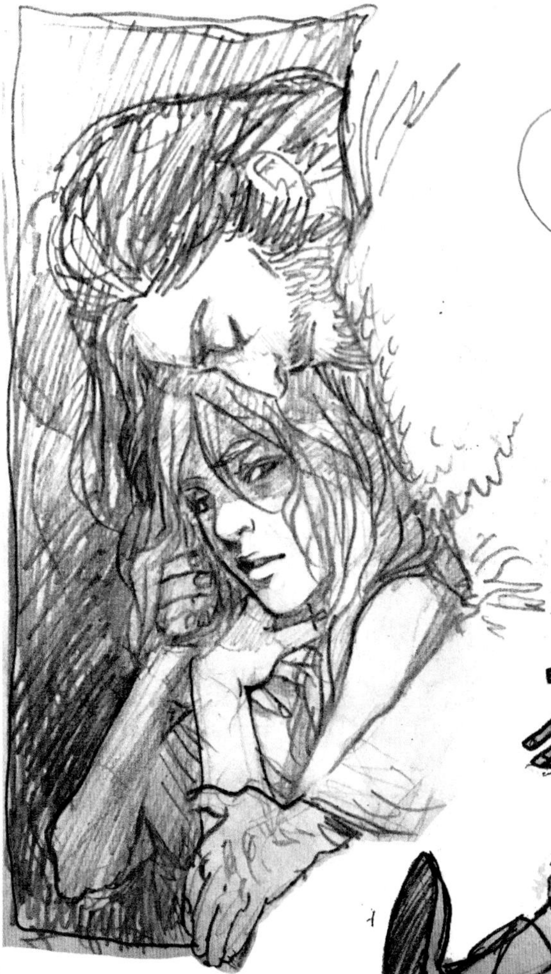
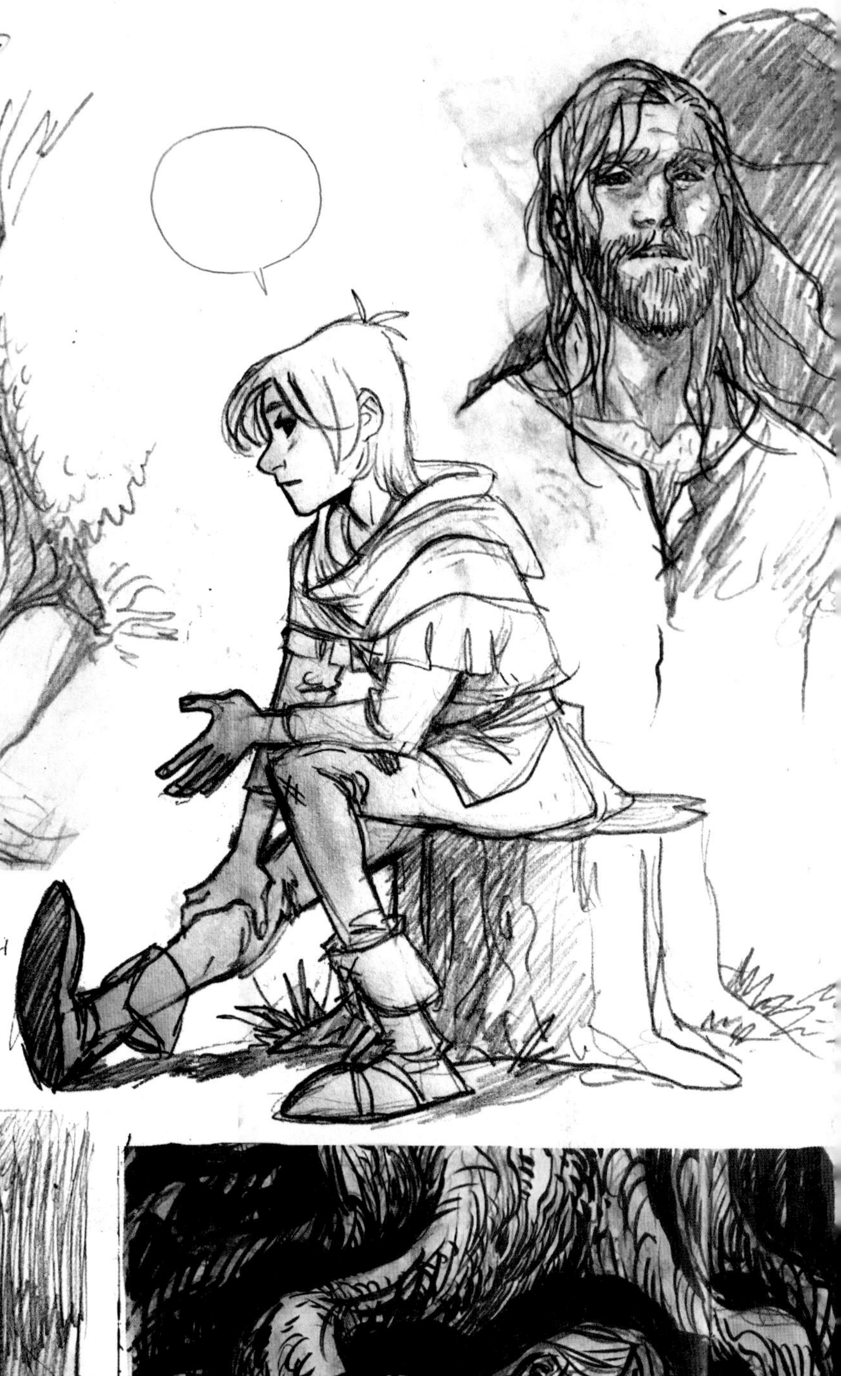
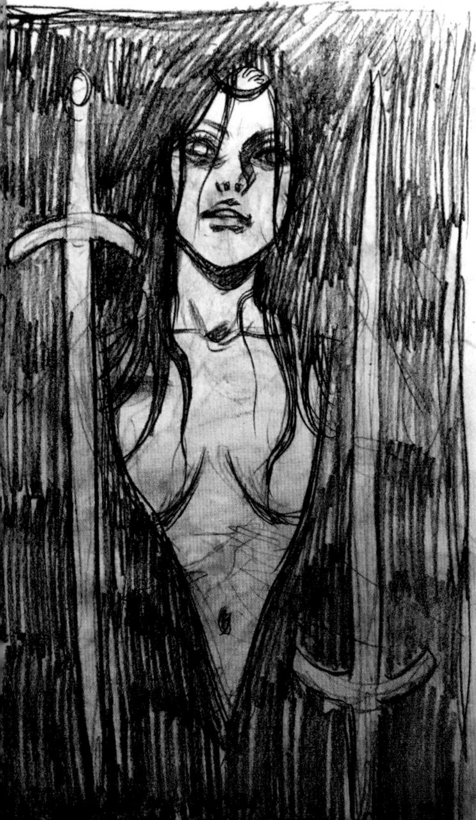
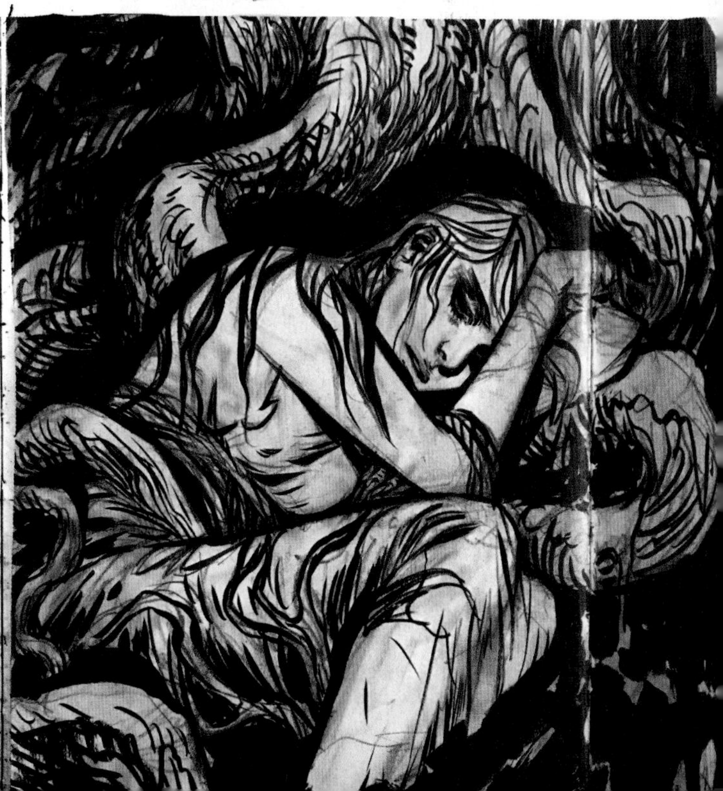

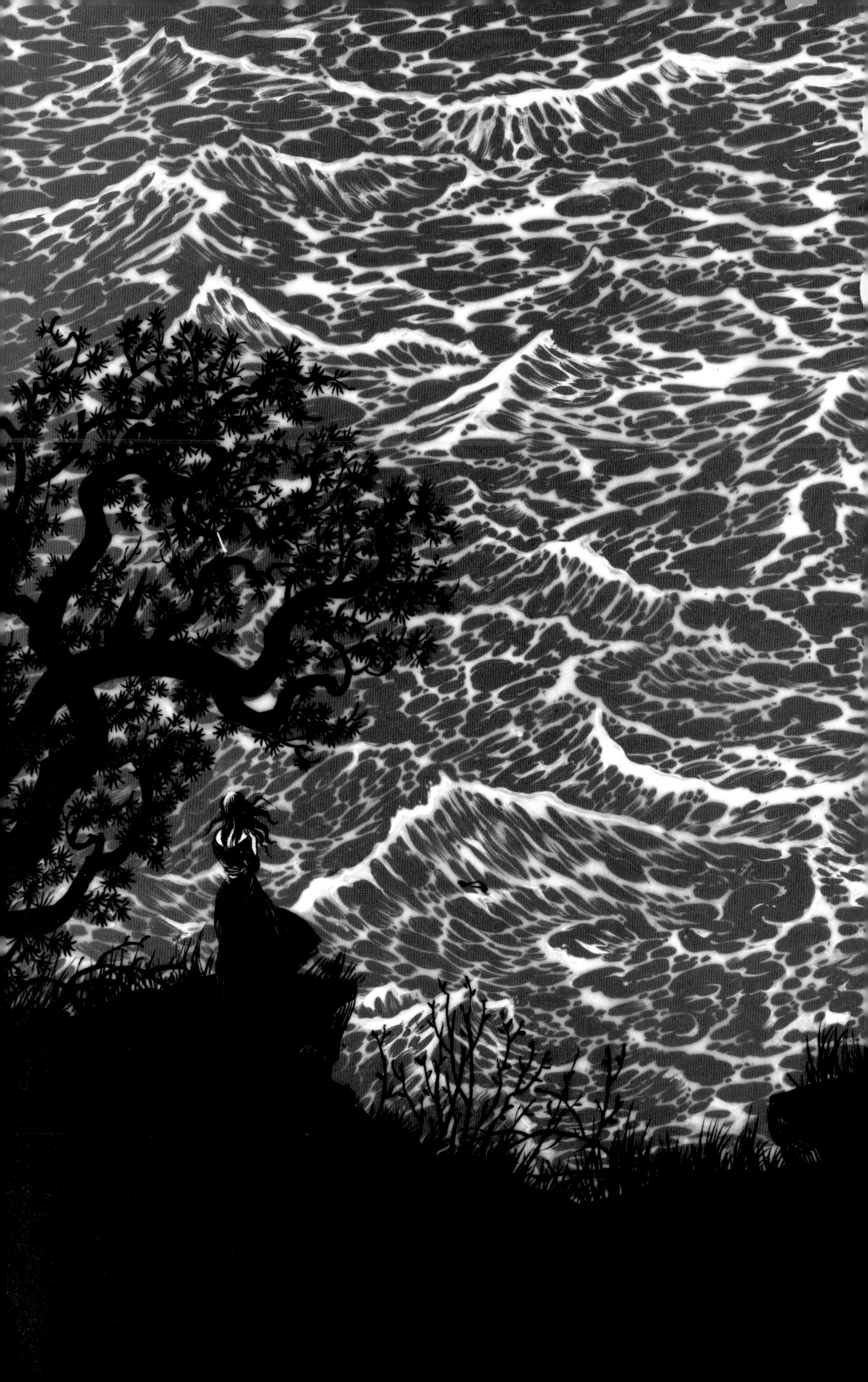

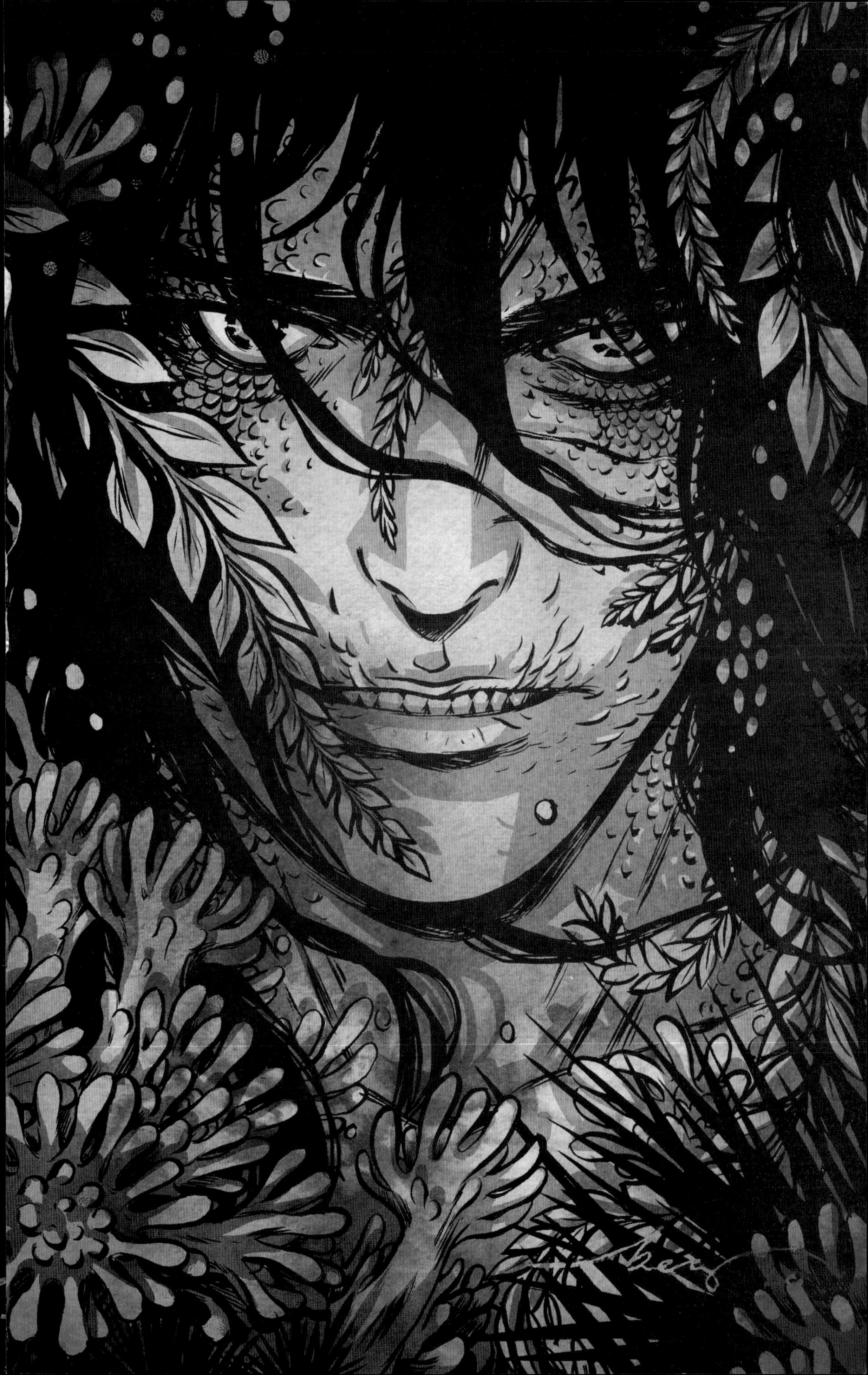

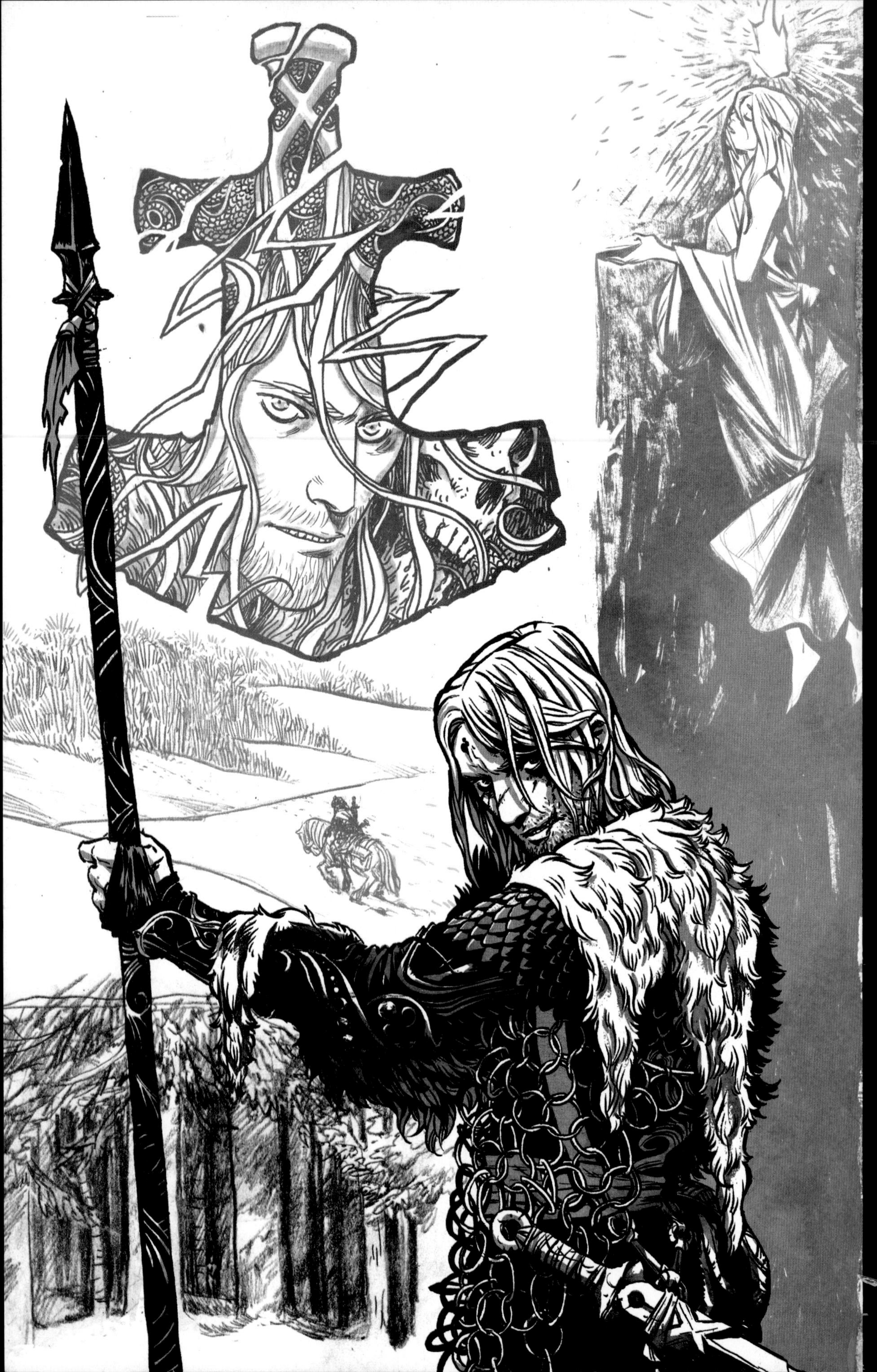

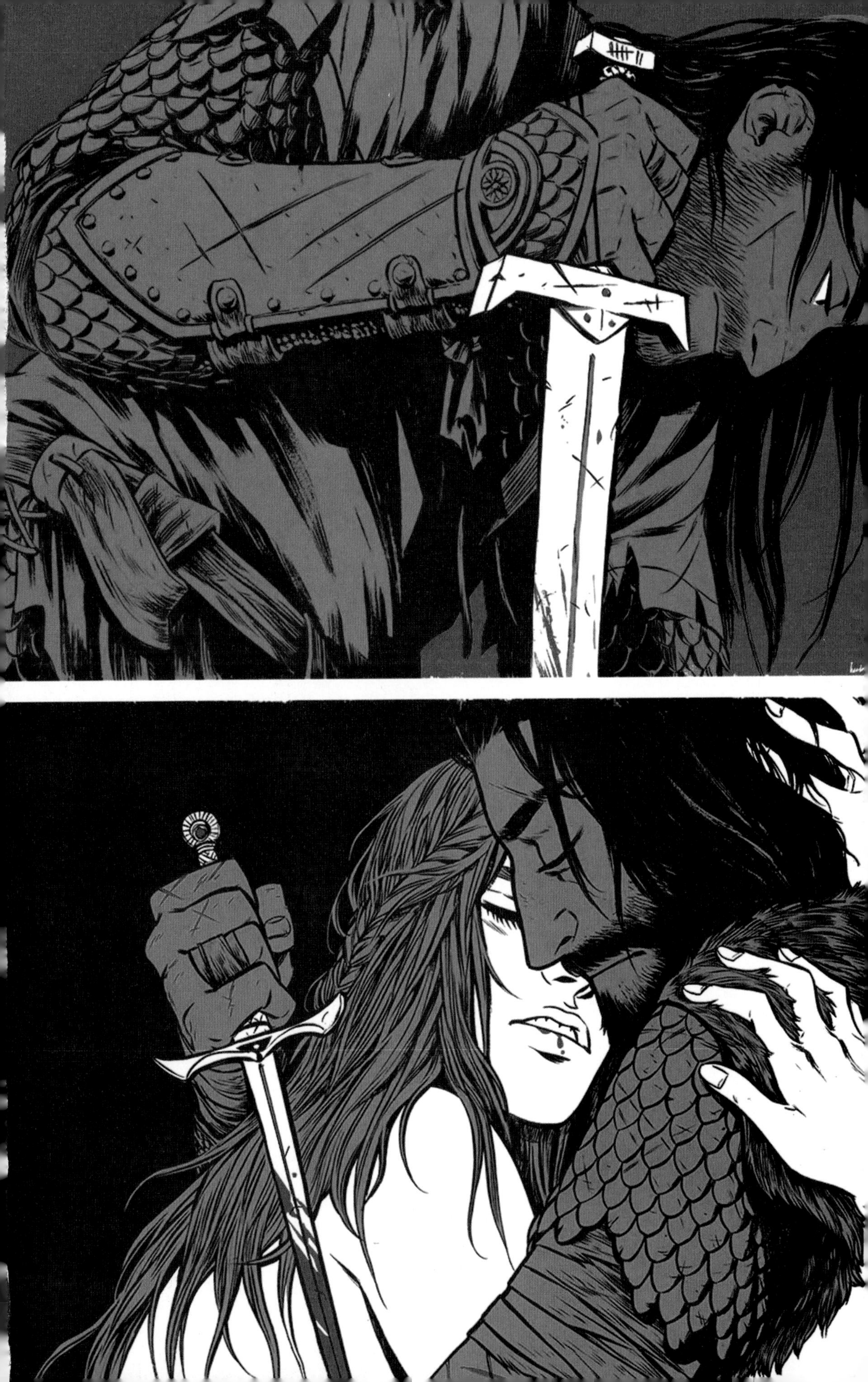

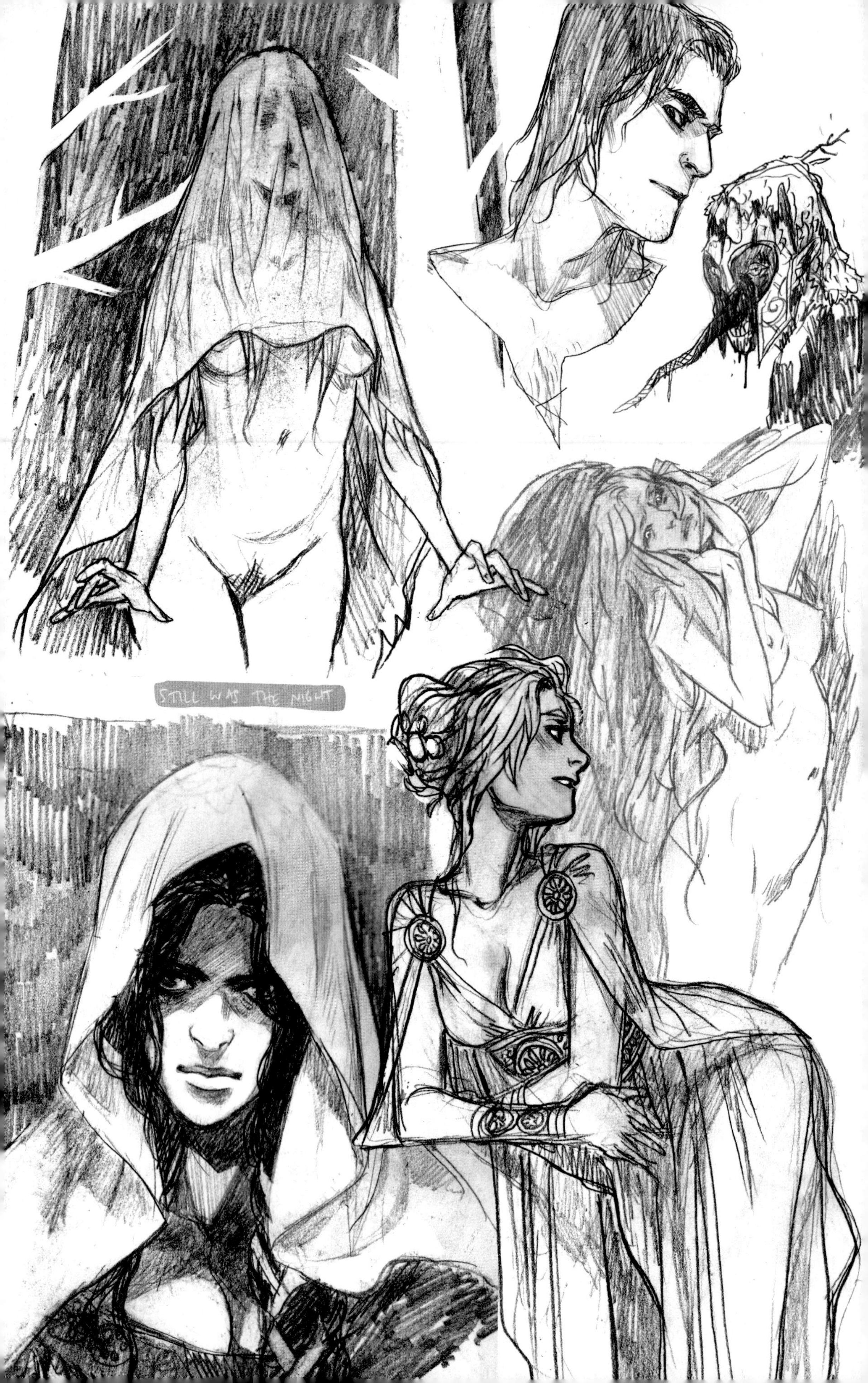
STILL WAS THE NIGHT

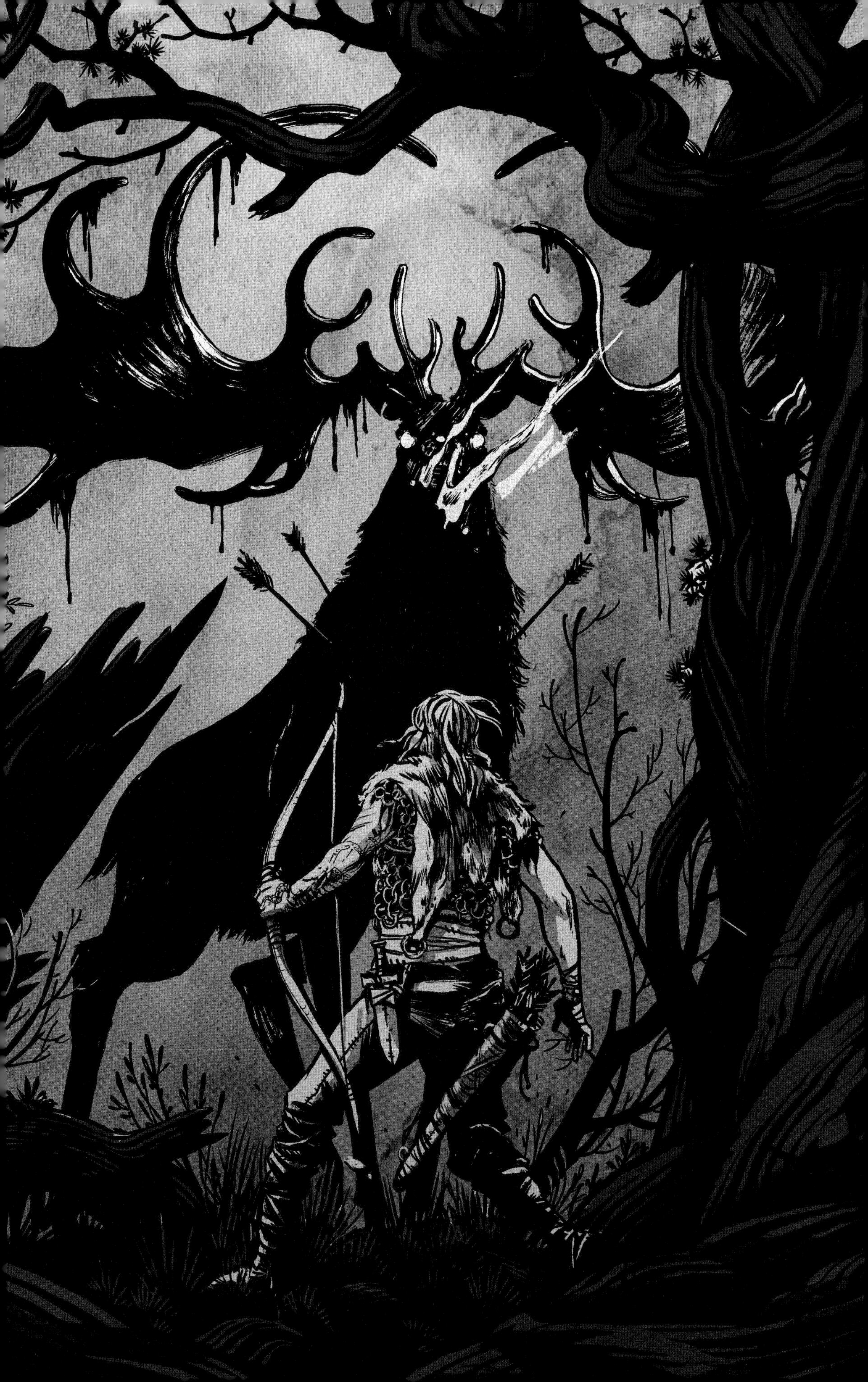

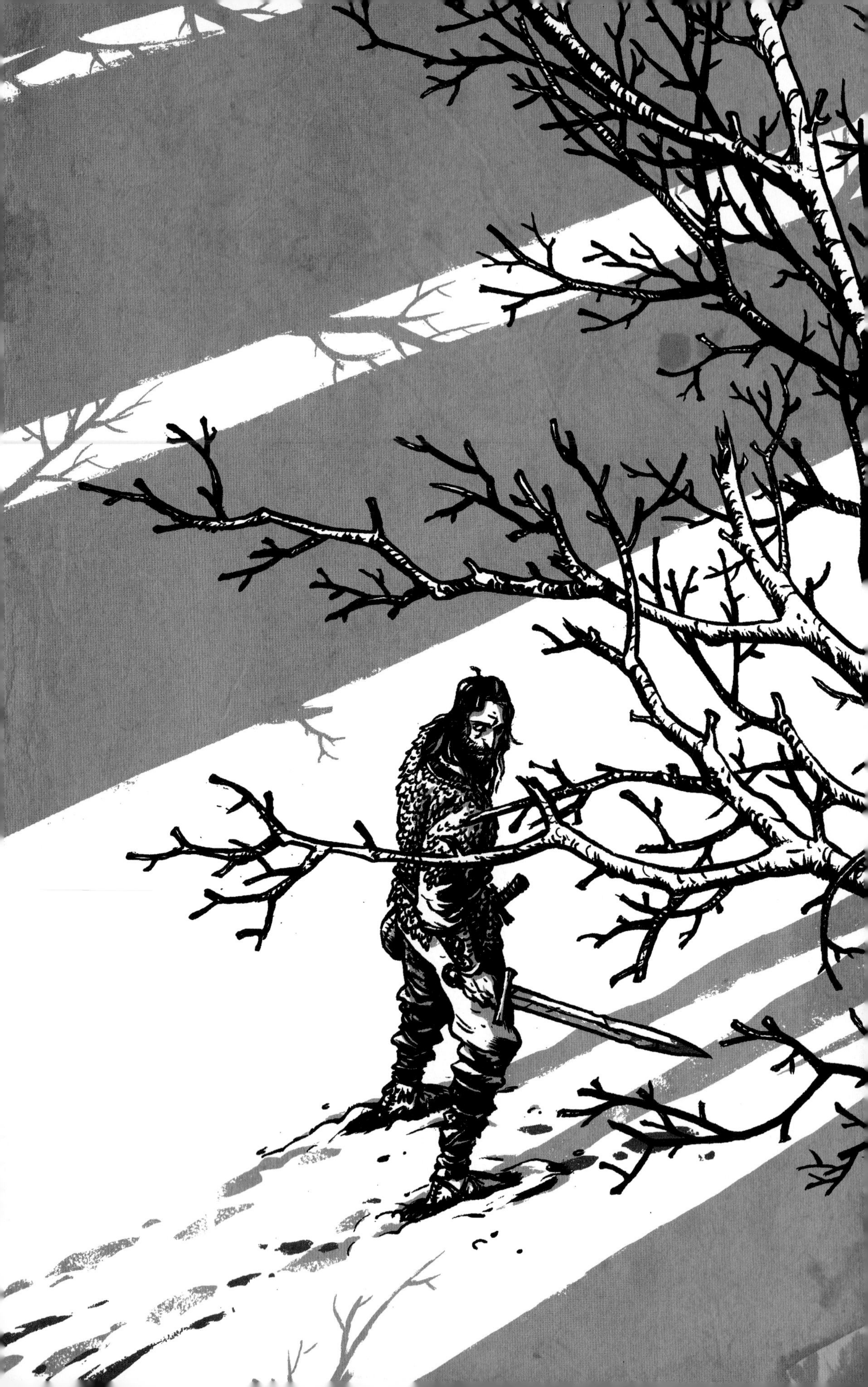

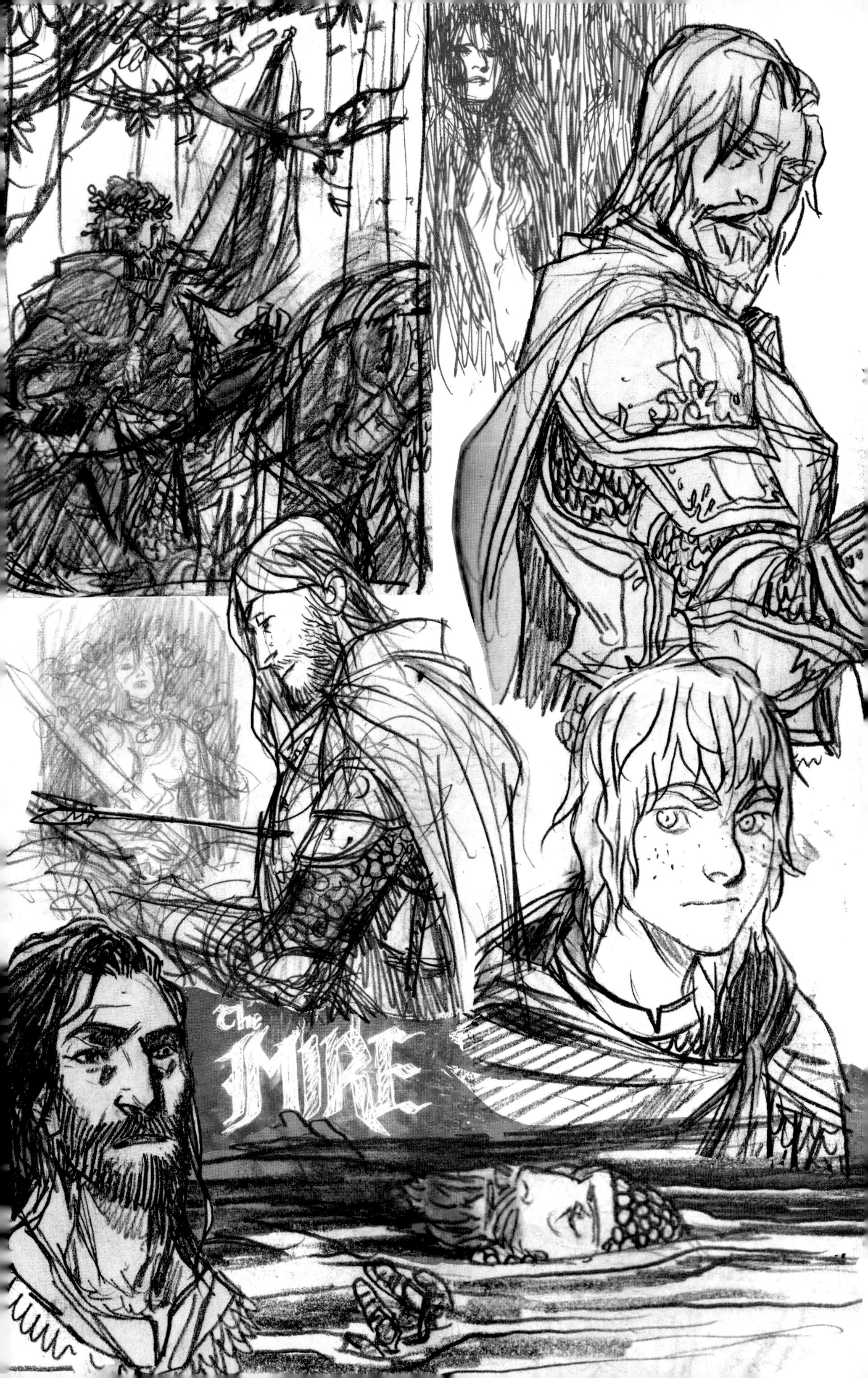
The MIRE

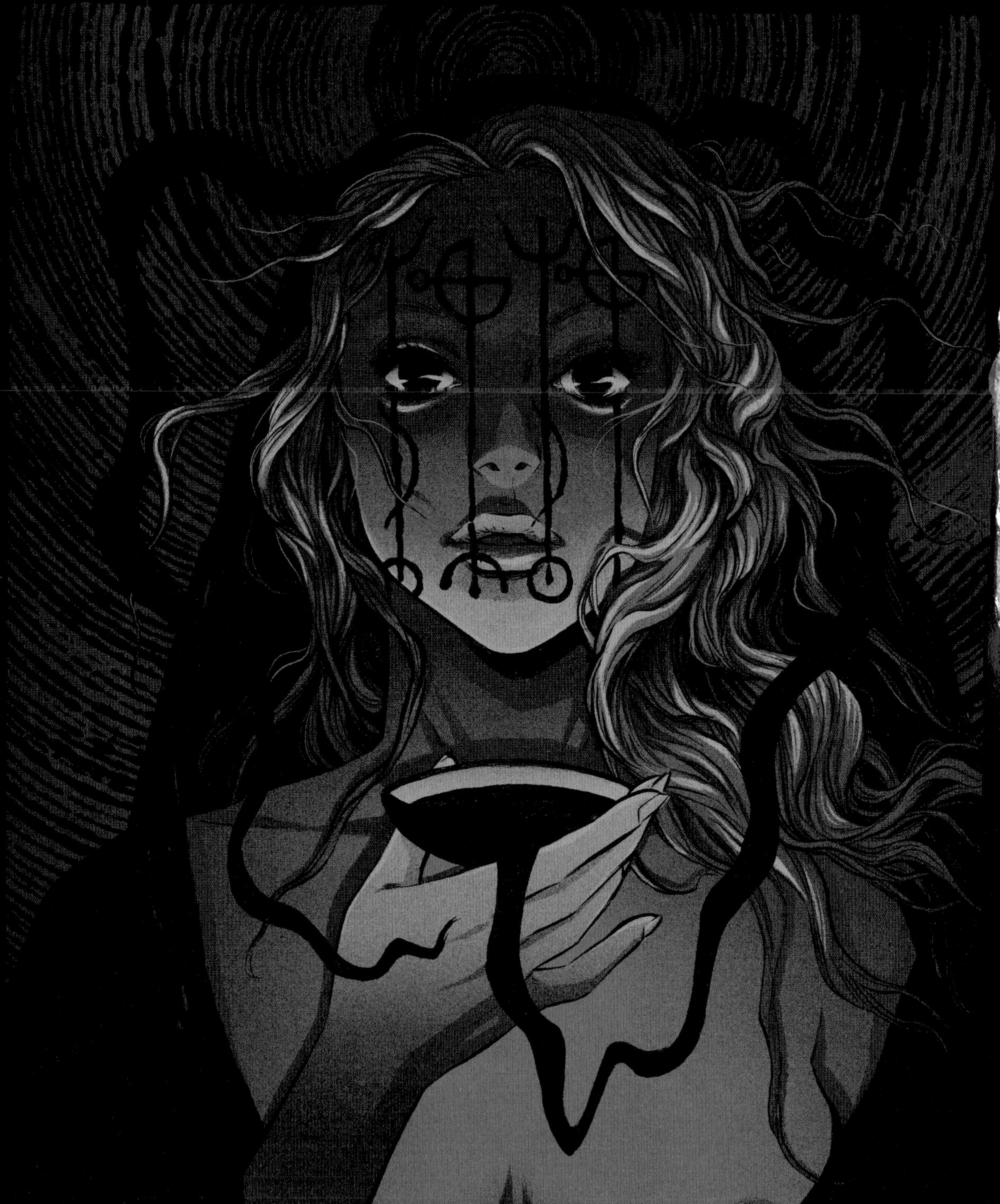

DRAUMSTAFIR—

TO DREAM OF UNFULFILLED DESIRES

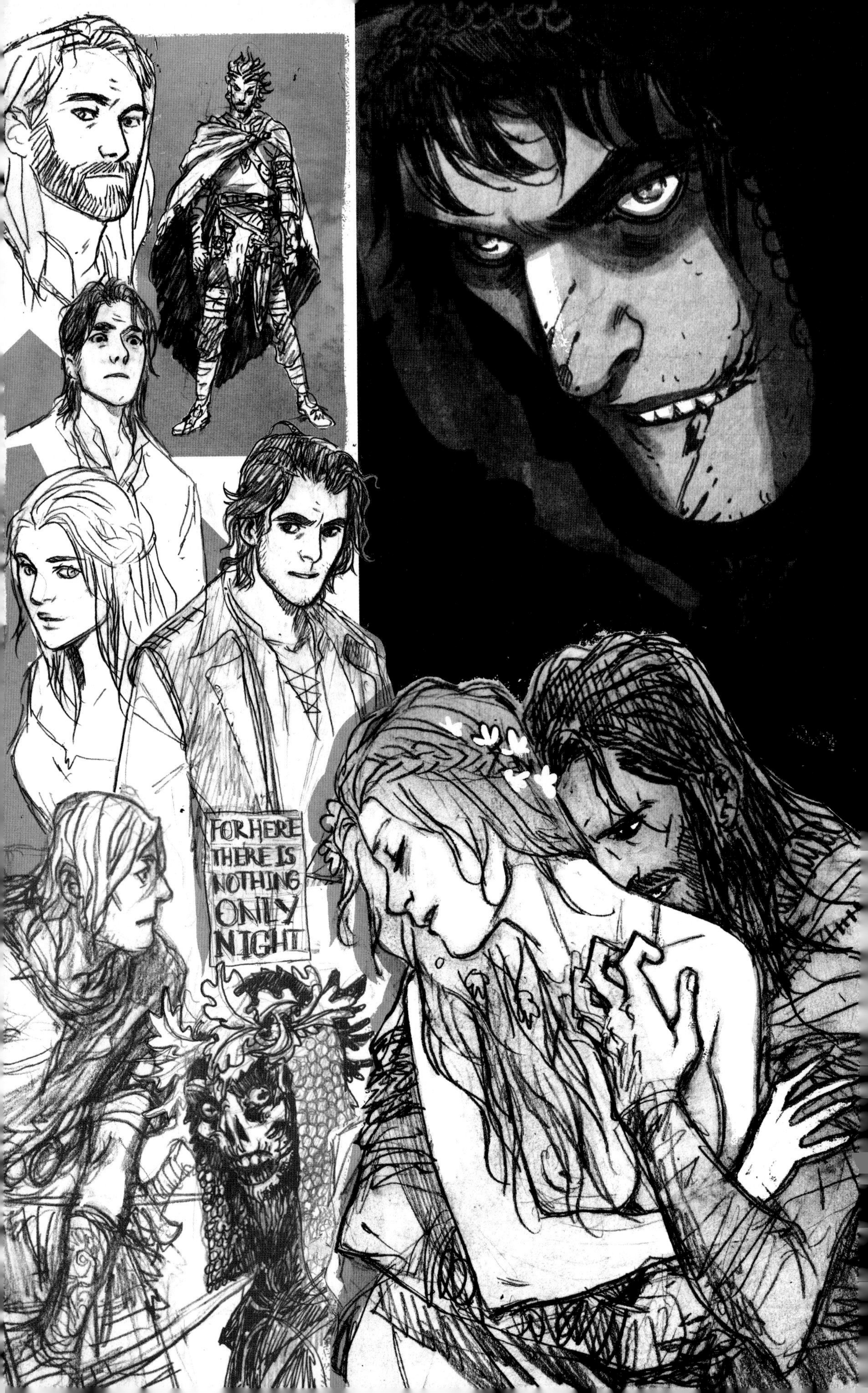

FOR HERE
THERE IS
NOTHING
ONLY
NIGHT

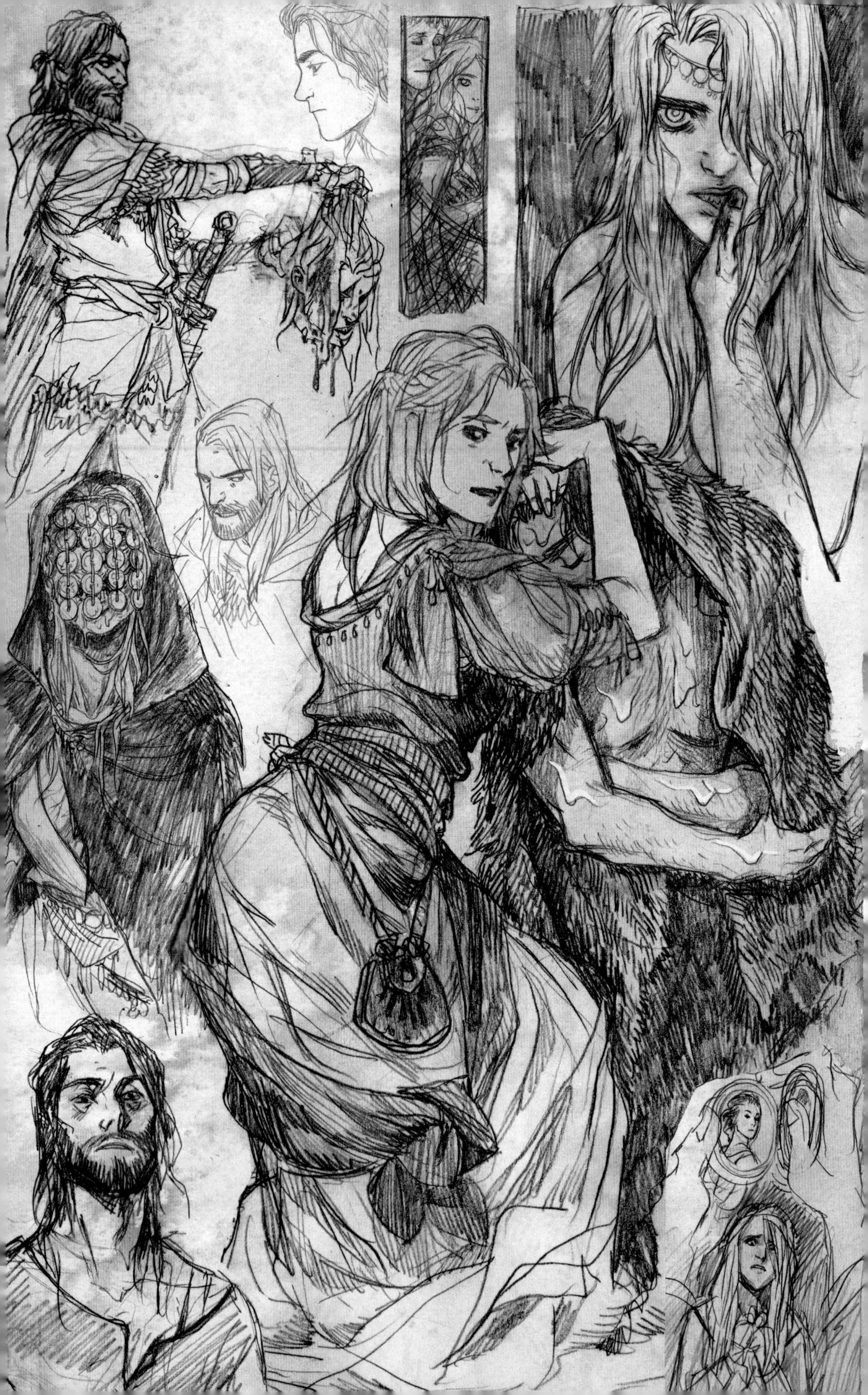

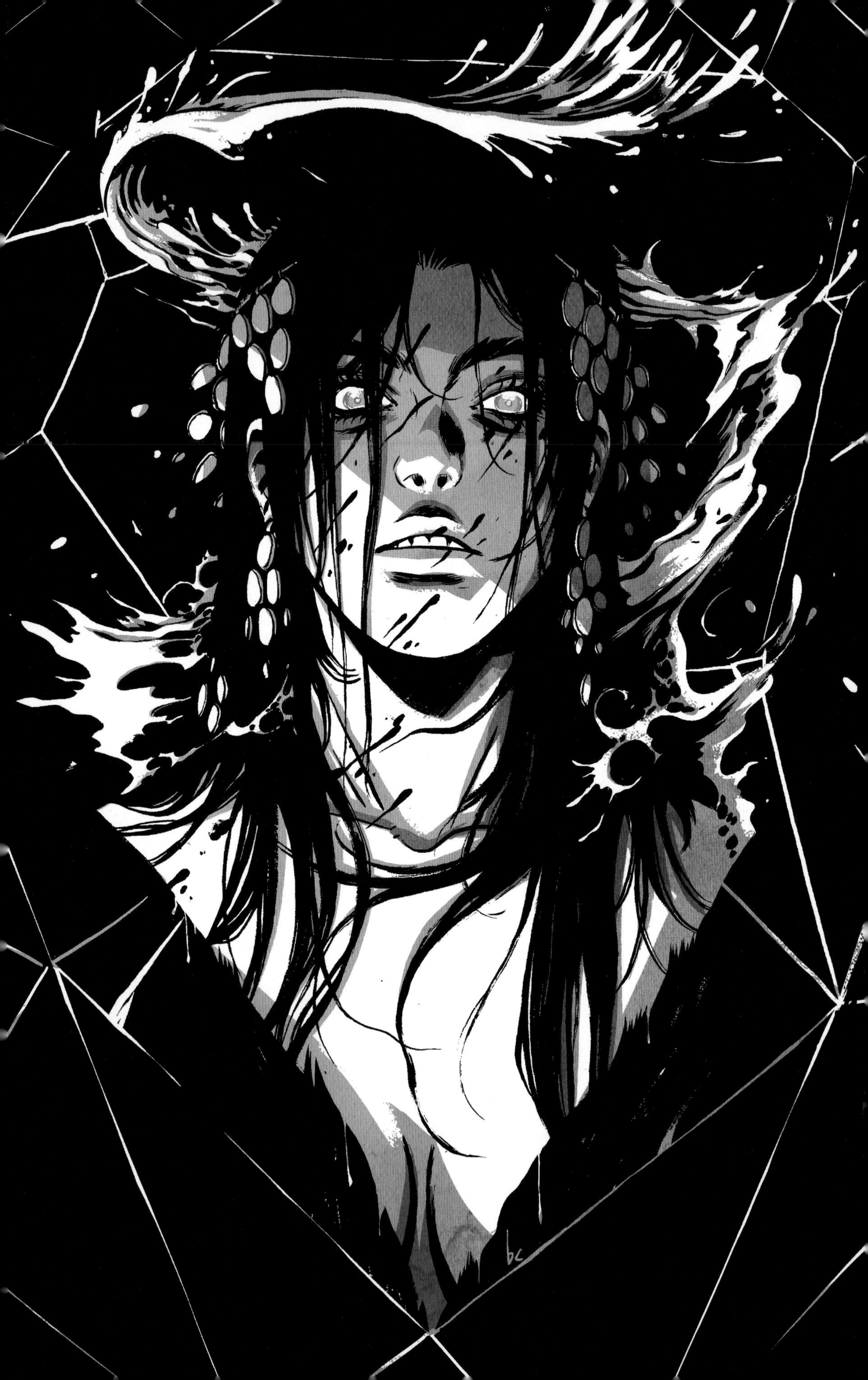

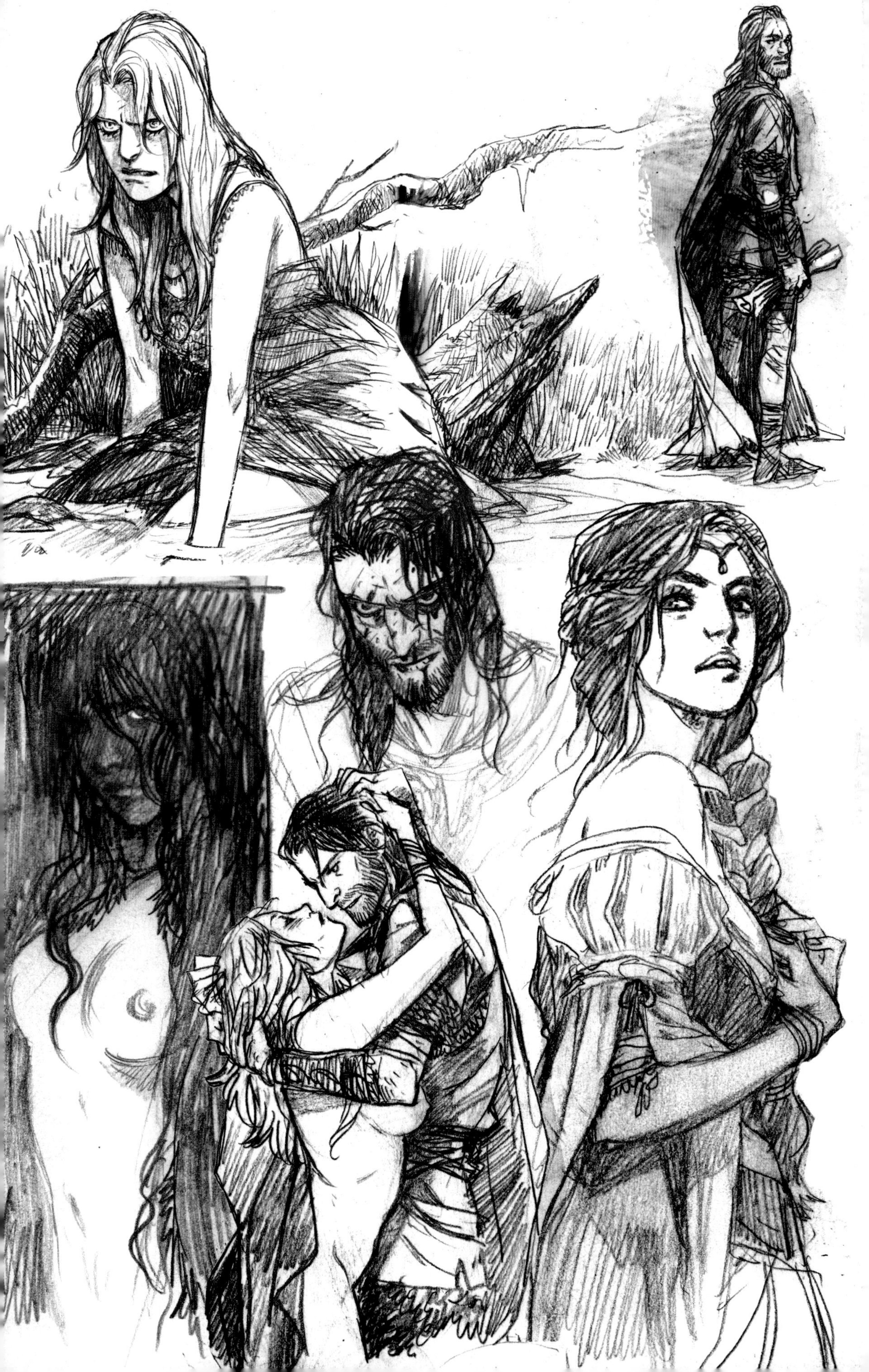

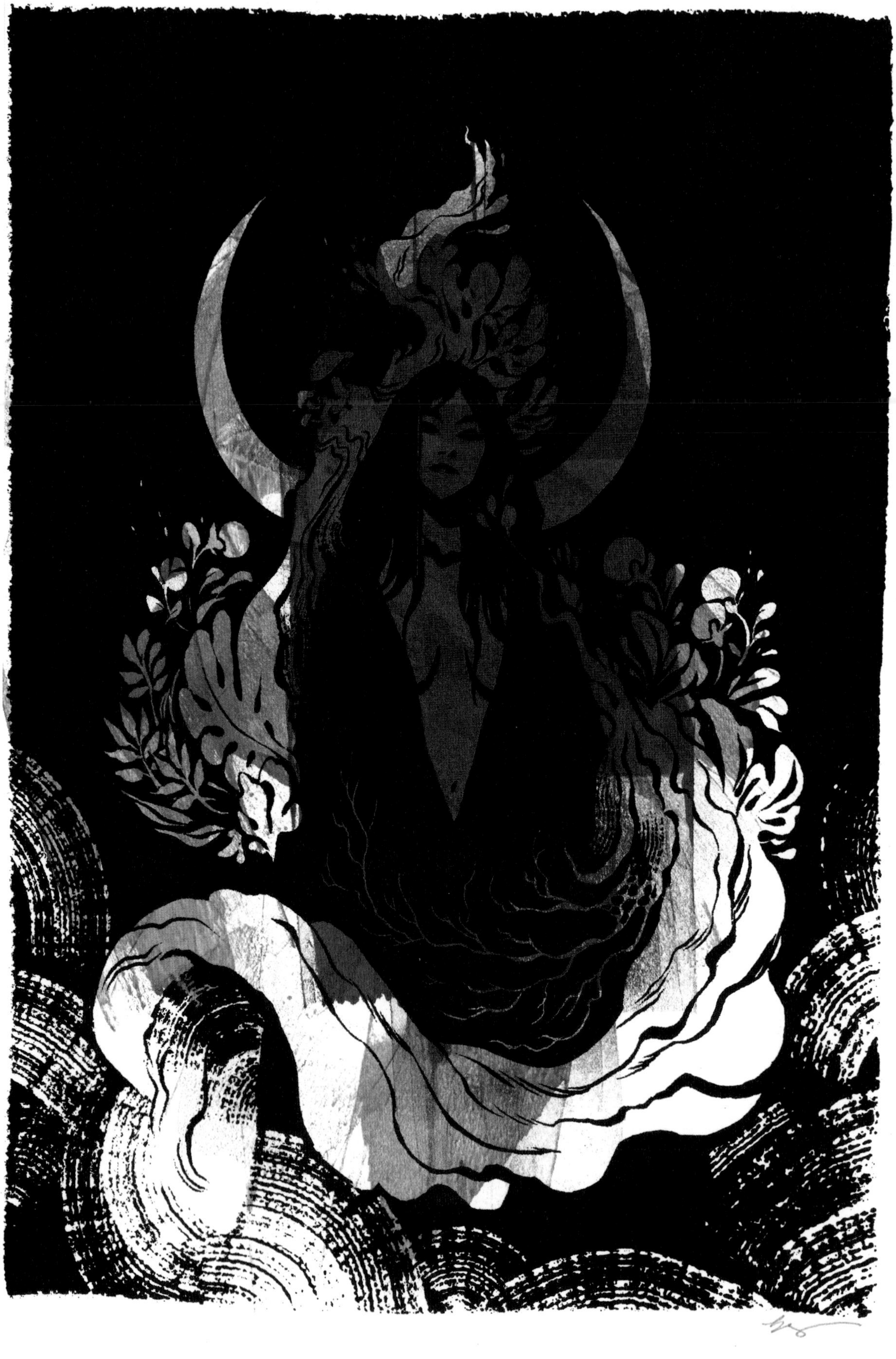

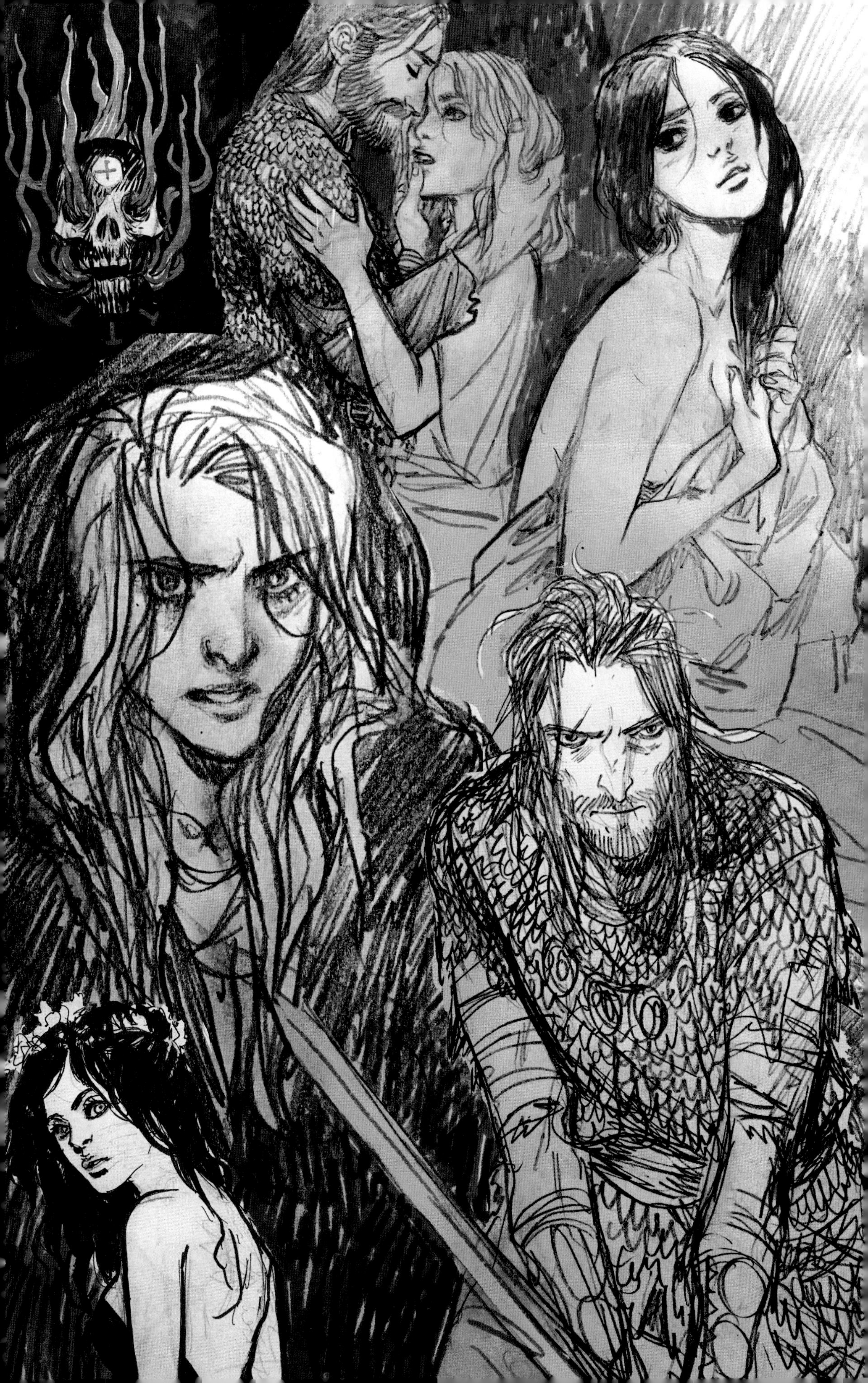

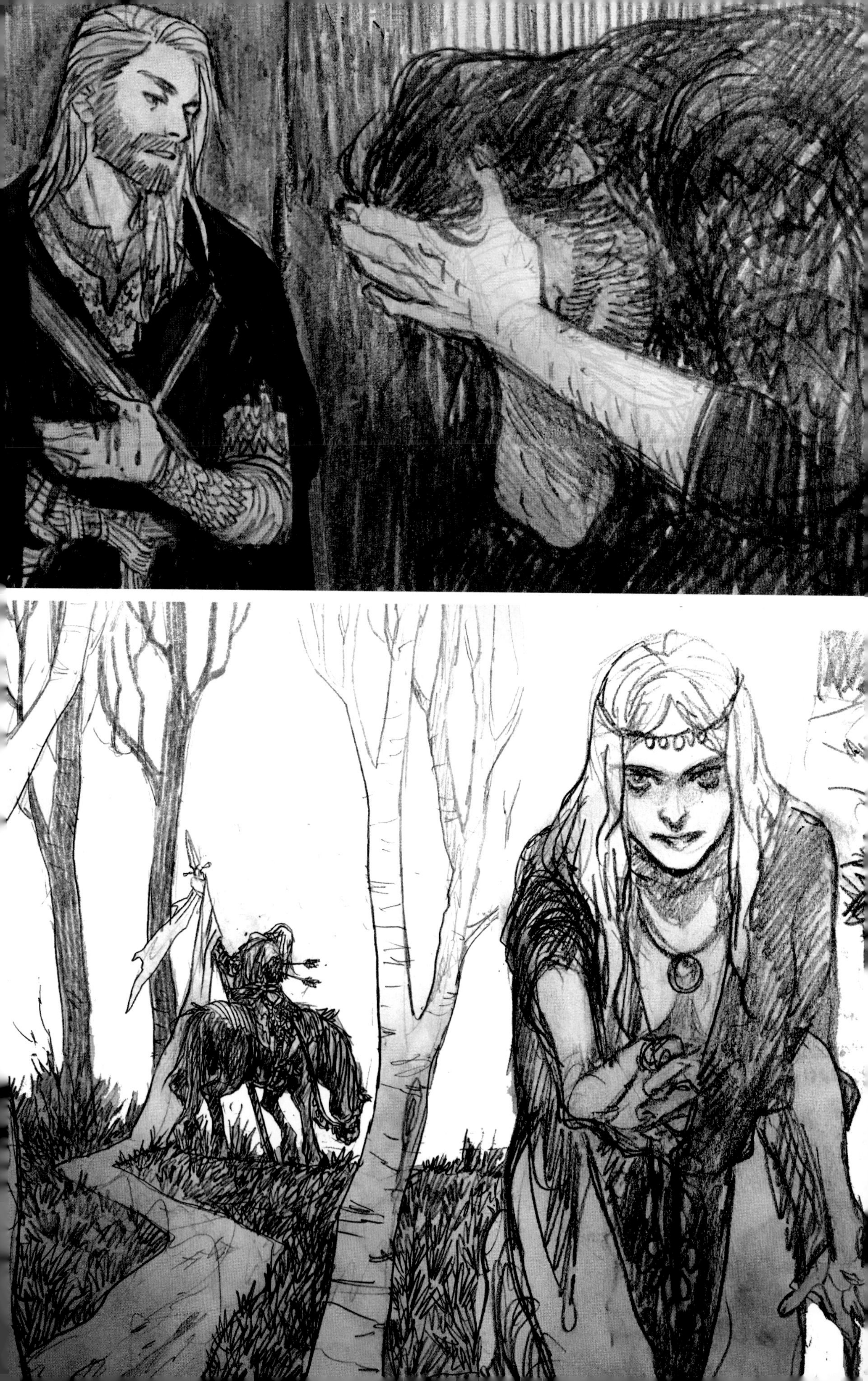

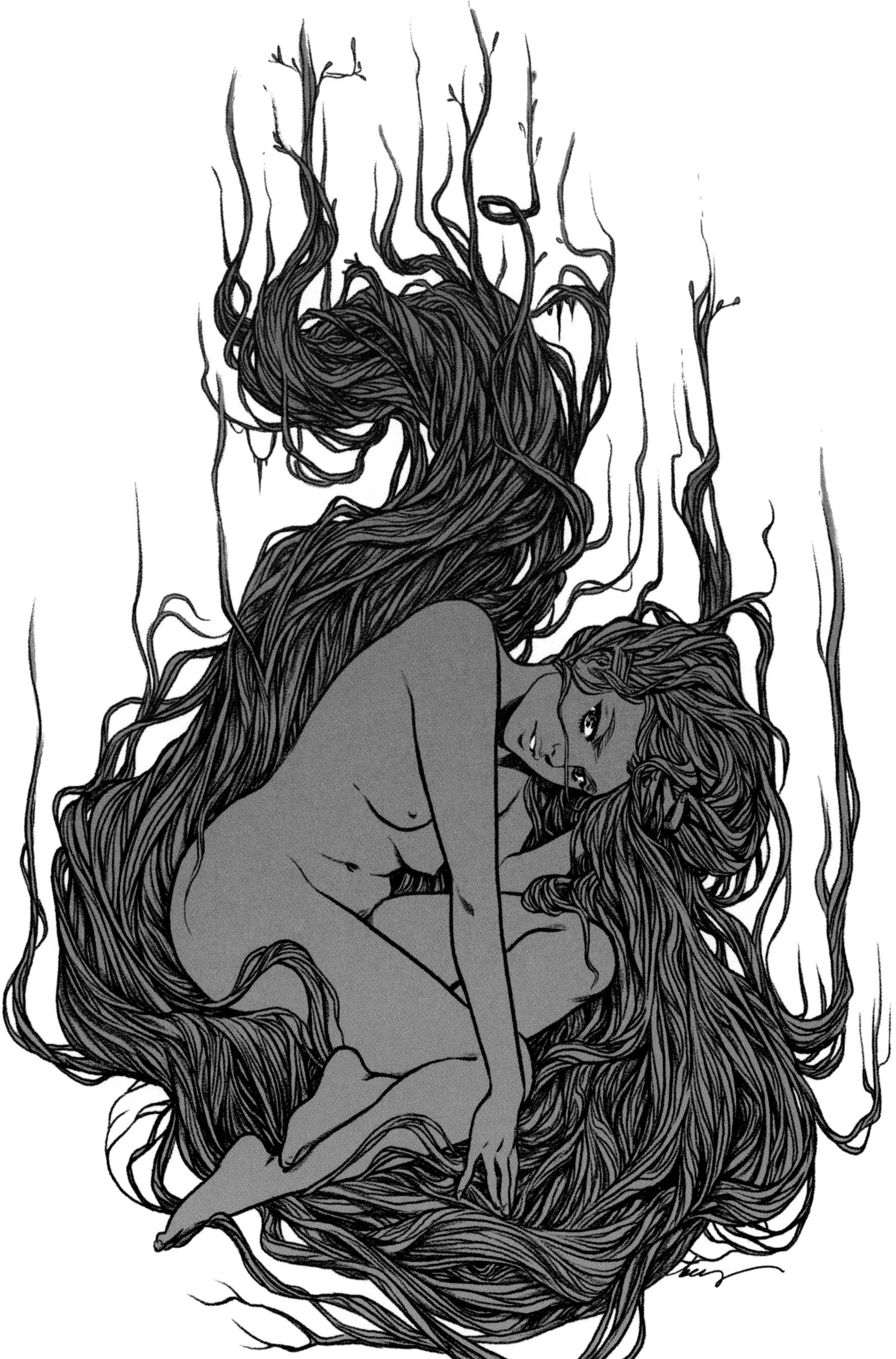

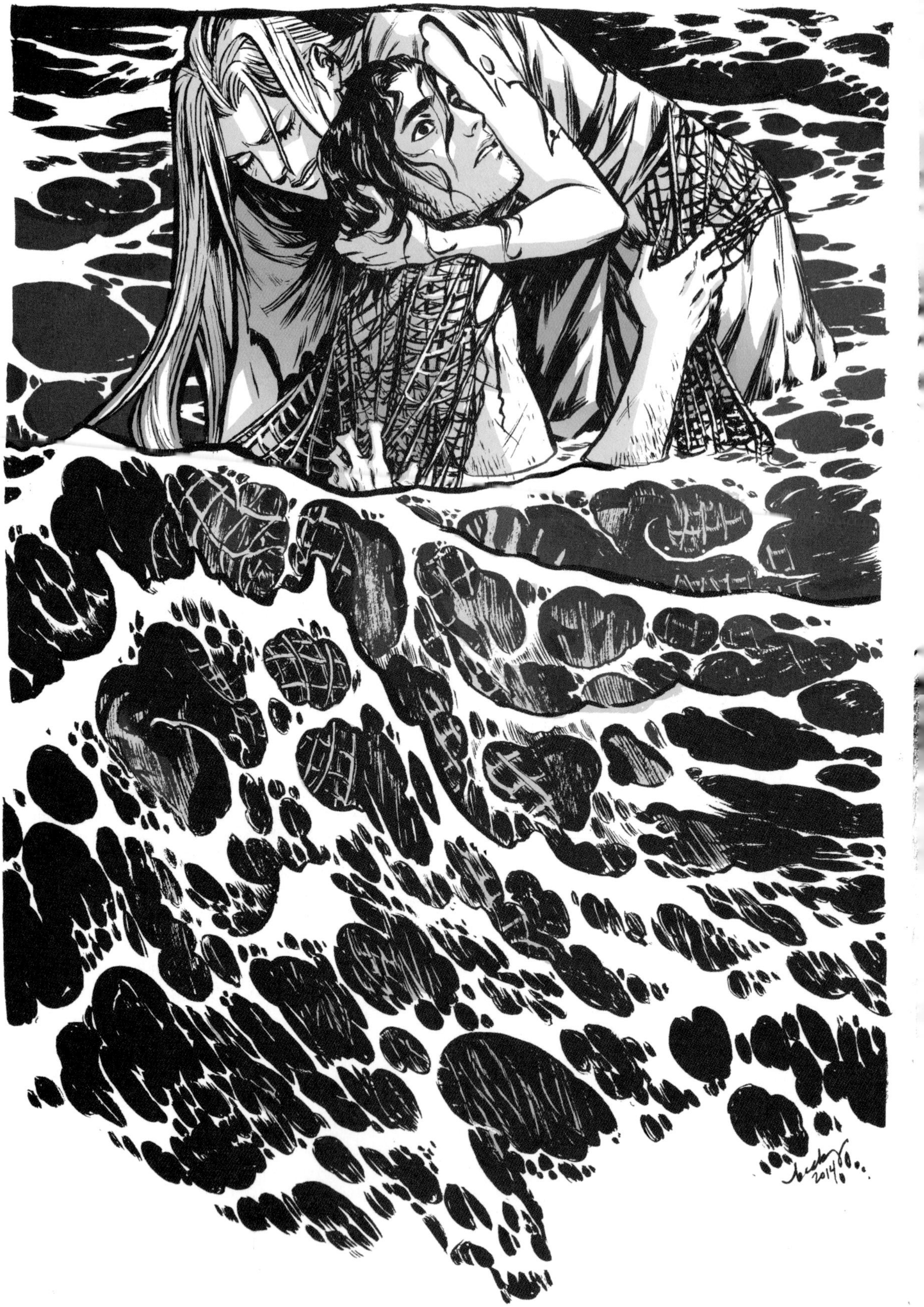

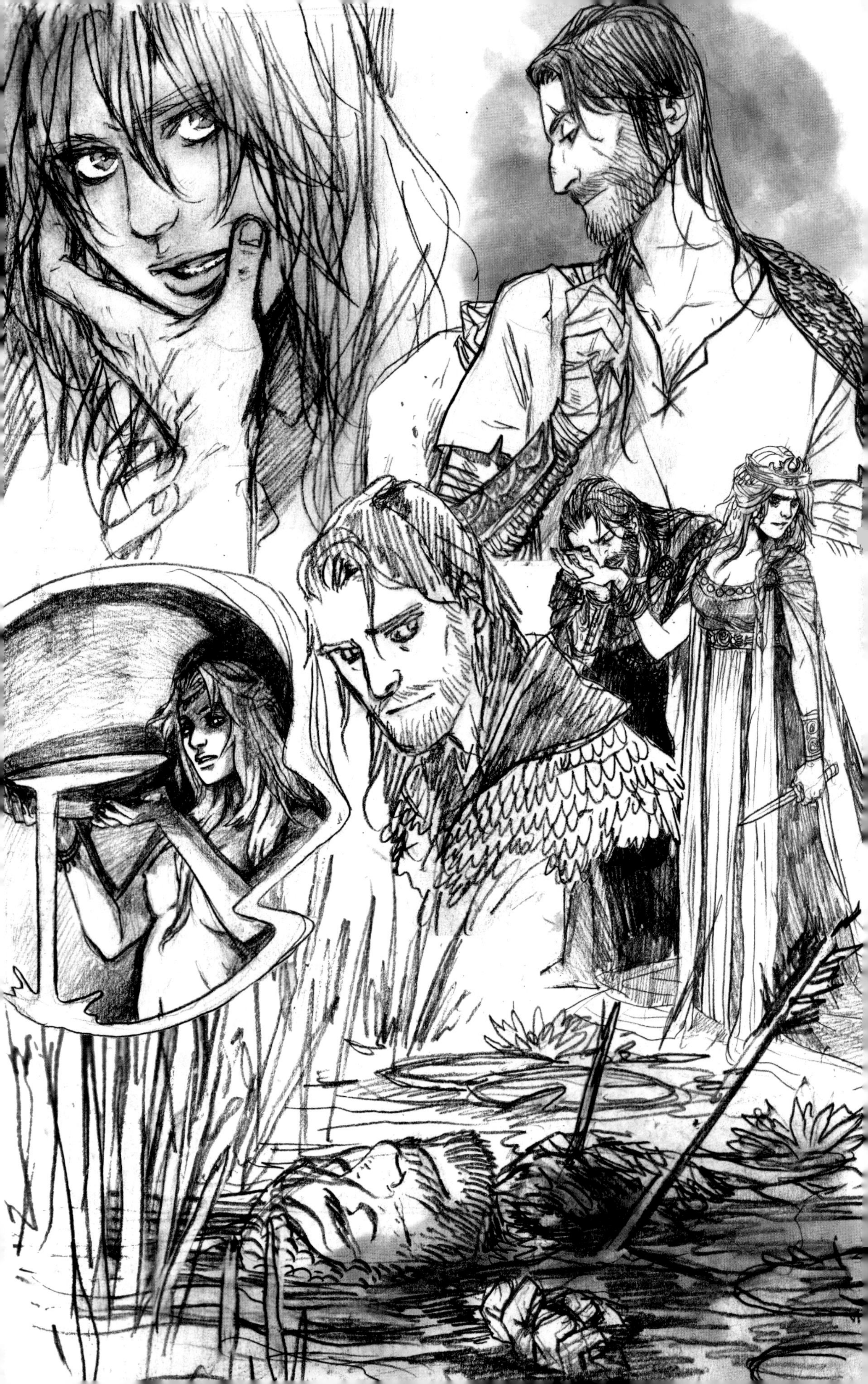

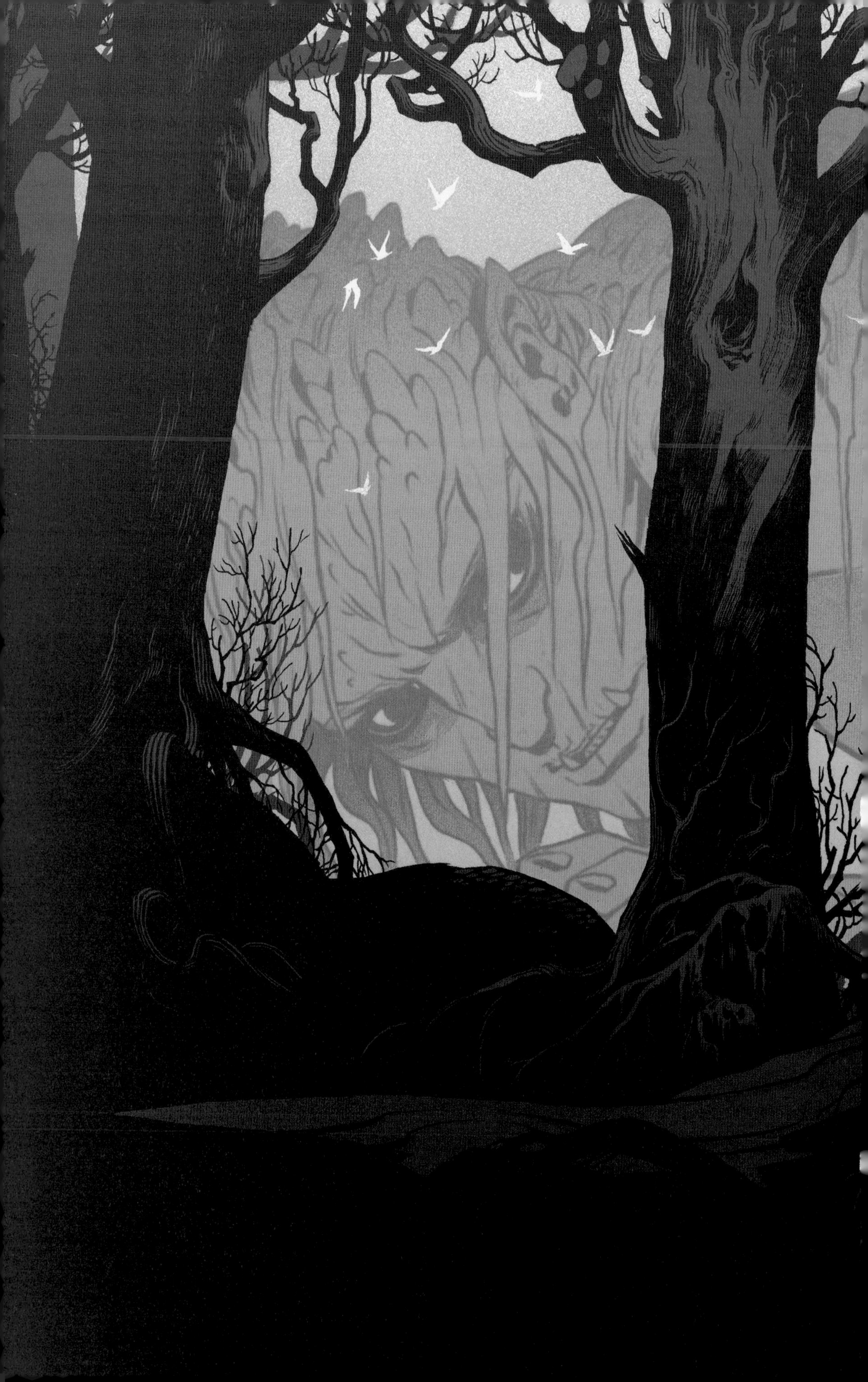

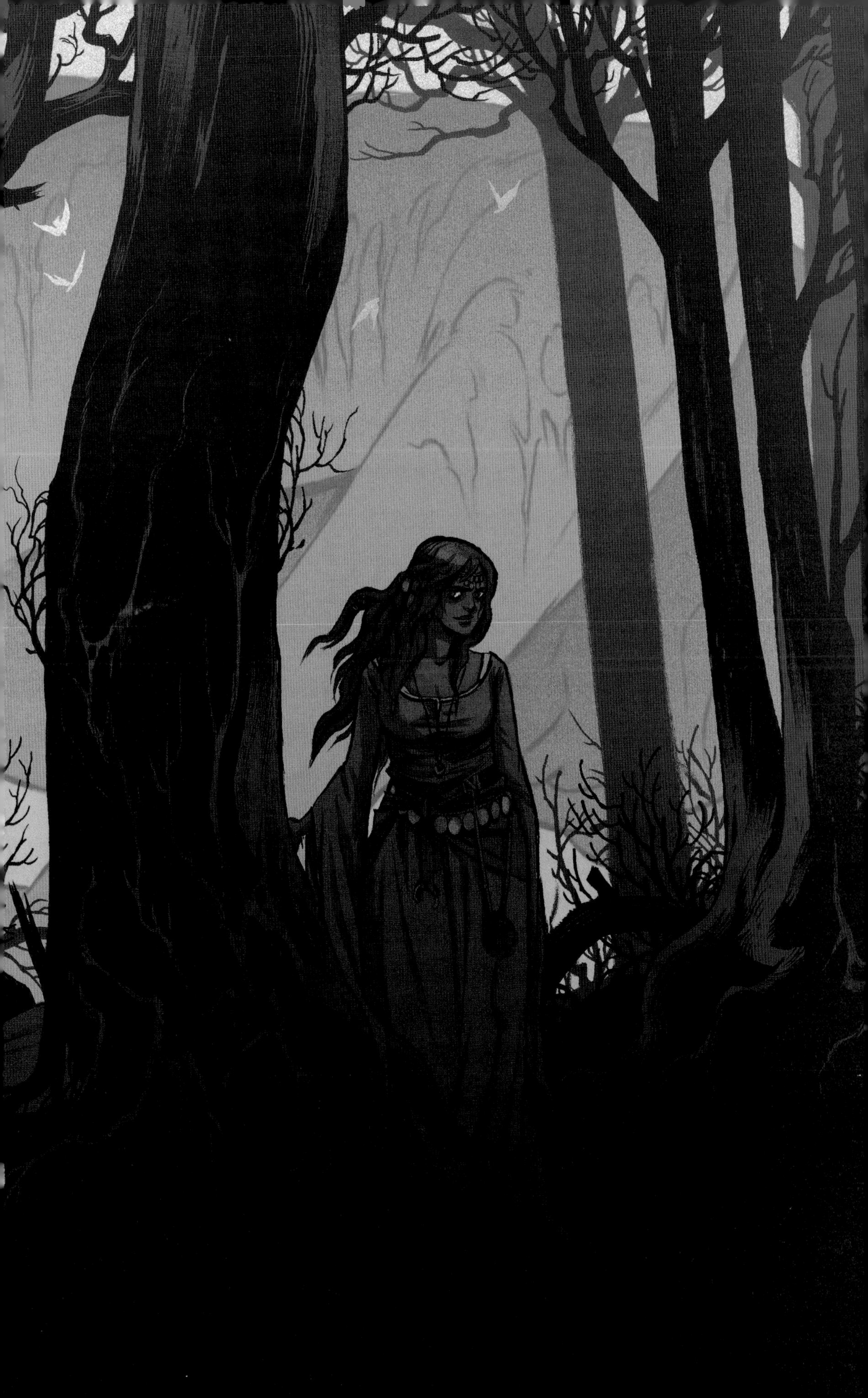

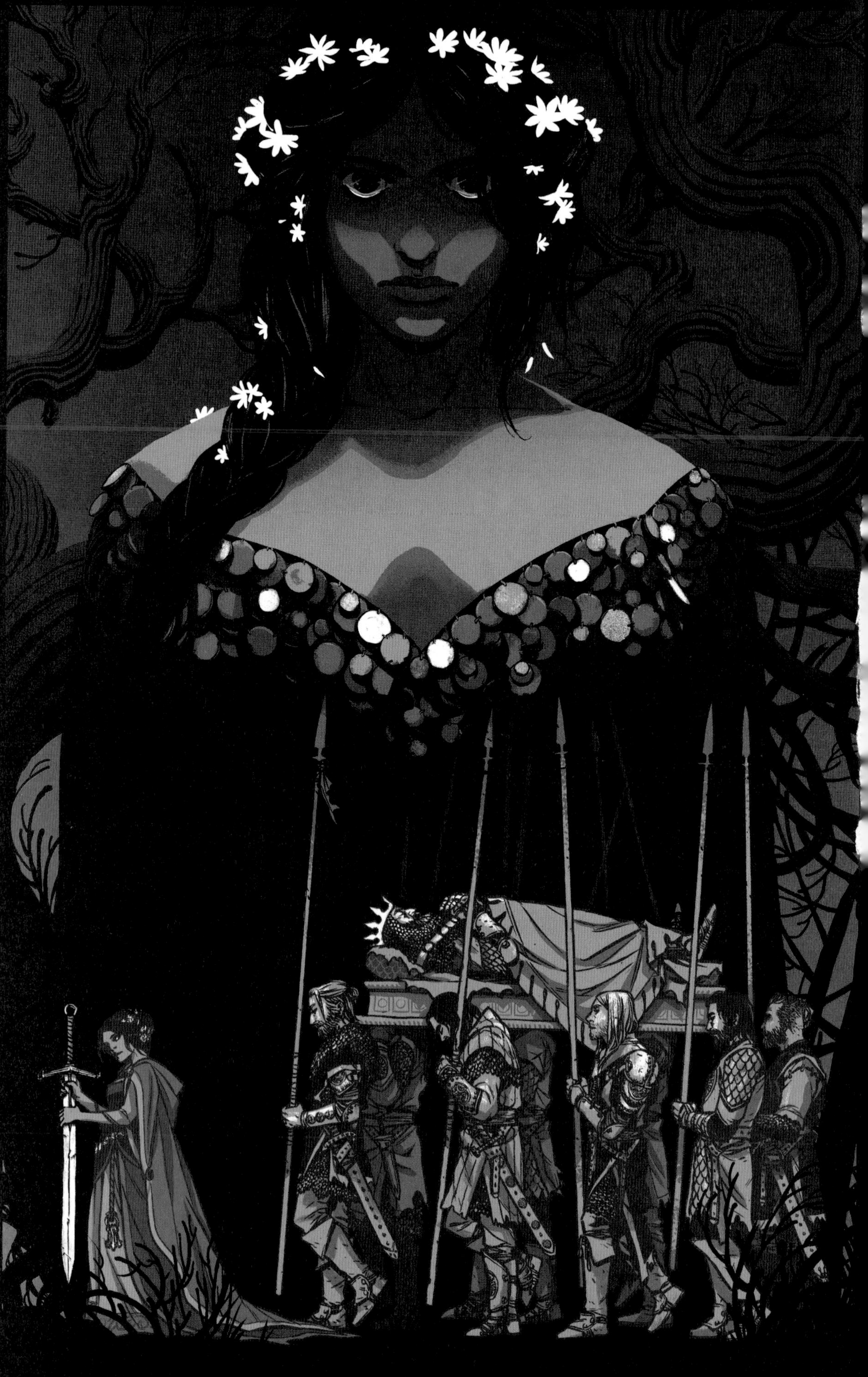

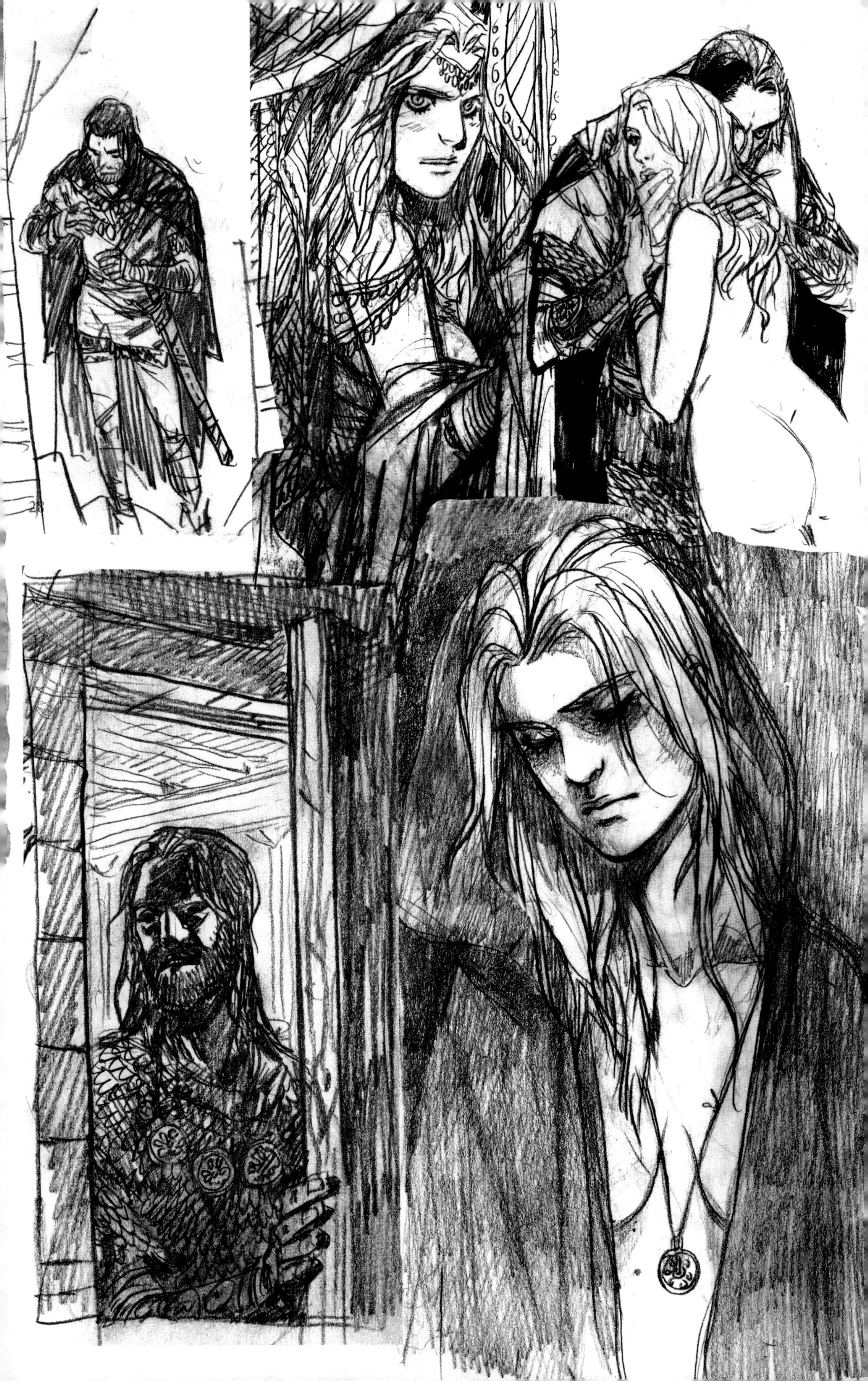

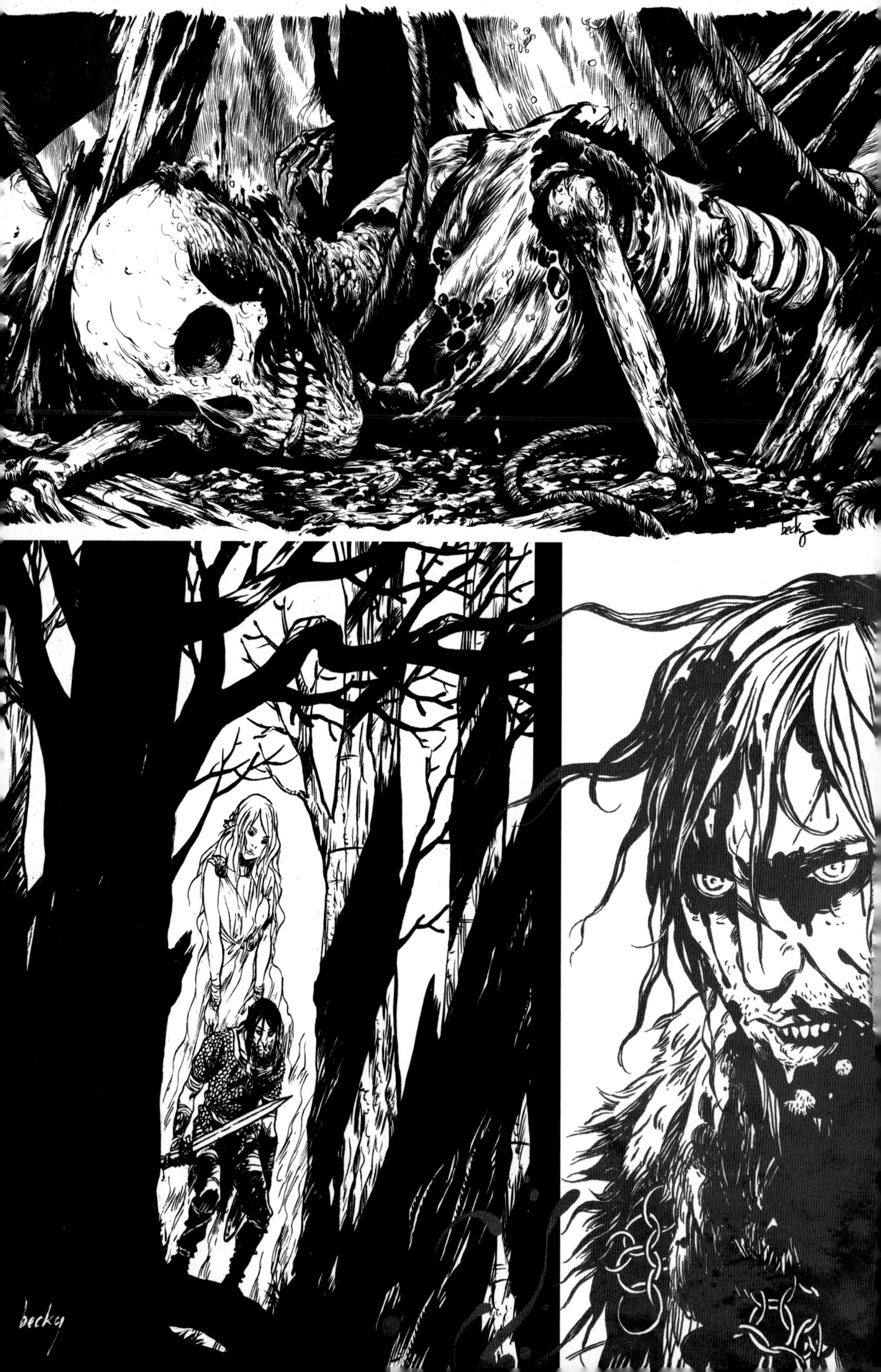
becky
becky

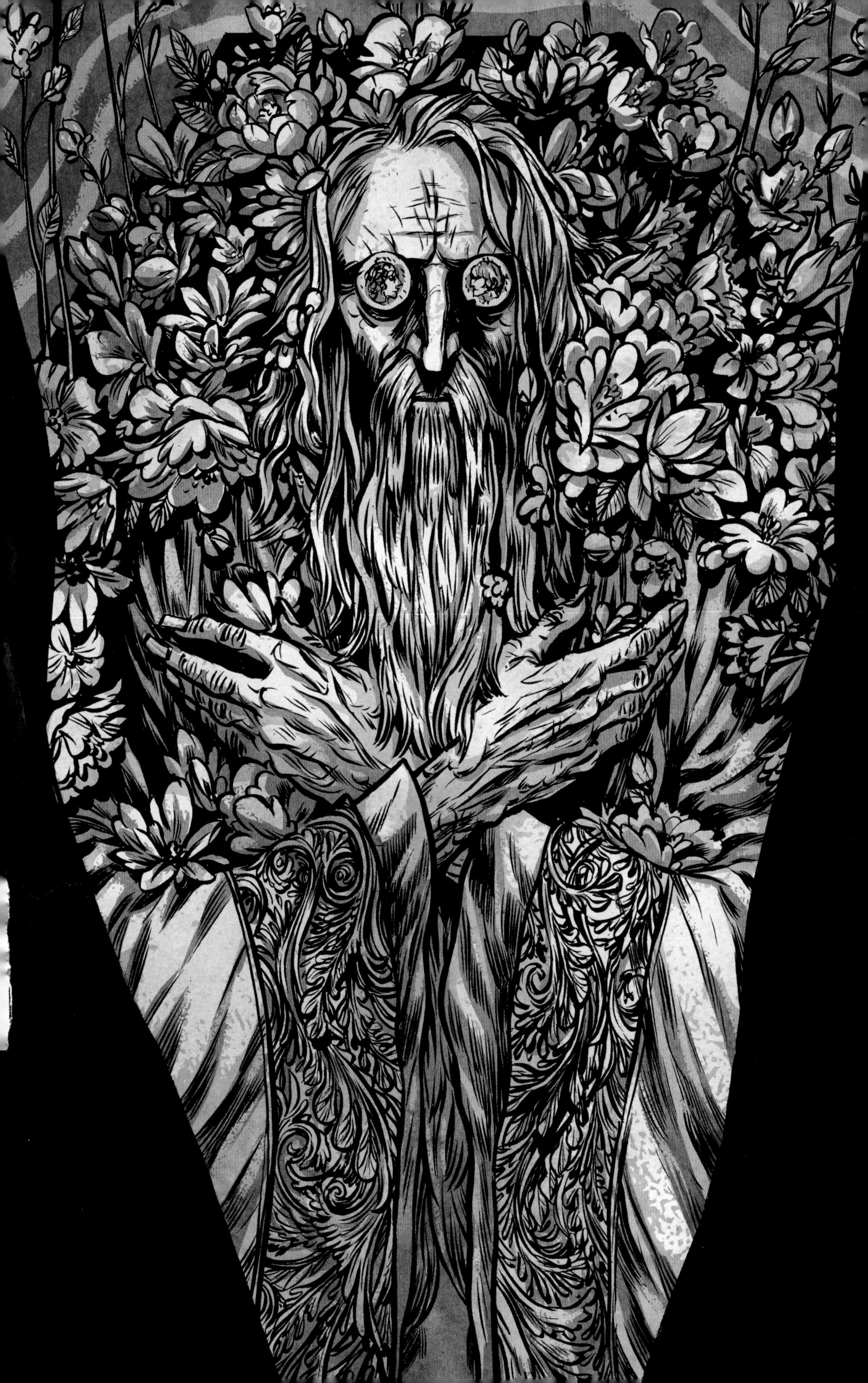

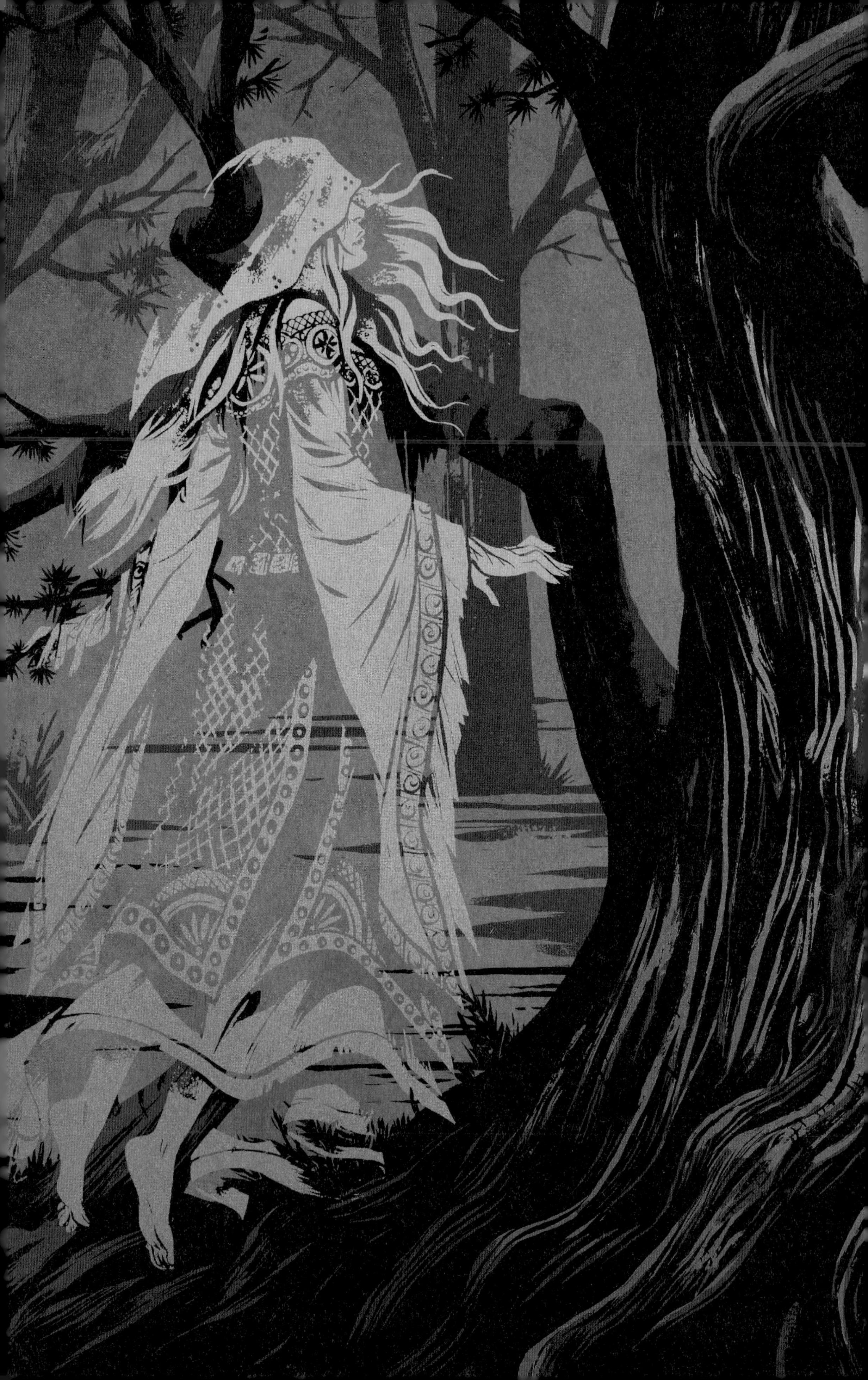

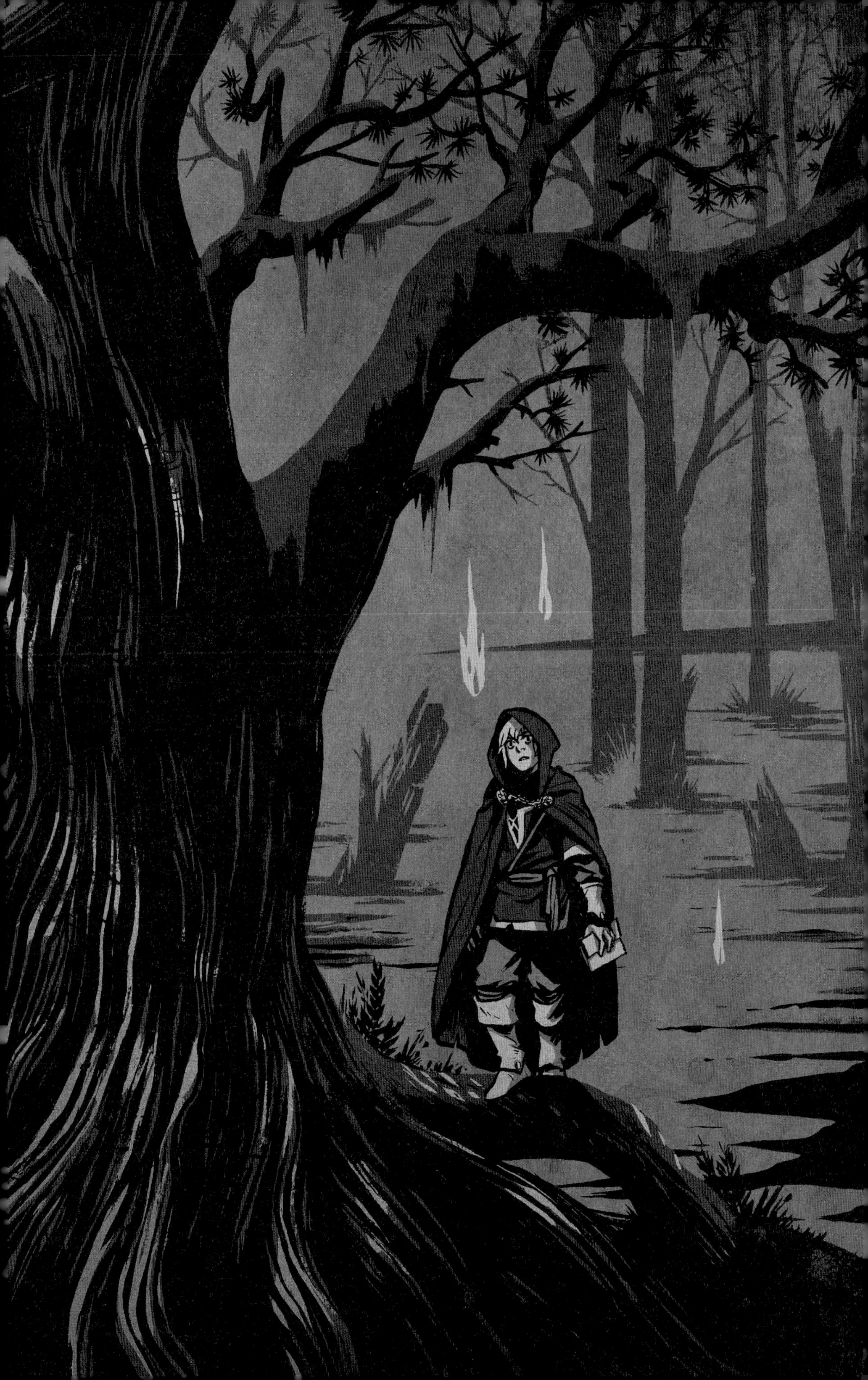

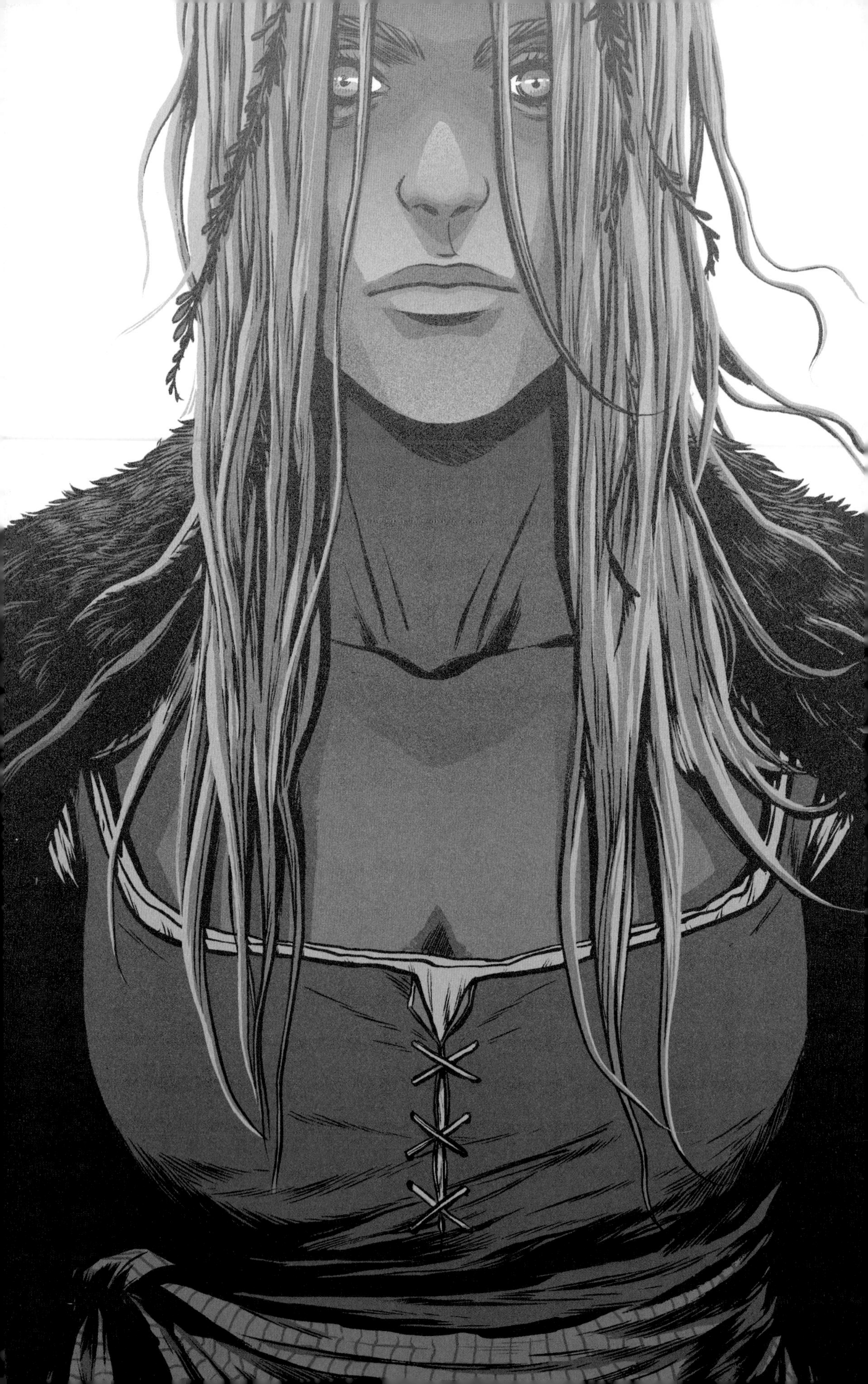

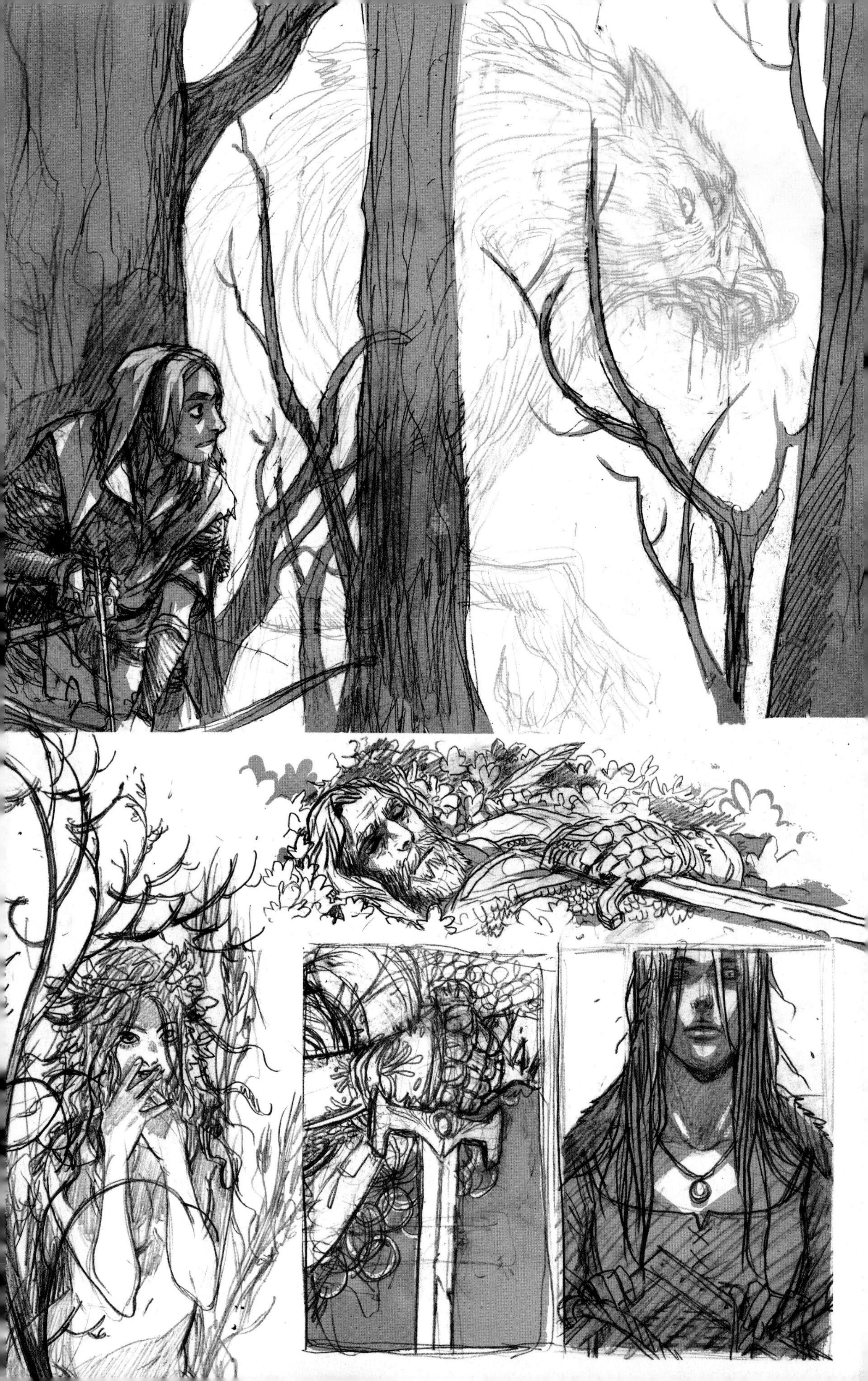

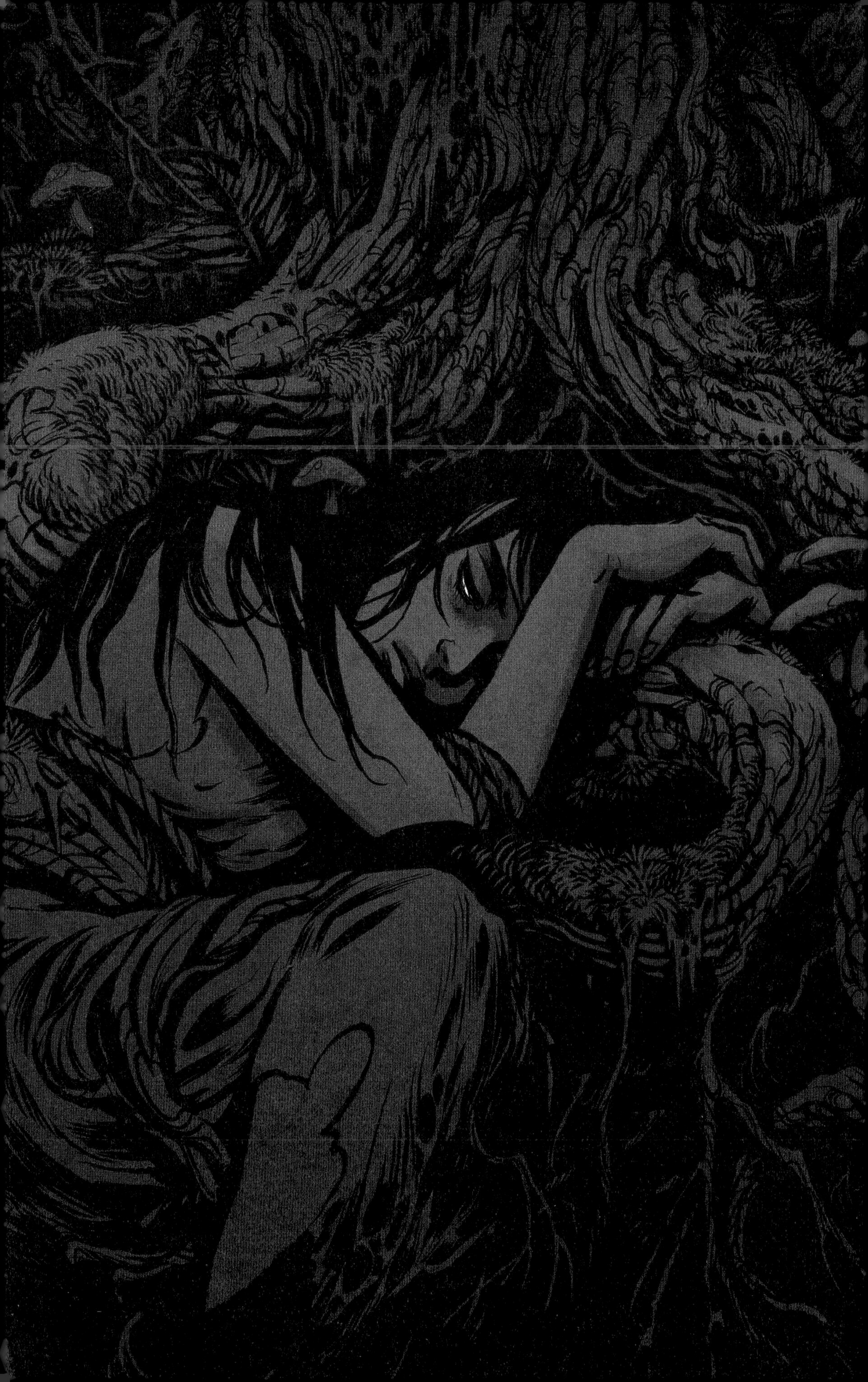